A VERY UNUSUAL AIR WAR

A VERY UNUSUAL AIR WAR

FROM DUNKIRK TO THE AFDU

THE DIARY AND LOGBOOK
OF TEST PILOT
H. LEONARD THORNE
1940–45

EDITED BY GILL AND BARRY GRIFFIN

Dedicated to the memory of F/Lt H.L. 'Len' Thorne, A.E. and all of the brave men of Fighter Command who took part in the Second World War and subsequent conflicts.

Photographs from Len Thorne's personal collection.
Edited and made ready for publication by the author's daughter and son-in-law, Gill and Barry Griffin.
Any errors are purely ours or Len's.

First published 2013

The History Press
The Mill, Brimscombe Port
Stroud, Gloucestershire, GL5 2QG
www.thehistorypress.co.uk

British Library Cataloguing in Publication Data.
A catalogue record for this book is available from the British Library.

ISBN 978 0 7524 9343 5

Typesetting and origination by The History Press
Printed in Great Britain

CONTENTS

Cadet Len Thorne, 1940.

Len and Estelle Thorne on their wedding day, 16th September 1941.

Len with Mustang 3 (P51b), 1944.

Len in September 1990, dressed for a church parade in Stratford-upon-Avon.

LIST OF PHOTOGRAPHS

THE LOGBOOK

Below is a photograph of a page in Len Thorne's logbook dated October 1941. The left-hand side has been copied almost exactly in the following pages of this book but the right-hand leaf has had to be condensed so that both can be displayed on one sheet. There are columns for Single-Engine and Multi-Engine aircraft, sub-divided into Day and Night Flying. This is further divided into Dual or Pilot in single-engine aircraft and Dual, 1st or 2nd Pilot in multi-engine aeroplanes. There are also columns for Passenger, Instrument or Cloud flying. These have all been condensed to three columns, Dual, Pilot or Passenger. The detailed notes on the right-hand leaf have been incorporated into the story told in the text.

The summary boxes occur at the end of each month. They give details of the hours flown on each type of aeroplane and are signed by the pilot, the officer in command of a 'Flight' and the squadron leader. In this case the O/C 'A' Flight was F/Lt Norman C. Macqueen, DFC. Six months after this, on 4th May 1942, he was killed when his aircraft was hit by tracer fire from an ME109, while he was flying with 249 Squadron over Malta. The 602 squadron leader who signed above was Al Deere. Some of the figures in the flying columns were written in red. This denoted night flying.

FOREWORD

This book was first conceived almost accidentally. Len Thorne was a Second World War fighter pilot. He still had his wartime logbook and it was one of his proudest possessions. It was originally to have gone to his younger daughter, who lives in Texas. When he was in his 85th year he decided that he did not wish it to leave England and so it was willed to the Imperial War Museum at Duxford. Because he could not keep his promise to give the logbook to his daughter, he felt guilty. This led him to make a handwritten copy of the book to give to her. When it was completed and handed over, he thought he should also give a copy to his elder daughter. She persuaded him that his reminiscences should be formalised so that we did not lose this first-hand history. Len found that the exercise of writing out his logbook had brought back many memories, so he created another manuscript copy, this time annotated with all his memories of the events which took place during his wartime RAF career and many of the people he had known. This book is the result.

It shows him to be one of the unsung heroes of the Second World War. He completed two tours of front line duty as a fighter pilot, when their life-expectancy was between two and four weeks. He then went to AFDU, the Air Fighting Development Unit, where he spent the rest of the war combat-testing new British, American and captured enemy aeroplanes.

Yet he was never decorated. He had been recommended for a medal and the citation had been written up but a change of commanding officer sent his medal elsewhere. I would not say he was bitter about it but the fact that he had no decoration did leave a scar. He was twice 'mentioned in dispatches', once for flight testing various Allied planes but mostly for flying comparative combat trials and demonstrations in the Focke Wulf 190A-3. His second mention was for flight testing, under operational conditions, the Spitfire Mk XXI in comparative trials against RAF, FAA and USAAF fighters to evaluate its suitability for service use and to prepare and submit a detailed report.

This was the man who held air speed records, setting a straight and level speed of 455mph in a Mustang, which made it the fastest operational airplane in the world at the time (see the entries for 5th March 1943 and 28th January 1944). He also made the first flight of a Spitfire as a fighter-bomber on 30th November 1942. Then, in late 1944 and early 1945 he was involved in the early operational testing of the Gloster Meteor Mk III, so his flying extended into the jet age. He always talked of himself as a 'hack' pilot, an ordinary Joe. Perhaps his lack of a medal left him with a feeling that he had done nothing special. He was always happy to talk about his time in the Royal Air Force but it was more to tell you about the aircraft and the people he had met than about himself.

Herbert Leonard 'Len' Thorne always denied being a Battle of Britain pilot. In British military eyes the 'Battle' started at the end of July 1940 and was over at the end of October 1940. He gained his 'wings' on his 21st birthday, 13th April 1941, went to the Operational Training Unit at Hawarden and was then posted to 41 Squadron, a front-line fighter squadron, starting active service on 11th June 1941. He always maintained that he missed being 'one of the Few' by six months. However, the Luftwaffe was still making bombing raids and by the end of June the RAF was sending attacking sweeps over occupied France and Belgium. The life of a fighter pilot was still measured in minutes in the air.

He flew and was friends with many of the top 'aces' of the war and his personal memories of these heroes add to our historical knowledge. Among others he talks about are Al Deere, Brendan 'Paddy' Finucane, T.S. 'Wimpy' Wade and James 'One Armed Mac' MacLachlan. He explains air combat tactics clearly. He describes technical details of the aeroplanes coherently and his lifelong love of those beautiful machines and of flying shines through.

This is the story, told through the medium of his pilot's logbook, of a man who so loved flying that, after making a full recovery from a cancer operation six months earlier, he performed an aerobatic display to celebrate his eightieth birthday.

This was no 'hack' pilot. He was an extraordinary one.

* * *

After his time in the RAF, Len returned to work for High Duty Alloys in Slough and Redditch. He later moved into rivet manufacturing with Pearson and Beck, a local Redditch factory. He moved on to Black and Luff, which became a subsidiary of Bifurcated and Tubular Rivet Company of Aylesbury, rising to the position of executive Managing Director of the Midland Division of that company.

He became a Freemason in Slough in 1948, being initiated into Industria Lodge No. 5421 and when he moved permanently to Redditch he joined a local Lodge, Ipsley Lodge No. 6491 in the Province of Warwickshire. He was also a member of Bordesley Abbey R.A. Chapter No. 4495, meeting in Redditch and in the Province of Worcestershire. He remained a Freemason for the rest of his life. He died just before he was due to receive his 60 Years Certificate.

He was a member and Past President of the Redditch Probus Club and delighted in telling anyone who would listen that his very 'correct' wife Estelle liked to explain the acronym as 'Poor Retired Old B***s Useless for Sex'. Len and his wife were also active members of the League of Friends of the Alexandra Hospital in Redditch. They worked together in the coffee shop for many years until Estelle became ill. Following her death in 1997 Len continued for a short time in the coffee shop, now working with his daughter Gill. He was also a member of the Committee and edited the League's quarterly newsletter.

He was a very gregarious man and was a member of the Bromsgrove branch of The Royal British Legion. He joined the Stratford branch of The Air Crew Association and became President and he was a life member of the Spitfire Society. For several years he was Chairman of the civilian committee of Studley ATC, 480 Squadron.

Len died on 6th June 2008 – D-Day. His interest in and love of flying never died. In his last letter, to the chairman of the local Spitfire Society, four days before he died, he wrote 'My interest in the Spitfire will never wane.'

Like many other pilots and ex-pilots, Len Thorne was deeply moved by this poem. He had a copy of it on a bronze plaque in his lounge.

> *High Flight (An Airman's Ecstasy)*
> Oh! I have slipped the surly bonds of earth
> And danced the skies on laughter-silvered wings;
> Sunward I've climbed, and joined the tumbling mirth
> Of sun-split clouds – and done a hundred things
> You have not dreamed of – wheeled and soared and swung
> High in the sunlit silence. Hov'ring there
> I've chased the shouting wind along, and flung
> My eager craft through footless halls of air …
>
> Up, up the long delirious, burning blue,
> I've topped the windswept heights with easy grace
> Where never lark, or even eagle flew –
> And, while with silent lifting mind I've trod
> The high untrespassed sanctity of space,
> Put out my hand and touched the face of God.

> *Pilot Officer Gillespie Magee*
> *No. 412 squadron, RCAF.*
> *Killed 11 December 1941*

INTRODUCTION

I was born on 13th April 1920 in the village of Waddesdon, Buckinghamshire, the fifth child born to Benjamin and Lydia Thorne. My sister Doris was fifteen years my senior, my brother Leslie thirteen years older and Gwen ten years older. My other sister, Sybil, died in infancy. I attended the C. of E. school in the village. Waddesdon is the site of Waddesdon Manor, a Rothschild home, now part of The National Trust. Mother and father were the landlords of The Five Arrows Hotel in Waddesdon. Sadly, my father Benjamin Thomas Thorne had died in 1927 and three years later my mother married a Birmingham man, Ernest Massey.

In 1931, having passed a scholarship, I moved to Aylesbury Grammar School. After Father's death my stepfather Ernest helped my mother with the hotel and garage business but in the year I started at grammar school, his health, too, became a problem and they were forced to give up the hotel and also the garage business which had been started by my father before the First World War. They moved to Birmingham. I remained at Waddesdon for the remainder of my year at Aylesbury, living with my 'second mother', Auntie Betty, one of my mother's younger sisters. At the end of that year I moved to Birmingham and for a brief six weeks attended Saltley Secondary School. In late September 1932, further deterioration in my stepfather's condition caused another move to Tewkesbury and I became a pupil at Tewkesbury Grammar School, where I spent two happy years. In the summer of 1934 my stepfather died, leaving mother in a very poor condition both financially and in health. It was decided that she would go to live with my younger sister Gwen at Poletrees Farm and for a time there was a strong possibility that, like my stepbrother, Gordon Massey, I would go into the Licensed Victuallers School, a type of orphanage, at Slough. My elder sister Doris, married to Percy Climer, a policeman, refused to accept this and I went to live with them and spent my final two grammar school years at Slough Secondary School. In 1936, having passed the Oxford School Certificate examination, I went to work as a junior clerk at High Duty Alloys, at the main factory on Slough Trading Estate and in 1938, I moved to the newly built shadow factory at Redditch.

I volunteered for aircrew training on Sept. 6th 1939 at the recruiting centre in Dale End, Birmingham. Because I was employed by High Duty Alloys Ltd., a company heavily engaged in production of aircraft components, I was deferred for three months. I was called to Cardington in January 1940 for medical and educational tests and accepted for pilot training as a cadet, rank AC 2. I again returned to Redditch, to await final call up. This came in May 1940 and summoned me to the receiving wing at Babbacombe in Devon.

Three weeks later I moved to No. 3 ITW at Torquay. With forty-nine others, I was billeted in the White House Hotel, situated high up the bank at the end of the harbour. During our stay we experienced some enemy bombing but suffered no damage. During the raids, mostly at night, we had to go down into the cellars; these cellars still contained an excellent store of wines but to our disappointment all were behind locked grills and remained untouched. My memory of ITW is of much polishing of buttons and buckles and much blancoing of webbing and, on evenings off, drinking Devonshire rough cider, all we could afford. Our officers and NCO instructors were a fine and efficient bunch of men, with whom we got on well. The WO in overall charge of 3 ITW was a super-efficient NCO who, we understood, had been transferred from the army. I remember his name as Warrant Officer Edsal, a much-feared disciplinarian who was not popular. Of course we were viewed as objects of interest and, dare I say, admiration, by the young ladies of Torquay. I expect the uniform had something to do with the attraction. Naturally, we took advantage of this whenever possible and I remember a pretty little girl who worked in the big store, Bobby's, in the High Street. It was strongly rumoured that to discourage our amorous activities, our tea was laced with bromide or some such chemical. If this was true it did not work on me!

After successful completion of the ITW course towards the end of September 1940, at the height of the Battle of Britain, I was posted to No. 7 EFTS (Elementary

Group photo of cadets under training at Babbacombe, late May 1940. Top row, Jonnie Timmis, shot down in September 1941 and became a POW. 2nd row, George Winter, crashed October 1941. Third row, Doug Hartwell shot down or lost, 1941, circumstances unknown and fourth from left, Len Thorne. Bottom row, John Walters from Studley, shot down in North Africa 1941/42.

Pilots under training outside the Norfolk Hotel, Torquay, 1941. Len Thorne far left.

Flying Training School) at Desford near Leicester, where I would be taught to fly the DH 82, De Havilland Tiger Moth, a small biplane training aircraft.

Pre-war, Desford had been a rather expensive private flying club owned by Reid and Sigrist, the instrument makers. At the end of 1939 it was taken over by the Air Ministry. The civilian flying instructors were 'invited' to stay on and those who did so were commissioned into the RAF. The school facilities were palatial, with a central block of buildings housing a large lounge with an adjoining dining room and kitchens. We cadets were treated like young gentlemen: pre-war habits had not yet died out. We had our own rooms in the nearby living quarters and even a batman to every four cadets.

A small number of the boys on this course were from wealthy backgrounds and had university or public school educations. These chaps were destined to become commissioned officers if they successfully completed the flying courses. The majority, like myself, were grammar school boys. To us, after the bare rooms of commandeered hotels at Torquay, Desford was pure luxury. Having entered the service as AC2s (Aircraftsman Second Class), popularly referred to as the lowest form of animal life in the Air Force, those of us who had passed the physical and ground training examinations were promoted to LAC (Leading Aircraftsman).

For the first few weeks there was no great sense of urgency and things moved at a leisurely pace. Our days were spent partly in flying and studying the Tiger Moth and partly in lessons and lectures. The latter included the theory of flight, aircraft engineering, Morse code signalling using an Aldis lamp or buzzer, navigation, meteorology and Air Force law. We studied engine starting procedure and safety precautions. Most light aircraft were started by swinging the propeller by hand. First

B Flight No. 2 Squadron, 3 ITW, September 1940. Signatures on the reverse of the photograph were annotated by Len Thorne during the 1940s as information came to him. There are notations for those who failed the course, those killed in training accidents and some missing or killed in action. Red ovals, 'halos', were sometimes used to indicate deaths.

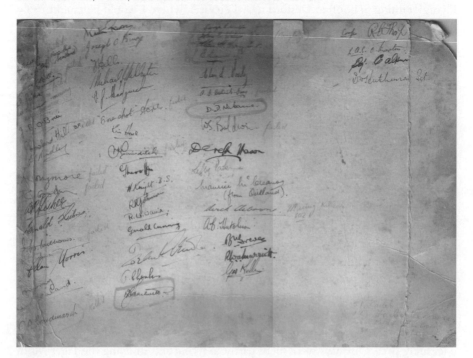

the engine was turned over in reverse (blow out), then turned over (suck in) with the magneto switches turned off, to draw fuel into the cylinders. Then, the pilot having shouted 'contact', the prop was pulled over sharply and hopefully the engine would start. In the event of a non-start, the pilot would shout 'switches off' and raise both arms to indicate that it was safe to proceed with a re-start. I well remember being told to keep a large spanner handy as the magneto contacts sometimes stuck but a sharp tap with the spanner would cause them to part. I passed the course with the rating 'average'.

Early in December I was posted to No. 9 SFTS, Hullavington, for advanced training, first on the Miles Master Mk 1, then to Hawker Hurricanes for all solo flying. I successfully completed the flying course, attended the passing out parade in April 1941 and received the coveted Silver Wings on April 13th, the date of my 21st birthday. I was then promoted to the rank of sergeant. My next posting was to No. 57 OTU, Hawarden, near Chester, for intensive training in the art of a fighter pilot, most of the instructors being those men who had survived the Battle of Britain. I experienced my first solo in a Spitfire Mk 1, flying from Speke airfield, now Liverpool airport.

I was posted to Catterick in late May, to become a member of 41 Squadron, flying the more advanced Spitfire Mk 2 and, after a period of flying patrols over the northeast coast, I moved to Tangmere to take part in operations over enemy-held France. Here I saw my first enemy aircraft and experienced my first anti-aircraft fire.

After a period with '41', I was posted to No. 602, City of Glasgow, Royal Auxiliary Airforce Squadron, to complete a full tour of operations lasting until May 1942. I flew under the command of many famous fighter leaders, among them Al Deere, Paddy Finucane, Francis Victor Beamish, Findlay Boyd and several others. In January 1942 I was promoted to Flight Sergeant and became senior NCO pilot in 'A' Flight, authorised to act, on occasions, as a flight leader. In the course of this service I was credited with five victories, three confirmed destroyed, two others probably destroyed and three damaged. In 602 we had Spitfire MkVb's armed with 20mm cannons.

In May 1942 I was posted, on rest, to the AFDU, the Air Fighting Development Unit, which was then at Duxford and after six months I was offered the chance to become an experimental test pilot and remain at AFDU as one of the permanent staff. The following year, in August, I was appointed Flight Commander of the unit. My most notable task at this time was to fly captured enemy aircraft, including the much-feared Focke Wulf FW 190. Apart from normal flights and comparative tests I took the latter machine all over the country giving demonstrations and mock combat to our own pilots. In the spring of 1945 I was briefly acting OC flying during the absence of S/Ldr. T.S. Wade. Also at that time I had a partial rest from flying and performed the duties of range instructing officer at the Selsey bombing and firing ranges.

At the end of the war, in August 1945, I was offered a posting to the Air Ministry in London and for the next three years I was attached to the Ministry of Supply as a liaison officer with the aircraft manufacturing companies. The end of my service career came in September 1948 when I returned to civilian life.

Ex RAFVR Flight Lieutenant No. 121518 (NCO No. 1164397) H.L. (Len.) Thorne.
One-time Flt. Commander of the Air Fighting Development Unit (AFDU) later, as part of
CFE, the Air Fighting Development Squadron (AFDS).

1

TRAINING

No. 7 E.F.T.S. (Elementary Flying Training School), Desford
No. 9 S.F.T.S. (Service Flying Training School), Hullavington
No. 57 O.T.U. (Operational Training Unit), Hawarden

YEAR	1940	AIRCRAFT		Pilot or 1st Pilot	2nd Pilot, Pupil or Pass.	DUTY (Including Results and Remarks)	Flying Time		Passenger
MONTH	DATE	Type	No.				Dual	Solo	
September	30th	DH 82	GADXT	P/O Hayne	Self	1. Air Experience			
						1a. Familiarity with cockpit layout			
						2. Effect of controls			
						4. Straight and level flight			
						5. Gliding	1-25		

Towards the end of September 1940, at the height of the Battle of Britain, I was posted to No. 7 E.F.T.S. (Elementary Flying Training School), Desford, near Leicester, to be taught to fly De Havilland Tiger Moth biplanes.

Explanation of exercises
The sequence of flying lessons is in accordance with the following numbers:

1.	Air experience
1a.	Familiarity with cockpit layout
2.	Effect of controls
3.	Taxiing
4.	Straight and level flight
5.	Gliding
6.	Medium turns
7.	Taking off into wind
8.	Powered approach
9.	Gliding approach and landing

10.	Spinning left and right
12.	Side slipping
13.	Precautionary landing
15.	Steep turns
16.	Climbing turns
17.	Forced landing
18.	Instrumentment flying
20. & 20a.	Night flying
22.	Aerobatics

I believe that 11, 14, 18 and 21 are lessons that apply to multi–engined aircraft training.

YEAR	1940	AIRCRAFT		Pilot or 1st Pilot	2nd Pilot, Pupil or Pass.	DUTY (Including Results and Remarks)	Flying Time		Passenger
MONTH	DATE	Type	No.				Dual	Solo	
October	1st	DH82	N6475	P/O Hayne	Self	2,4,5,3 and 6	1-40		
	2nd	DH82	N6475	P/O Hayne	Self	3,4,5 and 6	1-15		
	3rd	DH82	N6475	P/O Hayne	Self	4,5 and 6	-30		
	7th	DH82	N6475	P/O Hayne	Self	4,5,6,7 and 8	1-55		
						Grand total to date	6-45		
			N6475	P/O Hayne	Self	4,5,6 and 7	0-45		
			N6475	P/O Hayne	Self	6,7,9 and 10	1-10		
			R5039	F/Lt Hall	Self	6,7 and 9	0-20		
	15th	DH 82	R5039	F/Lt Hall	Self	6,7 and 9	1-10		
	16th	DH 82	R5039	F/Lt Hall	Self	6,7 and 9	40		
	18th	DH 82	R5039	F/Lt Hall	Self	6,7 and 9	25		
	25th	DH 82	R5039	F/Lt Hall	Self	6,7 and 9	-55		
	26th	DH 82	R5039	F/Lt Hall	Self	6,7 and 9	-40		
	28th	DH 82	R5039	F/Lt Hall	Self	6,7 and 9	-45		
	29th	DH 82	R5039	F/Lt Hall	Self	6,7 and 9	-20		
		DH 82	T5690	Sgt Males	Self	Solo test exercises:-			
						2 Effect of controls 3 Taxying 4 Straight and level flight 5 Gliding, climbing and stalling 6 Medium turns 7 Taxying into wind 8 Powered approach and landing 9 Gliding approach and landing Spins: 1 right 1 left	-40		
		DH 82	T5690	Self	——	FIRST SOLO	-	-10	

		DH 82	R5039	F/Lt Hall	Self	6, 7 and 9	-30		
		DH 82	R5039	Self	——	6, 7 and 9		1-05	
	31st	DH 82	G ADXT	F/Lt Hall	Self	6, 7, 8, 9 and 12	1-05		
		DH 82	G ADXT	Self		6, 7, 8, 9 and 12		1-25	
		DH 82	N-1077	Self		6, 7, 8, 9 and 12		-45	

7 October: In my logbook at this point is a pencilled note, as follows:–
Times at Desford
WEEK ENDING 4/10/40. 4 hours 50 minutes. A red stamp follows that says:
Certified correct, dated 5 Oct 1940 and signed by my instructor F/Lt Wardell, No.
7 EFTS. Desford.

29 October: Although we started out full of confidence, it still came as a surprise
when we achieved our first solo flight. On this day, after weeks of training, I made
the first flight of the day with F/Lt Hall, my usual instructor. There was nothing
untoward about it so it came as a surprise when, for my next flight, I was taken up by
Sgt Males who, although an NCO, was a very experienced instructor and he put me
through the complete list of exercises I had learned so far. After landing, we taxied
in to the dispersal point and he climbed out, leaving the engine running. To my
amazement he was holding the joystick (control column) from the second cockpit.
He shook it towards me and shouted, 'She's all yours; do one circuit and landing then
come in and switch off.' There is a song that originated in the Navy that starts:

'They say in the air force a landing's OK
If the pilot gets out and can still walk away.'

I could and I did – a wonderful feeling!
   On this day I had one more short flight with F/Lt Hall. He then sent me off again;
this time he had switched off and stopped the engine, so I had to go right through
the starting procedure before taking off for a solo flight of 1 hour and 5 minutes.
A wonderful day, I felt like one of the gods.
   Depending on possible previous experience (including manual dexterity
developed by an activity such as horse riding), most cadets would go solo in 12
to 14 hours, so my 14 hours 35 minutes was fairly average. 16 hours was crunch
time; those who had not made it by then were subjected to a CFI (Chief Flying
Instructor) Test, and his verdict was final. If he decided that a cadet was not going
to make the grade as a pilot, the unlucky chap would be offered a transfer to other
aircrew duties, i.e. navigator, observer, air gunner, radio operator and later the new
category of Flight Engineer. Refusal to accept usually resulted in a transfer to
ground duties. As far as I remember, roughly 10 per cent failed to clear this obstacle.

YEAR	1940	AIRCRAFT		Pilot or 1st Pilot	2nd Pilot, Pupil or Pass.	DUTY (Including Results and Remarks)	Flying Time		Passenger
MONTH	DATE	Type	No.				Dual	Solo	
November	1st	DH 82	G ADXT	F/Lt Hall	Self	12, 15 Steep turns and 16 Climbing turns	-55		
		DH 82	G ADXT	Self		12, 15 and 16		1-00	
		DH 82	G ADXT	Self		12, 15 and 16		-45	
		DH 82	G ADXT	Self		15 and 16		-20	
	2nd	DH 82	G ADXT	F/Lt Hall	Self	6, 7, 8 and 9	-10		
		DH 82	G ADXT	Self		6, 7 and 8		-50	
		DH 82	G ADXT	Self		15 and 16		-25	
	3rd	DH 82	G ADXT	F/Lt Hall	Self	19 Instrument Flying	-45		
		DH 82	R5109	Self		15 and 16		-50	
						GRAND TOTAL TO DATE 25 HOURS AND 35 MINUTES Signed By F/Lt W.E. Hall			
	5th	DH 82	N9272	F/Lt Hall	Self	12, 13, 17 Forced landing	-25		
		DH 82	N4475	Self		15 and 16		-50	
		DH 82	G AECT	Self		15 and 16		-50	
	7th	DH 82	G ADXT	F/Lt Hall	Self	12 Spins 1 left 1 right			
						17, 18 (action in the event of fire)			
						18A Abandoning aircraft			
						19 Instrument flying			
						21 Aerobatics		-40	
		DH 82	R5109	Self		10, 15, 16, 17 and 22		-55	
		DH 82	R5109	Self		10, 15, 16, 17 and 22		-55	
	8th	DH 82	R5109	F/Lt Hall	Self	Navigation	-50		
		DH 82	R5109	Self		15, 16, 17 and 22		1-20	
		DH 82	R5109	Self		15, 16 and 22		-45	
	13th	DH 82	R5109	F/Lt Hall	Self	13 Precautionary Landing	-10		
		DH 82	R5109	Self		10, 17 and 22		1-00	
		DH 82	R5109	Self		Cross Country Desford to Cosford		1-00	

Date	Type	Reg	Pilot	2nd Pilot	Duty		
	DH 82	R5109	Self		Cross Country Return to Desford		-35
	DH 82	R5109	Self		13, 15 and 22		1-00
14th	DH 82	R5109	F/Lt Hall	Self	19 Instrument Flying Turning on to and maintaining courses Spins:- 1 left 1 right	1-05	
	DH 82	R4946	F/Lt Hall	Self	14 low flying 20 taking off and landing crosswind	-40	
	DH 82	R4946	Self		13, 17 and 22		1-05
	DH 82	R5020	Self		13 and 22		-30
15th	DH 82	T7036	F/Lt Bamber	Self	19	-40	
	DH 82	T7036	F/Lt Bamber	Self	19	-40	
	DH 82	T7036	Self		10 and 22	-40	
	DH 82	G-ADOY	F/Lt Hall	Self	19 and 22	1-15	
	DH 82	G-ADOY	Self		10		55
	DH 82	G-ADOY	Self		10, 13, 17 and 22		1.00
16th	DH 82	R4900	F/Lt Hall		10, 17 and 22	-40	
	DH 82	R4900	Self				-30
	DH 82	R4900	Self				-50
					Instrument flying this month to date 4 Hours 10 minutes		

3 November: Through October and November there was no leave and the occasional day, or half day, off was spent locally. There were church parades on Sunday, otherwise just assemblies in the mornings, very relaxed, no 'bull'. There were infrequent visits to Desford village for a drink at the local pub, but these were not encouraged. Most of us were fairly short of cash or engaged in revision of lectures. There were also one or two evening trips to sample the wartime delights of Leicester. We had, of course, been given further lectures in personal hygiene and the dangers of VD, the ET (early treatment) room and how to use that little tube of ointment with the long, pointed nozzle.

It was after one of these trips to Leicester that three of us missed the last bus back to base. We had no alternative but to start walking the 10 miles back to Desford. When about halfway, foot sore and weary, a kindly motorist offered us a lift. It was only after our arrival at our quarters that we realised to our horror, that our benefactor was none other than the CFI (Chief Flying Instructor) F/ Lt Wardell. He pretended not to notice that we were cadets and said nothing but 'Good night'. We should, of course, have been back in camp by 2200 hours and it was then nearly midnight.

5 November: By this time the RAF's losses of fighter pilots in the battles over France, in the Dunquerque evacuation (operation Dynamo) and in the Battle of Britain, had become grave. Over 1,000 pilots were killed and many others were out of operation with wounds, burns, injuries from crashes and sheer fatigue. Most of these were pre-war trained, very experienced pilots. Replacements were a matter of great urgency and our flying training was stepped up to as many as six flights a day. (See 15 November.)

7 November: The flying lesson on this day was an exciting step forward. After running through various emergency procedures, I was given my first introduction to the joys of aerobatics. Incredibly, after just that one lesson, I was let loose to perform aerobatics on almost every following solo flight. As I remember, these in the Tiger Moth were limited to slow rolls right and left and straightforward loops. The rolls would have been really slow, around a level axis. I do not remember performing barrel rolls until much later and then probably by accident. In the perfect slow roll, when inverted, you would leave the seat and your weight would be taken by the shoulder straps or harness. It was therefore most important to ensure that the latter were properly tightened.

8 November: The next step forward was the navigation exercise on that day. Although only 50 minutes flying time it was the culmination of the many hours spent in the classroom. A destination having been selected, we had to complete a flight plan by laying out a line of flight on a map, allowing for wind speed and direction. We then calculated the compass direction, the IAS (indicated air speed) as shown on the ASI (air speed indicator), and the speed over the ground TAS (true air speed). Finally, we had to decide on the height at which we would fly and set the altimeter for air pressure at ground level.

13 November: Just five days after my dual navigation lesson came the high spot so far: I was trusted to fly solo to Cosford, land and check in to the duty officer in the control tower to record my safe arrival. Then refuel, take off again and return to Desford. Although it was only a distance of 30/35 miles, it felt wonderful to know that I could really fly alone, out of sight of the airfield.

There must have been quite a high head wind to account for the longer time on the outward flight. It should be borne in mind that the Tiger Moth cruised at only 75/80mph so a head wind would have made that much difference. I was filled with confidence that I could go anywhere I chose. Of course I had to give way to the urge to show off my prowess to my nearest family member, so two days later

I set a course of 290 degrees on the compass and flew the 20 or so miles, just over 20 minutes, to Streethay near Lichfield. I quickly located my elder brother's house and performed 10 minutes of aerobatics, slow rolls, a loop and a spin, and waved to my sister-in-law, Ivy, and my nephews, Terence and Robin. Leslie himself was, of course, in the RAF in India. Very pleased with myself, I returned to Desford. The trip was my secret but I always suspected that F/Lt Hall knew perfectly well where I had been.

16 November: Poor weather at the end of November curtailed our activities and terminated our flying at Desford. During the remainder of our time there, a matter of about a week, we took our examination in the ground subjects, with particular emphasis on navigation and instrument flying. Those cadets who failed or had failed their flying were 'washed out' and transferred to other duties. The lucky ones were transferred to further training in other aircrew categories.

17–25 November:
TOTAL HOURS

FLYING	SOLO	DUAL
	25-05	22-10
Instrument flying	4-10	
Proficiency as Pilot	*Average*	
To be assessed	Exceptional	
	Above average	
Ab initio as:-	Average	
	Below average	

Any special faults in flying which must be watched:-nil

Signed by	*J. W. A. Wardell* S/Ldr.
	Chief Flying Instructor.
	No.7 E.F.T.S. School
Date 17/11/40.	Desford

The one serious accident that I remember during the course involved a young man from Warwick or Leamington. He failed to recover from a spin and crashed into a wood near Leicester. I believe he was seriously injured and invalided out of the service. Bearing in mind that some days in October and November we had to contend with the early winter weather, it says a great deal for the quality of our instructors and the dedication of the members of our ground staff who serviced the aircraft, that we were able to complete the course in a little over six weeks.

On 30th November the Luftwaffe made their devastating bombing raid on Coventry, giving rise to the word 'Coventrated'. We stood on the airfield only six miles from the city and watched it all happen. Two days later I was given a weekend pass and decided to hitchhike the forty or so miles to Redditch to see my girlfriend Estelle Ludgate. There was very little chance of making the journey by public transport but I eventually got there, after many deviations for wrecked buildings and areas closed due to unexploded bombs. Searches were also continuing throughout the area for any inhabitants still alive but buried in the rubble.

Early in December I was posted to No. 9 SFTF (Service Flying Training School), Hullavington, Wiltshire, between the old towns of Malmesbury and Chippenham.

YEAR	1940	AIRCRAFT		Pilot or 1st Pilot	2nd Pilot, Pupil or Pass.	DUTY (Including Results and Remarks)	Flying Time		Passenger
MONTH	DATE	Type	No.				Dual	Solo	
December	11th	Miles Master	8402	Sgt Barrett	Self	6A Gliding turns with and without flaps	-55		
	12th	Miles Master	8402	Sgt Barrett	Self	5, 6, 7 and 8	-50		
	14th	Miles Master	8402	Sgt Barrett	Self	6, 7 and 8	-30		
		Miles Master	8386	Sgt Barrett	Self	6, 7 and 8	-50		
	17th	Miles Master	8386	Sgt Barrett	Self	6, 7, 8 and 8A Action in the event of overshooting	-45		
	22nd	Miles Master	8386	Sgt Barrett	Self	SOLO TEST	-15		
		Miles Master	8386	Sgt Barrett	Self	FIRST SOLO		-25	
	23rd	Miles Master	8386	Sgt Barrett	Self	15 and 23, Navigation	1-00		
	27th	Miles Master	8386	Sgt Barrett	Self	6, 7 and 8	-35		
	28th	Miles Master	8386	Self		6, 7, 8 and 15		-50	
		Miles Master	8386	Self		5 and 6 Gliding turns with and without flaps 8 Action in the event of overshooting 15 Steep Turns		-50	
		Miles Master	8386	Sgt Barrett	Self	5, 6, 7 and 8	-40		

22 December: For the training of those lucky enough to be chosen to become fighter pilots (every boy's ambition) our further training was on single-engine aircraft. The Miles Master was an all-wooden, low gull winged monoplane, powered by a Rolls-Royce Kestrel, liquid-cooled engine. Later versions were powered by the American Pratt and Whitney Wasp radial engine, as too were the American Harvard trainers which eventually took over the training role, particularly when the Empire training scheme came into being. The Master was a modern machine, a big step forward from the little Tiger Moth, with a retractable undercarriage, flaps and a controllable pitch airscrew. It was now that certain initial letters were imprinted in my heart and mind, indelible for ever. Before take-off:

TMPFFF standing for T – trim, M – mixture, P – pitch, F-fuel, F – flaps, and F – friction nut; these may be briefly explained:

T	trimming controls set neutral for take-off
M	mixture set rich
P	airscrew pitch of propeller fully fine
F	fuel on
F	flaps in the take off position (the Master did not require flaps for takeoff)
F	friction nut tightened to ensure that the throttle and pitch control was firmly held

After take-off a slightly different set of letters applied, UMPFFF:

U	undercarriage up and locked
M	Mixture set for flight
P	pitch set for flight
F	flaps up
F	fuel as before
F	friction nut loosened as required

Before landing, the same acronym, different meaning:

U	undercarriage down and locked
M	mixture rich
P	pitch fully fine
F	fuel as before (except that on some aircraft a particular tank had to be selected)
F	flaps down
F	friction nut tight

These letters were our bible and applied in varying form to all aircraft. (Do they still apply to modern jets or does a computer do it all?)

23 December: The two-day break for Christmas was very welcome and although there was not yet any snow, it was crisp and cold as Christmases used to be. I was invited to spend the holiday with my cousin Gladys Sawtell (née Fisher) and Geoff, her husband, at his family home in the country, near Bradford on Avon. He collected me at the main gate and I spent two very pleasant days with them. We had some excellent food and modest quantities of drinks but my main memory is of a very pretty young girl with the unusual name of 'Saramae'. It must have been the uniform and cadet flash that produced a real case of hero worship; she must have been all of 11 years old but it still made me feel good.

28 December: We cadets were billeted in an 'H' complex of wooden huts on the south side of the main quarters, away from the central buildings. The two uprights formed the dormitory areas, 'A' flight on one side and 'B' the other. The connecting bar housed the toilets. We had to rise at 6 a.m. and go to a nearby building for ablutions; it paid to be early before all the hot water had been used up. In the huts the only source of heating was a pot-bellied coke-burning stove. 1940/41 proved to be a very cold winter and fuel was in very short supply. We used to sneak out in the night to raid the station fuel dumps and it paid to be extremely careful because if caught the punishment was severe.

Apart from an iron-frame bed, we each had an upright plywood cupboard in which to keep spare clothes and personal belongings. These often included food and sweets and attracted various scavenging rodents. It was not unusual to wake in the night and find a rat sitting on one's chest, followed by a mad scramble of those nearby to catch and kill the offending creature; but they usually managed to escape.

We slept on 'biscuits', three square kapok (it used to be straw) filled mattresses. They were called palliasses. Each morning, before other duties, the sheets and blankets had to be folded in the exact manner laid down in regulations, placed on the three 'biscuits' laid at the head of the bed frame. Once a week there was an inspection by the duty officer and various service items, such as the 'hussif' (housewife) containing button and shoe cleaning items, etc. had to be placed exactly, ready to be checked. Woe betide any cadet who failed to meet the laid down standard or had anything missing.

Summary for:- December 1940   1 Miles Master
Unit:- No. 9 SFTS Hullavington
Date:- 1/1/41
Signature:- *G. Paul* F/Lt O/C 'A' Flight

We were given an occasional evening off, with an off-camp pass (we had to be back by 10 p.m., 22.00 hours). On one memorable evening, four of us went into Chippenham for a few drinks at one of the local pubs. Among our number was a very lively young Londoner, Benny Squires, a bit wild but great fun to be with. He was a talented mimic and leapt up on to one of the bar-room tables, with his hair brushed forward and a finger across his top lip. He gave a show of one of Adolf Hitler's speeches, raving and throwing his arms about, to general, although not universal, amusement.

On one or two evenings, particularly after I had acquired my first car, we went into Malmesbury for a few beers at a pub called The Bell. Benny was one of our party and one of his ideas of fun was to collect lavatory chains and the plugs from washbasins. On one such visit, towards the end of our time at Hullavington, he excelled himself. The pub sign was not one of the usual hanging shields but a handsome, highly polished, brass bell, about nine inches in diameter and quite heavy. On the way back to camp we were horrified when Benny pulled out the bell from under his tunic. Naturally, the people at The Bell were most upset and reported to the police that four cadets from Hullavington had stolen the bell. Our quarters were searched, so to prevent the SPs (Service Police) from finding it, Benny hid it in the roof space where the pot-bellied stove chimney went through the ceiling. It was not found then or later before we moved on. I wonder whether it was still there when the huts were demolished many years later. Benny completed the course and in April was awarded his wings but sadly, after joining a squadron, he was shot down and killed towards the end of 1941.

YEAR	1941	AIRCRAFT		Pilot or 1st Pilot	2nd Pilot, Pupil or Pass.	DUTY (Including Results and Remarks)	Flying Time		Passenger
MONTH	DATE	Type	No.				Dual	Solo	
January	1st	Miles Master	T8387	Sgt Barrett	Self	9 and 13	-35		
	2nd	Miles Master	T8390	Sgt Barrett	Self	7, 8 and 16	-25		
	3rd	Miles Master	T8390	Sgt Barrett	Self	10, 17 and 22	-55		
	5th	Miles Master	T8385	Self		9, 13 and 15		1-10	
	9th	Miles Master	T8400	Sgt Barrett	Self	17, Forced landing	-35		
	11th	Miles Master	T8389	Self		9, 13 and 17		-45	
		Miles Master	T8390	Sgt Porter	Self	19, Instrument flying	-30		
		Miles Master	T8390	Self		6, 7, 8, 15 and 16		-30	
	12th	Miles Master	T8393	Self		8, 15 and 16 10, Spinning		-30	
	13th	Miles Master	T8389	Self		13, 15 and 16		-45	
	14th	Miles Master	T8483	Self		13, 15 and 16		1-10	
	16th	Miles Master	T8385	F/Sgt Roberts	Self	20A, Night flying 6, Landings	1-00		

16 January: Night flying was one of the course highlights. At approximately 11 p.m. (23.00 hours) on a moonless night, we were taken in the three-ton Bedford pick-up trucks to Babdown Farm (near to where Prince Charles now lives at Highgrove). There were no electric landing lights, just a line of paraffin (kerosene) burning 'gooseneck' flares (ordinary steel watering cans with a length of rope stuffed down the spouts). See more about this later on April 7/8th.

Summary for:- January 1941   1. Master
Unit:- No.9 SFTS Hullavington   N/F 1.00
Date:- 1/2/41   Dual 3.00
Signature: - *G. Paul* F/Lt O/C 'A' Flight   Solo 4.50

In an earlier note I remarked that the winter weather was very severe, with much snow. We often had to clear it off the aircraft and muck in with the ground staff to clear the take-off paths (Hullavington had no runways at that time). When we were able to continue the training flights, it was a real pleasure to fly over snow-covered countryside, especially as Hullavington was towards the southern end of the Cotswold Hills. One notable landmark was the Fosse Way, the Roman road running north to south across the area.

For a period of three weeks there was almost no flying training, we concentrated on ground training and lectures. We had been introduced to the Link trainer during October while at Desford and during this period of bad weather the 'Link' kept us in touch with flying. Although I was assessed as average on it, I never really took to the Link but it certainly served a very useful purpose. It is still used today as a simulator for modern aircraft but is greatly improved and much more realistic than those early machines.

One dark and dismal morning we received a sharp reminder that there was a war on. A Heinkel 111 bomber came from the west out of low cloud; he dropped a stick of bombs in a line parallel with the hangars, at the same time spraying the area with machine-gun fire. When the air-raid warning siren sounded, all of us brave young budding fighter pilots made a rush for the nearest air shelter. A number of Tiger Moths of the EFTS on the far side of the airfield were destroyed and two of our Masters were damaged. I cannot remember if there were any casualties but we cadets escaped with a severe fright. The Luftwaffe aircraft was brought down by ground fire and crashed near Bath between the villages of Box and Corsham.

| YEAR | 1941 | AIRCRAFT | | Pilot or 1st Pilot | 2nd Pilot, Pupil or Pass. | DUTY (Including Results and Remarks) | Flying Time | | Passenger |
MONTH	DATE	Type	No.				Dual	Solo	
February	3rd	Miles Master	T8385	Sgt Nutter	Self	6, 7, 8, 13 and 19 (IF.)	-50		
	6th	Miles Master	T8387	Self		7, 8, 15, 16 and 17		-45	
		Miles Master	T8387	Self		7 and 8		-10	
	12th	Miles Master	T8483	P/O Roberts	Self	Formation positions 1, 2 and 3	1-30		
	14th	Miles Master	T8383	Sgt Nutter	Self	19, Instrument flying	1-00		
		Miles Master	T8483	Self		13 and 17		1-05	

	15th	Miles Master	T8387	Self		8, 13, 15, 16 and 17		1-05	
		Miles Master	T8387	P/O Roberts	Self	23, Navigation	1-20		
						Grand total to date: 72 hours 15 minutes			

6 February: The flight on February 6th was cut short by bad weather. Note that F/Sgt Roberts was commissioned at the end of January.

Summary for:– February   1. Master 4–40 dual

Unit:– No.9 SFTS Hullavington   3.05 solo

Date:– 28/2/41

Signature:– *B.B. Hallowes* pp O/C 'A' Flight

YEAR	1941	AIRCRAFT		Pilot or 1st Pilot	2nd Pilot, Pupil or Pass.	DUTY (Including Results and Remarks)	Flying Time		Passenger
MONTH	DATE	Type	No.				Dual	Solo	
March	6th	Miles Master	T86468	P/O Roberts	Self	7 and 8	-30		
		Miles Master	T8468	Self		7 and 8		-50	
	9th	Miles Master	T8385	P/O Roberts	Self	19, Instrument flying	-50		
	13th	Miles Master	T8385	Self		Navigation test		1-15	
		Hurricane	3116	Self		7 and 8 FIRST SOLO		-30	
	14th	Miles Master	T8401	Self	LAC Cadet John Timmis	19, Instrument flying "under the hood"		-45	
		Miles Master	T8401	LAC Timmis	Self	19, Safety pilot	-45		
	15th	Hurricane	3807	Self		7, 8, 13, 15 and 16		1-00	
		Miles Master	T8390	P/O Roberts	Self	22 and 19	1-10		
	16th	Miles Master	T8390	P/O Roberts	Self	Formations in positions 1, 2 and 3	-45		
	18th	Miles Master	T8400	F/Sgt Rowney	Self	19, Instrument flying	-25		
		Miles Master	T8385	F/Lt Paul	Self	Formation	-45		
	19th	Hurricane	3320	Self		15 and 16		-45	

		Miles Master	T8483	P/O Roberts	Self	22, Aerobatics and 19	1-10	
	20th	Miles Master	T8375	P/O Roberts	Self	Instrument flying Cross country (No. 2)	-55	
	21st	Miles Master	T8404	LAC Stevens	Self	10, Safety pilot		1-00
		Miles Master	T8404	Self	LAC Stevens	10, Instrument flying	1-00	
		Miles Master	T8404	LAC Drinkwater	Self	Safety pilot		-50
		Miles Master	T8404	Self	LAC Drinkwater	Instrument flying	-45	
		Miles Master	T8404	Self		Cross country	1-30	
		Miles Master	T8404	Self	LAC Drinkwater	19, Instrument flying	-30	
	22nd	Miles Master	T8401	Self		13, Precautionary landing		-55
		Miles Master	T8404	Self		Formation		-45
	23rd	Miles Master	T8401	P/O Russell	Self	6, 7 and 8	-45	
		Hurricane	3211	Self		Formation		-55
	25th	Hurricane	3211	Self		Formation		-45
	26th	Miles Master	T8391	P/O Rowley	Self	Formation flying		-40
		Miles Master	T8393	P/O Rowley	Self	Formation flying		-4-
		Miles Master	T8387	P/O Harding	Self	Formation flying		-30
		Hurricane	3211	Self		Formation flying as leader		-45
		Hurricane	1742	Self		Formation flying		-45
	27th	Hurricane	2548	Self		Cross country No. 2		1-30
	30th	Miles Master	T8482	Self		Cross country No. 3		1-50
		Miles Master	T8375	P/O Roberts	Self	20a, Night flying, 5, Landings	-50	
		Miles Master	T8375	Self		20a, Night flying, 5, Landings		-30
	31st	Hurricane	3807	Self		Use of radio, air to ground		-35

13 March: Up to this time in the RAF, advanced training after going solo on the Miles Master had been carried out on the obsolete Hawker Hart biplane. Due to the urgent need for newly trained fighter pilots as replacements for those lost the previous year and to man the many newly formed squadrons, our No.28 course was the subject of a drastic (or dramatic) experiment. After only a few hours, in my case 4 hours 5 minutes, I soloed in the Master. After a further 10 hours of solo training I, like the other cadets, transferred straight on to a front line fighter, the renowned Hawker Hurricane, for the remainder of my solo training.

This drastic step resulted in a crop of minor accidents and some more serious ones; three resulted in fatalities. One of these was an army captain who had transferred to the RAF and another was one of the group of Indian Air Force officers who were members of the course.

In an attempt to tighten up, and bring about an improvement, the CFI instituted a 'black list' displayed in the operations tent. It was my bad luck to be the first to qualify for my name to head the list after holding off a little too high when landing. The Hurricane stalled when still a few feet from the ground, dropped the starboard wing, which brushed the ground, and was slightly damaged. Other names followed but the idea backfired, causing a drop in morale and a loss of confidence. The list was dropped but it had in fact brought about an improvement.

14 March: For instrument flying practice the pupil in the rear cockpit was 'under the hood', a cowl which pulled forward totally enclosing the cockpit. Initially one of the instructors occupied the front cockpit but as the course advanced another cadet would act as safety pilot (see March 21st). On one of these flights I was 'under the hood' flying blind completely on instruments. My safety pilot must have taken a nap as, when my time was up, I emerged into daylight and to my horror found we were in the middle of the Wolverhampton balloon barrage. By the grace of God we escaped unscathed but my comments to the other cadet are unprintable.

21 March: When acting as 'safety pilot' our flying time was booked as passenger, when actually we had to remain alert and in control. I see, in my mind's eye, those other young men as they were 66 or so years ago.

26 March: Our early lessons in formation flying were based on what was known as VEE or VIC formation:

```
              X
            XXXXX
    X         X         X
  XXXXX       X       XXXXX
    X                   X
    X                   X
```

The tight VEE formation left little chance of watching our tails, the direction from which the most lethal of enemy attacks came. A relic of World War 1, it was continued until 1940 by the RAF. As a result many of our aircraft were unnecessarily lost. By mid-1941, when I joined a squadron, the lesson had been learned the hard way and the outdated VEE gave way to the 'finger four' used so successfully by the Luftwaffe fighters:

X

X   X

X

In the open 'finger four' the aircraft were well apart, allowing all pilots to weave back and forth to maintain a constant watch to the rear and also to allow individual freedom of action.

27 March: The cross-country No. 1 was from base to a single destination and return with or without landing. Cross-country No. 2 would have been a triangular course and No.3 a rectangle. On one of these cross-country trips I acted as leader and flew to Poletrees Farm between Bicester and Aylesbury, the home of my younger sister, Gwen, and my mother. When I made one or two low passes, Mother appeared, waving her apron and, according to Gwen, shouting, 'Get up Len! Get up Len!' My brother-in-law, Joe Cooper, always swore that on one pass I almost knocked him off the hayrick that he was building.

Summary for:- March 1941   1. Master N/F -50 mins
Unit:- No. 9 SFTS. Hullavington   Master Day 8-30
Date:- 1/4/41   2. Hurricane 7-30
Signature:- *G. Paul* F/Lt O/C 'X' Flight

YEAR	1941	AIRCRAFT		Pilot or 1st Pilot	2nd Pilot, Pupil or Pass.	DUTY	Flying Time		Passenger
MONTH	DATE	Type	No.				Dual	Solo	
April	5th	Miles Master	T8434	F/O Davies	Self	WINGS TEST		2-10	
	6th	Miles Master	T8484	P/O Harding	Self	10, IF take off (1)	-30		
	7th	Miles Master	T8833	P/O Harding	Self	19, Instrument flying	-20		
		Miles Master	T8837	P/O Harding	Self	19, IF take off (1)	-15		
		Miles Master	T8837	Self		13, 15 and 17		1-45	
		Miles Master	T8444	P/O Harding	Self	20A, NF, 7 landings		1-10	

		Miles Master	T8444	Self		20A, NF, 2 landings		-10	
	8th	Miles Master	T8376	P/O Russell	Self	20A, NF, 2 landings	-30		
		Miles Master	T8376	Self		2 70A, NF, 4 landings		1-00	
		Miles Master	T8392	Self		7		-15	
	9th	Miles Master	T8404	P/O Mehta	Self	8 IF 'under the hood'	-15		
		Miles Master	T8404	Self		Safety pilot	-45		
	10th	Hurricane	7444	Self		R/T air to ground and air to air	-40		
		Miles Master	T8404	Self		Instrument flying		-50	
		Miles Master	T8404	P/O Dutt	Self	Safety pilot		-40	
	11th	Hurricane	1742	Self		Formation		1-30	
	12th	Miles Master	T8834	Self		13, precautionary landing and formation		1-30	
		Miles Master	T8538	Self		13, 15 and 16		1-40	
		Miles Master	T8736	F/Lt Barrett	Self	CFI. Test. The big one!	-35		
		Miles Master	T8381	Self		Formation		1-25	
	13th	Miles Master	T8404	Self		13, 15, 16 and 17		1-35	
		Miles Master	T8385	P/O Roberts	Self	Advanced formation	1-45		
		Miles Master	T8538	Self		13, precautionary landing		1-10	
						Night flying	3-30	1-40	
						Day flying	54-00	60-50	3-30
	25th	Miles Master	T8635	Sgt Wynn	Self	Local reconnaissance	-45		
		Miles Master	T8635	Self		Local reconnaissance		-15	
	26th	Spitfire	AG	Self		FIRST SOLO, Local reconnaissance		1-10	
	27th	Miles Master	T8635	Sgt Wynn	Self	Circuits and landings	-25		
	29th	Miles Master	T7985	Sgt Wynn	Self	Circuits and landings	-15		

		Miles Master	T7833	Self		Circuits and landings	-40	
		Miles Master	T7833	Self		Circuits and landings	-40	
		Miles Master	T7833	Self		Circuits and landings	-50	
	30th	Spitfire	AB	Self		Circuits and landings	-50	

5 April: My 'wings test' on this date was, to say the least, interesting! P/O Davies was, I believe, another of those officers who had themselves been trainees only two or three courses earlier. The 'wings test' was a three-leg cross-country flight, from base to a map reference in the hills of South Wales, using a normal map. The second leg was to a point somewhere near Northampton, with only a map circle of 10 miles radius. From there we had to set course and fly by instruments and dead reckoning back to base. It happened that on this day the weather was extremely poor but considered good enough to make the test flight. Setting out in rain and low cloud, together with poor visibility, we were not too sure that we correctly identified the point in one of the South Wales valleys. We pressed on but got lost on the middle leg and failed to hit the map circle. After reaching our ETA (estimated time of arrival), we turned back and my instructor told me to land on any airfield we spotted. Sure enough, an airfield appeared and I landed, narrowly missing a steam-roller! We found that it was a new field under construction, with only the contractor's workmen in sight. They told us where we were so we took off and, at the right ETA, landed back at Hullavington. As no one there knew the true facts, we 'cooked the books' and so I passed my test.

7 April: Although not recorded, I believe that our night flying on April 7th was at a small grass airfield near Castle Combe, alleged to be the prettiest village in England, whilst that on the 30th March was at Babdown Farm. On the latter date a Luftwaffe bomber, I recollect that it was again a Heinkel 111, dived across the landing area and machine-gunned the line of goose-neck flares, causing no damage. Fortunately, he dropped no bombs; otherwise the story might have had a different ending. Night flying was perhaps the most dangerous part of our training but most of us thoroughly enjoyed it. The highlight of the proceedings was a midnight breakfast by lamplight, bangers, bacon, eggs, baked beans and chips in abundance. As the weather improved, the pressure increased to get us into operational readiness. The number of flights per day was stepped up, my record being five on April 7th.

10 April: I can truthfully say that after my wings test on April 5th I never got lost again although I frequently called flying control for a homing, i.e. a magnetic bearing to base. It was usually laziness on my part, although it was always welcomed by the WAAF plotters and flying control officers. The young ladies of the WAAF staff got a lift from hearing the voices of their heroes, the young and dashing 'Brylcreme boys'. Much later, in 1943/44, when flying test missions, I had several emergencies and had to call for priority landing. My friend F/O Vic Merritt said that he always recognised my call, so quiet and calm whatever the circumstances; little did he know!

P/O Mehta and P/O Dutt were two of the Indian Air Force officers who were with us on course No.28. The Sikhs stood out particularly, as they wore their usual turbans but in pale air force blue, with the small wing emblems on the side.

12 April: This was the final flying test, on the results of which we were awarded those coveted silver wings.

13 April: In my logbook opposite the final entry for April 13th is a pencilled note: 'My 21st. birthday & my wings.' During that afternoon, the successful cadets attended the 'Wings Parade' and that eagerly awaited wings badge was pinned to our tunics, for me to wear with pride for the following seven years. What a 21st birthday present.

Summary for:- April 1941	Master: N/F	1-40	1-10
Unit: No.9 EFTS	Master: Day	4-35	10-10
Date: 13/4/41	Hurricane:		2-10
Signature: *G. Paul* F/Lt			

Summary for: N.28 Course 1941	Master: N/F	3-30	1-40
Unit: No.9 SFTS	Master: Day	28-55	29-00
Date: 13/4/1941	Hurricane:		9-40
Signature: *G. Paul* F/Lt			

Proficiency	
as Pilot	Average
On Type.	
To be assessed:	Exceptional,
Above the average,	Average,
	Below average

Any special faults which must be watched: Nil

SIGNED:- *T.A.BIRT*
G/Cpt. O/C
No. 9 SFTS RAF Hullavington
Date: 16/4/1941

GRAND TOTAL TO DATE   120 hours 0 minutes
I certify that LAC Thorne has had 10.40 hours instruction and has completed
the General Instrument Flying Course on the Link Trainer with the exception of
Exercises
A.C. Wilson F/Lt   Date: 16/4/41

Following the presentation of my wings another welcome event took place: I
was promoted to the rank of Sergeant, a welcome step forward. During the initial
training period at Babbacombe RW (Receiving Wing) and at Torquay ITW (Initial
Training Wing), we cadets had the rank of AC2 (Aircraftsman Second Class),
popularly known as the lowest form of animal life in the RAF. The pay was two
shillings (10p) per day. We were permitted to make an allotment of not more than
50% to a dependent relative, which was matched by the Air Ministry. Mother, a
widow, therefore received two shillings a day, most of which she saved to help me in
my moments of need.

On commencement of flying training we were promoted to the rank of LAC
(Leading Aircraftsman) with a pay increase to three shillings and nine pence per
day. Promotion to the rank of Sergeant brought a much greater increase to twelve
shillings and sixpence per day, about £4/7/6d per week. On top of this our
uniforms, flying clothing, food and accommodation were provided by the service.
Suddenly we were rich!

Gaining our wings marked the end of our SFTS training at Hullavington. We
were granted a seven-day leave to go home in order to show off our stripes and
wings; in my case I went first to visit Mother and sister Gwen at Poletrees Farm
with trips into Aylesbury and my home village of Waddesdon. Two days later I
travelled on to Redditch to see fiancée Estelle and visit members of her family.
Of course, with my bright new wings in evidence everyone treated me as if I was
already an Ace, all of which was wonderful.

The seven days passed quickly and my orders came through to report to No.
57 OTU (Operational Training Unit), at Hawarden near Chester. At this time
Hawarden was an all-grass airfield with, on the south side, a Vickers Armstrong
factory where first Wellington and later Stirling bombers were assembled.
Conditions were not ideal for Spitfires so, after one or two flights in Miles Masters,
most of our training was done at nearby aerodromes.

26 April: After two refresher flights in a Miles Master we were considered to be
sufficiently experienced to be let loose in a Spitfire, a day that will stay in my memory
for as long as I live, the culmination of all those months of training. There were no
two-seaters in those days; an experienced instructor saw us seated comfortably in the
cockpit, first to ensure that our parachute was properly fitted and the straps good and
tight, safety straps done up and tightened, secondly to check that radio and oxygen
were plugged in, and we were all set to go. The instructor stood on the wing and
explained the controls, the take-off and landing speeds, then off you went.

As our airfield at Hawarden was out of action due to a heavy smoke pall and poor visibility following the heavy bombing raids on the Mersey towns of Birkenhead and Liverpool, we travelled by coach through the Mersey tunnel to Speke, then a small grass airfield on the north bank of the river some four or five miles east of Liverpool.

The take-off run was slightly downhill towards the river. When safely airborne it was necessary to retract the undercarriage by placing the selection lever in the up position. There were no hydraulics in the early (Mk 1) Spitfires so the pilot had to use a hand pump, a long cranked lever on the right side of the cockpit. To do this he had to change hands, operating the control column with the left hand, having tightened the throttle friction nut. Meanwhile he worked the pump with his right hand. This resulted in a take-off rather like a kangaroo; incredibly, we all made it safely. A steady circuit of the airfield, then back for my first Spitfire landing, a curved, semi-glide, final approach to keep the landing path in sight past that long nose. Level out, ease throttle closed and the touchdown proved easy. Prior to the actual landing we put into use those letters so carefully learned: U – undercarriage down and locked, M – mixture full rich, P – pitch fully fine, F – fuel on, F – flaps down (a Spitfire used full flap for landing), and F – friction nut loosened for easy throttle control movements. The Spitfire flew like a dream and despite the narrow undercarriage, landed without any problems. A few more sessions of landing practice in a Master (circuits and bumps), then it was Spitfire all the way. At long last I really felt like a fighter pilot.

YEAR	1941	AIRCRAFT		Pilot or 1st Pilot	2nd Pilot, Pupil or Pass.	DUTY (Including Results and Remarks)	Flying Time		Passenger
MONTH	DATE	Type	No.				Dual	Solo	
May	1st	Spitfire	AO	Self		Navigation		1-10	
	3rd	Spitfire	AB	Self		Height test to 25,000ft		1-10	
		Spitfire	AO	Self		Ranging		1-30	
	9th	Spitfire	AB	Self		Formation		1-30	
	10th	Spitfire	AI	Self		Formation		1-10	
	11th	Spitfire	AA	Self		Ranging		1-00	
	12th	Spitfire	CB	Self		Circuits and landings		1-10	
		Spitfire	CB	Self		Formation		1-25	
	13th	Spitfire	CV	Self		Formation		1-25	
		Miles Master	T8044	Self	Sgt Ingle	Instrument flying		-50	
		Miles Master	T8044	Self	Sgt Ingle	Safety pilot, instrument flying		-50	
	16th	Spitfire	CY	Self		Formation		1-30	
		Spitfire	CA	Self		Formation		1-30	
	17th	Spitfire	CA	Self		Formation		1-35	

	20th	Miles Master	J	Self	F/Lt Baldie	Ferrying		-20	
		Spitfire	CJ	Self		Formation		1-30	
	21st	Spitfire	CG	Self		Aerobatics and low flying		1-25	
		Spitfire	B(CJ)	Self		Formation and ranging		1-20	
	22nd	Spitfire	CH	Self		Formation		1-20	
		Miles Master	B	Self	Sgt Garden	Map reading		1-20	
	24th	Spitfire	CJ	Self		Formation and target for camera gun practice		1-20	
		Spitfire	CG	Self		Formation, cross country and camera gun practice		1-25	
	25th	Spitfire	CD	Self		Formation and aerobatics		1-20	
		Spitfire	CD	Self		Formation and camera gun practice and evasive action		1-30	
	26th	Spitfire	CA	Self		Formation and aerobatics		1-30	
		Spitfire	CC	Self		Formation		-25	
	27th	Spitfire	CD	Self		Ranging practice		1-10	
	29th	Spitfire	CJ	Self		Formation and aerobatics		1-25	

3 May: This was my first experience of climbing to a height above 4 or 5,000 feet and my first use of oxygen.

13 May: When we were 'comfortable' in a Spitfire the training was increasingly aimed at operational needs, hence lots of formation flying (sadly still the obsolete VIC formation, battle climbs, air drill, etc.) We all agreed that the 'Spit' was a delight to fly, a lady with no vices. Care was needed when taxiing on the ground, due to the narrow undercarriage and poor visibility past the long nose. With the small radiator, overheating was always a problem. It was vital not to hang about once the engine was running but to get airborne as soon as possible. The joy of flying, particularly in a Spitfire, is well described in the poem 'High Flight' by John Gillespie Magee Jnr: 'Oh! I have slipped the surly bonds of earth/And danced the skies on laughter-silvered wings'.

21 May: Although my logbook entries show very few aerobatic sessions, it is misleading. On most flights, in the spirit of joie de vivre, we threw our willing steeds through the air. I well remember flying along the North Wales coast, doing continuous slow rolls, left and right alternately.

26 May: Following the first of the two flights on the 26th I made a mistake and collected the following endorsement:

BLUE ENDORSEMENT Landed down wind.
Signed by J.R. Dunsworth S/Ldr
CFI. 57 O.T.U.   dated 31/5/41.

At this time we were using the small airfield at Sealand, normally an EFTS operating Tiger Moths. On a windless day I had taken off from West to East. Returning after some exhilarating aerobatics, I failed to note that the 'Landing Tee' had been changed through 180 degrees and landed the same way I had taken off. I finished my landing run among the Tigers! Fortunately I missed them all and no damage was done, except to my reputation and ego.

| YEAR | 1941 | AIRCRAFT | | Pilot or 1st Pilot | 2nd Pilot, Pupil or Pass. | DUTY (Including Results and Remarks) | Flying Time | | Passenger |
MONTH	DATE	Type	No.				Dual	Solo	
June	1st	Spitfire	CJ	Self		Formation and battle climb		1-10	
	2nd	Spitfire	CM	Self		Formation		-35	
	3rd	Spitfire	CL	Self		Formation and air drill		1-45	
		Spitfire	CD	Self		Formation		1-30	
		Spitfire	CN	Self		Formation		-40	
	4th	Spitfire	CD	Self		Formation, battle climb and air drill		1-40	
	5th	Spitfire	CJ	Self		Formation, Sealand to Hawarden		-10	
	7th	Spitfire	CC	Self		Formation attack and evasive action		1-20	
		Spitfire	CK	Self		Formation and dog fighting		1-30	
		Spitfire	FI	Self		Air firing, air to ground		-25	
							3-30	1-40	
							55-25	110-25	4-40

7 June:
Unit 57 OTU. Hawarden
Summary for May/June 1941   Master   1-25   5-05
                                   Spitfire   44-30
Signed:- *H.L. Thorne* Sgt

| O/C 'C' Flt Summary for 20 Course | Master | 1-25 | 5-05 |
| | Spitfire | | 44-30 |

Signed:- *H.L. Thorne* Sgt

Signed:- *J.W. Baldie* F/Lt O/C 'C' Flight
       J.R. Dunsworth S/Ldr. O/C Training 57 OTU

This concluded my training as a fighter pilot. It seems incredible now that only on the final flight, that on June 7th, did I experience firing the eight machine guns and then only air to ground. On the same day I had my one and only lesson in dog fighting. Perhaps even more unbelievable is that I had only 1 hour 40 minutes flying solo at night and that in a Miles Master trainer within sight of the flarepath. On joining 41 Squadron, on June 12th, I was ordered off for a night reconnaissance of the Catterick sector. My Spitfire was fully armed and operational in case I ran across the odd German bomber. We had only the old TR9 radio with poor reception and limited range and, apart from the magnetic compass, no navigation aids. It still seems absolutely amazing that we supremely confident youngsters got safely back to our bases. Of course there were some who were not so lucky.

At OTU most instructors were veterans of the Battle of Britain just a few months earlier, on rest from their battle experiences or recovering after being wounded or injured in crashes. Some of them still showed the stress and trauma of their operations. They taught me as much as time permitted, to improve my flying and how to hold my own in combat; they also taught me to play bridge.

Having a car made me popular with the other cadets and I made particular friends with four of them. Ron Rayner came from Manchester and being quite near, we spent a weekend with Ron's parents. Desmond O'Connor (Dessie) came from the north of England and was a quiet, likeable youngster. Later we both became members of 602 Squadron and I was most upset when in the hard fought battles of the next year, on March 8th, he was shot down; later it was confirmed that he had died. Ronnie Rayner and I first joined 41 Squadron at their home base of Catterick, although my stay there was only two months. Ron remained with the squadron and after a full tour was posted to Malta and North Africa. He converted back to Hurricanes and later still went to Yugoslavia, instructing Tito's airmen. He was awarded the DFC and survived the war. Ron passed away in 2001.

John Niven joined 602 squadron straight from OTU, like me as a sergeant. He and Jimmie Garden were both Scotsmen. Johnnie was commissioned early in 1942 and became my flight commander in 'A' Flight. He survived being shot down later in the war and was, I believe, badly wounded. Awarded a DFC, he attained the rank of squadron leader, but some years after the war he, like Ron, developed heart trouble. We met at the Hendon RAF Air Museum in 1976 and he invited Estelle and me to visit him at his home in Inverness but he died before we could take up the invitation.

2

41 SQUADRON, HOME BASE CATTERICK

| YEAR | 1941 | AIRCRAFT | | Pilot or 1st Pilot | 2nd Pilot, Pupil or Pass. | DUTY (Including Results and Remarks) | Flying Time | | Passenger |
MONTH	DATE	Type	No.				Dual	Solo	
June	11th	Spitfire	B	Self		Local reconnaissance		1-30	
		Spitfire	D	Self		Air firing; Air to ground		-55	
	12th	Spitfire	E	Self		Night flying. Local		-25	
		Spitfire	C	Self		Squadron formation		-55	
		Spitfire	D	Self		Formation and DF homing		-35	
		Spitfire	D	Self		Night flying. Circuits and landings		-35	
	13th	Spitfire	D	Self		Night flying test		-10	
	14th	Spitfire	H	Self		Formation and cloud flying		1-10	
		Spitfire	H	Self		Local flying		-25	
	15th	Spitfire	H	Self		Cloud formation and dog fighting		-50	
		Spitfire	H	Self		Squadron formation and climbs		1-3-	
		Spitfire	H	Self		NIGHT FLYING. Circuits and landings		1-00	
	16th	Spitfire	D	Self		Aerobatics		1-05	
		Spitfire	D	Self		Squadron formation to Acklington		-30	
		Spitfire	D	Self		Air firing		-25	
		Spitfire	D	Self		Acklington to base		-30	
	17th	Spitfire	D	Self		Night flying, Army co-operation		1-20	
		Spitfire	D	Self		Formation to Leeming. Crashed on landing		-10	
	18th	Spitfire	G	Self		Night flying test		-10	

	19th	Spitfire	G	Self		Night flying. Army co-operation		1-45	
		Spitfire	G	Self		Night flying test		-20	
	20th	Spitfire	C	Self		Air test		-45	
	21st	Spitfire	C	Self		Squadron formation and climb		1-05	
	22nd	Spitfire	F	Self		Night flying. Army co-operation		-55	
		Spitfire	F	Self		Night flying. Army co-operation		-40	
		Spitfire	C	Self		Camera gun attacks on Spinning		-55	
	23rd	Spitfire	C	Self		Army co-operation		1-10	
		Spitfire	C	Self		Cloud flying and Spinning		1-05	
	24th	Spitfire	C	Self		To forward base (Thornaby)		-25	
		Spitfire	C	Self		Return to Catterick		-15	
	25th	Spitfire	C	Self		Army co-operation		1-15	
		Spitfire	C	Self		Authorised 'beat-up' of Gun posts at Leeming		-25	
		Spitfire	C	Self		Formation and cloud flying		-50	
	26th	Spitfire	C	Self		Squadron formation		1-00	
		Spitfire	C	Self		To forward base		-10	
		Spitfire	C	Self		Return to Catterick		-10	
		Spitfire	C	Self		Catterick to Redhill		1-15	
		Spitfire	C	Self		Operational sweep		2-00	
	28th	Spitfire	C	Self		'Flap', an operational Scramble		-30	
		Spitfire	C	Self		Redhill to Catterick		1-15	
	29th	Spitfire	D	Self		Aerobatic		1-05	
	30th	Spitfire	D	Self		To forward base		-10	
		Spitfire	D	Self		Return to Catterick		-10	
		Spitfire	D	Self		Flap Scramble		1-00	
		Spitfire	D	Self		Flap Scramble		-55	

11 June: I do not remember firing at a towed drogue target; we just pointed the aircraft's nose and fired out to sea.

12 June: The letters DF stood for direction finding, in this instance by a short radio transmission (we usually counted up to 10 but some chaps used their own variations, 'Mary had a little lamb' being popular). This was my first experience of calling control for a homing to base.

15 June: At Catterick our Squadron Leader was Donald Finlay, a time serving regular airman who had trained as an engineer at Halton near Aylesbury. Donald was a natural, enthusiastic athlete and a member of the pre-war British Olympic team as one of the hurdlers. As can be seen from the logbook entries he worked us hard at Catterick and when not flying there was plenty of PT with cross-country runs in the fields adjoining the airfield.

16 June: This really was my only experience of firing at a towed drogue target. I presume that I must have hit it, as the exercise was not repeated (or perhaps I hit the towing aircraft).

17 June: My night flight was as a target for searchlight units carrying out radar calibration. In anticipation of our brief visit to Redhill we flew to Leeming Bar to exchange our Spitfire Mk 2s, with the original armament of only 8 x .303 machine guns, for Spitfire Mk Vs, which had two x 20mm cannons in addition to the four machine guns.

The squadron commander decided that we would show off by arriving at Leeming in squadron formation and land in pairs. My section leader made his final approach too low over an earth bank (due to the runway being under construction) and when concentrating on maintaining station, I hit the earth bank, leaving my wheels stuck in the top. I made a wheels-up (belly) landing on the grass with surprisingly little damage.

18 June: In addition to the improved armament, the Spit. Mk Vb had other improvements. The much more powerful Rolls-Royce Merlin 45 engine gave a higher speed and a service ceiling close to 40,000 feet. Another great improvement was the introduction of TR9 radio, which was very clear and covered our flights well into France and Belgium.

21 June: About this time I was introduced to the use of oxygen. It was a standing order that, when we intended to fly above 15,000 feet, we breathed pure oxygen through our face masks. If we operated above 25,000 feet we had to go on to oxygen from ground level upwards.

22 June: On these army co-operation exercises we flew fully armed, ready to be vectored (directed) into an interception if an enemy aircraft was detected.

24 June: For much of my time at Catterick I flew the same Spitfire – C for Charlie. Many of our flights at this time were spent patrolling over the towns and cities of the North East coast, partly as an extension of our OTU training and partly to restore the confidence of those pilots who had been through the mill in the Battle of Britain. The pilots of 41 Squadron were a very mixed bunch; as well as men from all the home counties we had two Australians, one New Zealander and one young Dutchman.

A flight of two Spitfires was maintained on full readiness at all times, armed and ready to go, as we fully expected the Germans to resume their onslaught on Britain. We took turns to take on this duty and I was paired with Sergeant Frank Usmar. He was popularly known as 'Itma', after Tommy Handley's radio comedy programme. (I.T.M.A. stood for 'It's that man again'). We flew to a forward base nearer to the coast, usually Thornaby, ready to do or die. It was lovely summer weather, so we sat around near our own aircraft, wearing our bright yellow life jackets (Mae Wests), with parachutes and helmets ready to hand. There was a river, the Tees, along one side of the airfield and the area abounded with rabbits at which we potted with a .22 rifle. It says something for our fighter pilots' skill that I do not remember that we ever hit one.

It was during my flight on the night of June 24th that I had my first brush with death. The weather was clear when I took off but fog rolled in from the sea and blanketed Catterick and all local airfields. Things looked really bad and baling out became a strong possibility. Flying control homed me into the Catterick circuit and at this point the squadron commander, Donald Finlay, took up a position in the runway control hut. With the help of main control and the sound of my Spitfire, he talked me down to a safe landing. He almost certainly saved my life that night, so – thank you Donald.

As well as Thornaby we sometimes used Middleton-St George, near Darlington, at what is now Teeside Airport, as forward base.

26 June: I believe 'Squadron formation' was our first practice of the 'finger four' formation in readiness for our coming first operation over enemy territory.

'Operational sweep' was my first operation over enemy-held territory. 41 Squadron augmented the Kenley Wing in conjunction with Biggin Hill, Tangmere and North Weald Wings. Twelve squadrons of fighters escorted one squadron of 12 Bristol Blenheim light bombers to attack road and rail junctions near St. Omer in Northern France. The close escort wing flew Hurricanes and the Kenley Wing flew escort cover. For the first time I saw enemy flak some way in front, in bursts coloured red, blue and green. We learned later this was 'marker' flak, which indicated our position to enemy fighters. As it happened, no enemy fighters were seen. On the 27th, happy and confident with our new Spitfire Mk Vb's, we flew to Redhill in Surrey, part of 11 Group in the south of England. At this time it was the only way we could carry the fight to the Germans. We had been disappointed not to meet the Messerschmitt 109s. We learned later that they were fully occupied by Operation Barbarossa, the German invasion of Russia. We had fully expected to engage in aerial combat but had to wait another four weeks and a change of squadron for that 'pleasure'.

28 June: Enemy aircraft had been reported off the South Coast, our squadron was scrambled to attempt an interception. It proved to be a false alarm and we were told to 'pancake' (land again).

30 June: Flap scramble 1. A number of hostile aircraft were picked up on radar approaching the east coast and 602 was one of a number of squadrons scrambled to intercept. I briefly saw a Luftwaffe Heinkel III but once again it escaped into cloud before I could intercept. This proved to be my last chance to get at an enemy bomber.

Flap scramble 2. Yet another false alarm, I reckon the radar boys were getting a bit 'twitchy'. This was the first occasion I had a car accident, when we were called to readiness at short notice. Driving from the sergeants' mess to dispersal, I drove too fast round a perimeter bend and did a complete roll, upside down then back on my wheels. The surrounding grass was long and lush, the car and its occupants were undamaged and we carried on safely to dispersal.

As can be seen from the daily entries, this was a time of great activity, flying every day as many as four flights, some at night. I remember only one afternoon off, when we went into Richmond.

YEAR	1941	AIRCRAFT		Pilot or 1st Pilot	2nd Pilot, Pupil or Pass.	DUTY (Including Results and Remarks)	Flying Time		Passenger
MONTH	DATE	Type	No.				Dual	Solo	
July	1st	Spitfire	D	Self		To forward base		-10	
		Spitfire	D	Self		Return to Catterick		-10	

Summary for June/July 1941   1. Spitfire   6-00 – night flying
Unit: 41 Squadron   Spitfire   41-45

Date: 1/7/41
Signed: – *A.L. Winskill* P/O   *D.O. Finlay* S/Ldr
Act. O/C A Flt. 41 Squadron   O/C 41 Squadron

It was unusual for a Pilot Officer to be a flight commander or even an acting flight commander. I presume that in this instance it was due to the losses in the Battle of Britain. Many years later, in the 1990s, through my membership of the Duxford Airfield Society, I made contact with the then P/O Winskill. In answer to my letter I was amazed and delighted to learn from his reply that he remained in the RAF after the war. He reached the high rank of Air Vice Marshal and received a knighthood for his expertise and dedication. A few months after I left 41 Squadron, Archie was shot down over St. Omer but successfully evaded capture and returned to England at the end of 1941.

My time at 41 ended on July 4th (no fireworks), after 'routine' short flights on the 2nd and 3rd. Sadly I said goodbye to Ron Rayner, my friend from training days; we were not destined to meet again until many years after the war, actually in 1991, at a reunion with him and Johnny Timmis at Hullavington. I was posted to 602 City of Glasgow Squadron, one of the pre-war squadrons of the Royal Auxiliary Air Force, at their home base of Ayr. Only three days later, the squadron, having received a number of new, recently trained youngsters like myself, was up to the full strength of 19 pilots and was moved to Kenley in Surrey, near Biggin Hill, for the squadron to take part in the increasingly intensive operations against the Luftwaffe. Those of us who had cars were allowed extra petrol coupons to drive from Scotland to the new base, on condition that we took another squadron member with us. The other pilots flew the squadron Spitfires. So with Johnnie Bell-Walker, I set out at lunchtime on the 8th and had to report by mid-day on the 10th. Johnnie and I decided that if I drove through the night we could sneak a day at home. At 4am on the morning of the 9th, approaching Kendal in the Lake District, I took a right-hand bend a little too fast. The front nearside tyre burst, we skidded off the road, hitting a couple of telegraph poles, a 30 miles an hour sign and scraping a stone wall. The car turned over back into the road, finishing upside down through the stone wall on the opposite side. The car was a write-off but, incredibly, we crawled out of the wreck with minor scratches and a few bruises. We gathered up our belongings, found a small garage in the town, sold the wreck for £8.00 (the value of four new tyres and a new battery) and continued the journey by train. We still managed to sneak those few hours at our respective homes and arrived at Kenley with 5 minutes to spare.

There was a bizarre follow-up to this story. A few weeks later the garage owner was found to have aviation petrol in his possession (it had a colour dye added). The police phoned my given home address, Poletrees Farm, and asked for my whereabouts as the garage man claimed to have found the petrol in my crashed car. My brother-in-law, Joe Cooper, said he was unable to give my address as I was away on active service, engaged in operations against the enemy. Nothing more was heard about the matter but I still wonder where that coloured petrol came from and whether some kind-hearted member of the ground staff had put a few gallons into my tank to be helpful.

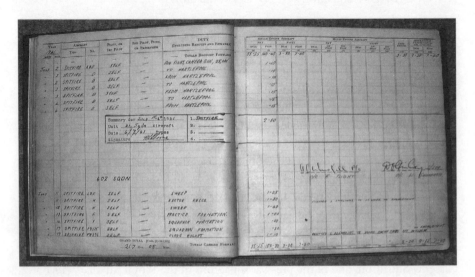

Logbook, July 1941.

602 Squadron, 1941. Left to right, back row: Max Charlesworth, J.R. Denehey, Johnny Busbridge, Len Thorne, Al Watson, Les Scorer, Ken Murray, J.A. Nicholson, D.V. Osborne, A.'Ted' Meredith, Johnny Niven, Stan Caterall, Desmond O'Connor, M. Maltin. Front row: A.N.'Doc' Hands, 'Adj' Hargreaves, F/Lt Johnny Williams, C.O. Al Deere, F/Lt E.V. 'Mitzi' Darling, J.G. Ozanne, Intelligence Officer, F/Lt N.C. MacQueen.

Johnny Niven.

A cartoon of Al Deere given to Len some years after the war.

3

602 SQUADRON

YEAR	1941	AIRCRAFT		Pilot or 1st Pilot	2nd Pilot, Pupil or Pass.	DUTY (Including Results and Remarks)	Flying Time		Passenger
MONTH	DATE	Type	No.				Dual	Solo	
July	11th	Spitfire	LO X	Self		Sweep		1-05	
		Spitfire	H	Self		Sector reconnaissance		1-30	
	12th	Spitfire	H	Self		Sweep		1-40	
	13th	Spitfire	F	Self		Practice formation		1-00	
	14th	Spitfire	Y	Self		Squadron formation		-20	
	17th	Spitfire	P8375	Self		Squadron formation		-30	
		Spitfire	P8396	Self		Close escort		1-10	
	20th	Miles Magister	R1915	Self	AC2 Gee & A.N. Other	A joy ride for two of the ground staff		1-15	
	21st	Spitfire	P7818	Self		To North Weald		-30	
		Spitfire	P7818	Self		Bomber escort		1-45	
	22nd	Spitfire	P7818	Self		Bomber escort		1-45	
		Spitfire	P7818	Self		To Merston, advanced base		-25	
		Spitfire	P7818	Self		Operational sweep		1-20	
		Magister	P1915	Self	Sgt Osbourne	Fun flip		-40	
	24th	Spitfire	P8047	Self		To Merston		-25	
		Spitfire	P8047	Self		Operational. Escourt		1-20	
		Spitfire	P8375	Self		To Tangmere		-30	
		Spitfire	P8375	Self		Patrol off Cherbourg		1-15	
	27th	Spitfire	P7297	Self		Aerobatics		-45	
							3-30	7-40	
							55-25	162-25	4-40

12 July: We flew close escort to three Short Stirling four-engined bombers; we saw plenty of flak but still no enemy engagement.

17 July: We flew close escort to six Bristol Blenheim bombers for an attack on enemy shipping off Boulogne. Bombing was accurate despite plenty of flak but still no sign of the Luftwaffe.

20 July: Actually two flights, when I landed to change passengers. The Magister was a tandem two-seat training aircraft with open cockpits. It was used as an alternative to the Tiger Moth at some EFTSs. Operational squadrons usually had, on strength, a two- or four-seat light plane for communication and passenger flying including flips, which were always appreciated by members of the ground staff.

21 July: For deep penetration we usually flew to an advanced base nearer the coast. On the 21st the note in my logbook reads: 'Flew as bomber escort cover, taking three Stirlings to Lille. When nearing the target we were attacked by five ME.109Fs but they were too eager and overshot as they opened fire. But unfortunately our Wing Leader, W/Co. John Peel was hit and forced to return to base. The bombing was completed with bursts near the target. Accurate ack-ack fire on the return journey. F/Lt Glyn Richie, our A flight commander was missing.' It was later confirmed that he was killed, our first casualty in our first brush with the enemy. We were most upset by the loss of F/Lt Richie, our well liked 'A' flight commander. He was 602's first casualty since the Battle of Britain.

On one of the occasions when we escorted Stirlings, we were operating at about 12,000 feet and the sight of those three big machines flying majestically in close VIC formation was a sight to see. Suddenly the situation changed dramatically. The leading machine received a direct hit by an anti-aircraft shell and in an instant it just disappeared; one moment it was there and the next just what looked like dust falling to the ground; the crew must have been killed immediately.

22 July: We patrolled mid-channel to cover return of Blenheims. No engagement. The Spitfire carried only 90 gallons of fuel, enough, with care, for approximately 2 hours 15 minutes flying at maximum economical throttle settings. In combat, this time could be reduced to little more than an hour. It will be appreciated that, on operations like this, we were running it a bit close.

Having arrived at Kenley on July 10th we hardly had time to draw breath before being thrown in at the deep end. In the remaining 21 days of July we flew operations on 11 of them, as many as four flights on the 24th.

We patrolled near the French coast, north of St. Valery; saw no sign of the enemy. Kenley, like other Fighter airfields, suffered badly in the Battle of Britain, many of the permanent buildings were destroyed, including the living quarters of both the Officers' and Sergeants' messes. In the latter the kitchen, dining room, lounge and bar area, after extensive repairs, were the only parts usable. Most of the staff, cooks and serving girls were members of the WAAF (Women's Auxiliary Air Force). These girls, most of them youngsters like ourselves, looked after us pilots with great care and, although warned to avoid close relationships with pilots who might well be shot down and killed, inevitably some friendships, perhaps short-lived, developed. I had a particular friend up to the time of my marriage in September. Elsie, I often wonder what happened to you.

The officers and NCOs of the Kenley squadrons were billeted in large private houses just outside the aerodrome boundaries, the former in Red House and the latter at 'Hillhurst'. I slept in a large first-floor bedroom that I shared with four others.

When I joined 602 squadron, the commanding officer was S/Ldr Meagher; he was then in poor health and had to leave for treatment. He was replaced by newly promoted Alan (Al) Deere, a New Zealander, who had joined the RAF some time before the outbreak of war. He was a fine man, a first class sportsman and athlete, the pre-war middleweight boxing champion and a keen rugby player. He was one of the Battle of Britain aces, credited with 19 confirmed victories. On operations he was a great leader, brave but not foolhardy; he never led us into a situation where we would be at an obvious disadvantage.

One of the real heroes, we met many years later, after he retired from the RAF with the rank of Air Commodore. He was then living at Wendover, a few houses away from my company's fellow director, Graham Luff. Knowing of my association with Al, Graham invited him to lunch with us in the boardroom at our group headquarters in Aylesbury. Although during my service with him I was still an NCO pilot, we remained friends until his death in 1990.

24 July: Merston was one of the Tangmere satellites, right on the coast near Chichester used, in this instance, as a forward base.

We escorted 18 Bristol Blenheims from Merston to Cherbourg. Arriving off the French coast we watched a *gruppe* of ME 109s climbing up behind us, but they did not engage our squadron (they knew I was there). On the return I saw an aircraft plunge into the sea north of the objective; the pilot had baled out. I landed back at Kenley. 'To Tangmere'. The Cherbourg, Normandy coastal area was almost due south of the point where we left England. If returning at low altitude, the sea seemed to go on for ever and on occasions I started to get a bit worried in case I had set course too far south and missed England.

27 July:
I wonder where I went to show off my skill? Probably Slough.

Summary for: July 1941	1 Spitfire	18hrs 15mins
Unit: 602 Squadron	2 Magister	1hr. 55mins
Date: 1/8/41		
Signature: H.L. Thorne		

J.D.Williams Flt Lt   *A.C. Deere* S/Ldr
O/C.A Flight   O/C 602 Squadron

GRAND TOTAL TO DATE.
229 hours 00mins.

YEAR	1941	AIRCRAFT		Pilot or 1st Pilot	2nd Pilot, Pupil or Pass.	DUTY (Including Results and Remarks)	Flying Time		Passenger
MONTH	DATE	Type	No.				Dual	Solo	
August	2nd	Spitfire	P8791	Self		Air test and cannon test at 34,000ft		1-10	
		Spitfire	P8791	Self		Cannon test		-40	
		Spitfire	P3638	Self		Air test and cannon test at 35,100ft		1-05	
	5th	Spitfire	P8423	Self		Bomber escort		1-25	
	7th	Spitfire	P8791	Self		Operational sweep		1-35	
		Spitfire	P8799	Self		Gun and air test		-35	
		Spitfire	P8799	Self		Gun test		-40	
	18th	Spitfire	P8787	Self		Bomber escort		1-20	
	19th	Spitfire	W3622	Self		Bomber escort		1-35	
	20th	Spitfire	W3407	Self		Gun and air test		-30	
	21st	Spitfire	W3622	Self		Bomber escort		1-25	
		Spitfire	W3622	Self		Bomber escort		1-05	
	24th	Magister	R1915	Self		To Merston		-30	
		Magister	R1915	Self		To White Waltham		-30	
	25th	Magister	R1915	Self		Return to base		-50	
	26th	Spitfire	W3756	Self		Cannon test		-40	
		Spitfire	W3622	Self		Operational sweep		-50	
	27th	Spitfire	W3622	Self		Bomber escort		1-15	

		Magister	R1915	Self		Flip		-10	
		Magister	R1915	Self		To White Waltham		-30	
	28th	Magister	R1915	Self		Return to base		-30	
	29th	Spitfire	W3622	Self		Operational sweep		1-40	
	30th	Spitfire	W3736	Self		'Pansy' squadron formation and aerobatics		1-35	
	31st	Spitfire	W3622	Self		Operational sweep		1-20	
							3-30	7-40	
							55-25	185-40	4-40

2 August: The unbelievable thrill of making my first flight to over 30,000 feet, using oxygen from the ground upwards, taking a little over 10 minutes to reach that height. I could see the whole sweep of the south coast and most of London and fly over or through the fleecy white tops of billowing cumulus clouds, the best way to appreciate the aircraft's speed.

When 20mm cannons were first installed in Spitfires, stoppages caused frequent problems. We carried out regular tests particularly at high altitudes.

7 August: My first taste of real action. I flew as Red 4, otherwise known as tail end Charlie or more rudely as arse-end Charlie, in the central leading section. My function was to weave backwards and forwards across the rear of the other three Spitfires in the section to give them maximum cover against attacks from above and behind.

602 Sqdn were flying Bomber escort cover, slightly above and to starboard of six Blenheims. When we were about ten miles west of St. Omer, Red Section (that's us) were attacked by four 109 Es. As they overtook us in their diving attack Wing Commander Johnnie Kent attacked the leading enemy fighter. He followed it down. I attacked the second 109, firing a short burst with guns and cannons, from dead astern and slightly below. The enemy aircraft turned on to its back and went down vertically leaving a thick trail of white smoke. I claimed it probably destroyed. Sergeant Jimmie Garden attacked the third ME 109 with a short burst and claimed it damaged. P/O Thornton failed to return but I have no memory as to whether he survived. He was flying as Red 2 and must have suffered severe damage in the initial burst of enemy fire, so his chances were not good. My victim was seen to crash and I was credited with 1 destroyed. My first kill.

Looking back, it is difficult to believe that my combat that day was only the seventh time I had fired my guns. The earlier times were mostly air to ground, just to hear and experience what it felt like. It was the first time I had actually shot at another aircraft and it felt great, although I did not really feel that I was firing with the intention of killing the enemy pilot. At last I felt that I really was a fighter pilot, the culmination of all those months of training. The credit for my 'kill' should really go to Wingco. John Kent who put me in the right position; I only had to press the firing button.

On one of the early August operations Al Deere's Spitfire was severely damaged when he was attacked by a pair of 109s. Quite a number of strikes were in the engine area but surprisingly the coolant system escaped damage. Al's story is told in his biography *Nine Lives* and this operation certainly saw him use up one of them.

19 August: We escorted six Blenheims to attack a target in the St. Omer area. I was attacked by a single, very determined enemy fighter, which dived on me as I was crossing the French coast. It was only by taking evasive action in a series of tight turns that I managed to shake him off so I escaped without damage.

I believe that this operation by six Blenheims to bomb an enemy-held airfield north-east of St. Omer, was when a new tin leg was dropped to replace the one damaged when Wing Commander (later Group Captain) Douglas Bader was shot down and captured. The Germans had offered free conduct but would have used it for propaganda purposes so the leg was dropped in the course of a normal operation. It was carefully packaged to avoid damage and was dropped by parachute from a fighter of Bader's own 616 Squadron.

21 August: Once again, we escorted six Blenheims to a target between St.Omer and Lille. I was attacked by a single ME 109, which fired a short burst from astern which caused minor damage to the elevators and rudder. In taking violent evasive action I lost the squadron formation and returned alone. The slight damage to the tail unit was discovered after I landed.

In the operations of early and mid-1941 our objective was to draw the enemy into combat and to 'show the flag' to encourage the French and Belgians. I suppose that it was also felt necessary to prove to the Americans that not only had we not been defeated in 1940 but were also ready and willing to carry the fight to the Germans. The Bristol Blenheim twin-engine light bombers were comparatively slow and it was not easy for a Spitfire to maintain station. Initially, Hawker Hurricanes flew as close escort and escort cover. They had to stay close and so were more vulnerable to enemy attacks. As more and more Spitfires came off the production lines, losses from the earlier years were quickly replaced and many new squadrons were formed. The Hurricanes were phased out and Spitfires took over close escort duties in the daylight role. The Hurricanes continued to participate as fighter bombers and came to be known as Hurribombers. They were extensively used in the middle and far eastern theatres; for increased fire power they were armed with four 20mm cannons as well as the original four .303 machine guns and proved to be very effective. They were also the first replacements of the Gloster Gladiator biplane fighters of 'Faith, Hope and Charity' fame, which fought so gallantly over Malta and were more than a match for the Italian fighters.

21 August: Escorted three Beaufighters to attack enemy minesweepers off Calais. No engagement.

24 August: I managed to hitch a lift from White Waltham to Slough for a quick overnight visit to my eldest sister, Doris, and her family, to confirm arrangements for my wedding the following month.

26 August: After the bombing, my section leader, who had been hit by flak, left the formation. I saw him clear of danger. I returned to escort the Blenheims as far as the French coast, then returned to base. They all returned safely.

27 August: Escorted six Blenheims to bomb 'Long Nez' airfield in the Pas de Calais. No engagement. Then another chance for an overnight visit to the Climer family at Slough.

29 August: Flew cover escort for six Blenheims to bomb Hazebrucke; we saw numerous vapour trails. Six ME 109s came down out of the sun to attack our centre (red) section. We took evasive action by turning sharply into the direction of the attack; they gave up the attack and dived away.

30 August: An exercise intended mainly to boost the morale of the local population.

31 August: Saw no sign of enemy activity, not even any flak, so no fun at all.

Summary for: August 1941   Spitfire   20-15
Unit: 602 Squadron   Magister   3-00
Date: 01/09/41
Signature: H.L. Thorne

S. Rose F/O For T.D.W. Flt/Comm   *A.C. Deere* S/Ldr
O/C A Flight   O/C 602 Squadron

YEAR	1941	AIRCRAFT		Pilot or 1st Pilot	2nd Pilot, Pupil or Pass.	DUTY (Including Results and Remarks)	Flying Time		Passenger
MONTH	DATE	Type	No.				Dual	Solo	
September	1st	Spitfire	W3638	Self		Convoy patrol		1-35	
	2nd	Spitfire	W3622	Self		Operational sweep		1-25	
	3rd	Spitfire	W3622	Self		Local flying, formation		-45	
	7th	Spitfire	W3622	Self		Formation to 31,000ft		1-20	

		Spitfire	W3622	Self		Aerobatics		-35	
	10th	Spitfire	W3622	Self		Formation practice, dog-fights and aerobatics		1-40	
	11th	Spitfire	W3622	Self		Rhubarb		1-40	
		Spitfire	W3622	Self		Convoy patrol		1-20	
		Spitfire	W8791	Self		Aerobatics		1-00	
	22nd	Spitfire	P3796	Self		Calibration tests		-55	
	27th	Spitfire	P3756	Self		Operational circus		1-00	
	28th	Spitfire	P8791	Self		Practice formation		1-05	
							3-30	7-40	
						Total hours to date	55-25	200-00	

11 September: After the glorious autumn weather of 1940, 1941 reverted to form with dull, wet weather and operations were severely curtailed, particularly in the first two weeks. On the 11th it was worse than usual with low cloud and rain. It was decided that each of the Kenley squadrons would carry out a 'Rhubarb' at different times throughout the day. Rhubarbs were notoriously dangerous so volunteers were called for. A Rhubarb was a low-level offensive patrol by a pair of our fighters over enemy-held territory to attack targets of opportunity, particularly road and rail transport such as lorries and army vehicles. We were under strict orders not to attack airfields as they were always heavily defended by light and heavy flak. A number of Battle of Britain aces who tried it were shot down – hence the ban. They were known as Rhubarbs because of the effect on the bowels of eating too much of it, the operation having much the same effect.

On this day Sergeant Osborne of B Flight and I were the suckers who volunteered. We took off mid-morning and wandered around the Pas de Calais for some time and, being at tree-top level, were never really sure of our exact position. Suddenly we found ourselves crossing the perimeter of Calais Marck, one of the main Luftwaffe fighter air bases in the area. We had no alternative but to carry on; it would have been fatal to attempt to turn back. So we streaked across the flying field heading for the far boundary, firing at a steam-roller which was working on the runway. Due to the bad weather and our low altitude, we caught the Germans literally with their pants down. Approaching the hangars we saw large numbers of the ground staff enjoying their mid-morning *Kaffee und Kuchen* at the German equivalent of the NAAFI wagon. As they streamed back towards their gun positions, we opened fire with guns and cannons and caught many of them as they ran.

We saw many bodies thrown to right and left but whether they were hit or just trying to avoid our fire we did not wait to enquire; but it is almost certain that there must have been many casualties. As we roared over the hangars and boundary hedges, streams of 'flaming onions' were already looping over and round our aircraft. By the Grace of God and extreme good luck, plus the suddenness of our arrival and departure, neither Spitfire was hit and we escaped unscathed. Although we had not deliberately attacked the airfield, the C/O gave us both a severe telling off for our escapade.

13 September: As far as Kenley was concerned, 13th September had been my stag night, which I celebrated by flying my Spitfire to Waddesdon, the village of my birth, to show off to family and friends my skill as a pilot. It was nearly my last flight as, in the course of my aerobatic display, I performed a slow roll at very low altitude over the village. While inverted I almost hit the old windmill that stood just south of the village. Luck was with me and I got away with it. Back at Kenley there was time for a few drinks with the boys, goodbye to Elsie and the girls, then down to Whiteleaf station in the evening and back to Waddesdon, this time by train, to begin a seven-day leave from the 14th to the 21st of the month.

Estelle and I were married at Waddesdon Church by the vicar, the Rev. George Dixon, who had baptised and confirmed me many years before. We spent our wedding night at the farm. Then it was off by train for a short four-day honeymoon, spent in a small hotel at Paignton in Devonshire. Days were spent enjoying local beauty spots and strolling along the seafront, admiring the barbed wire defences that lined the beaches.

On the 21st it was back, first to the farm then, for Estelle, on to Slough, where she lived with Doris, my eldest sister and her family, until June of the following year. During that time she worked as a secretary in the CID (Criminal Investigation Department) office of the local police force. I, of course, travelled back to Kenley to resume my efforts in the defeat of Hitler and his Nazis.

During my week's leave the Squadron had run into trouble on several occasions and was badly mauled. Seven pilots were missing, together with their aircraft. Three of the five relatively new boys, with whom I had shared a bedroom, were among those lost. The Spitfire, Squadron letters LOA, which I regarded as 'my' Spitfire, was one of those lost. I always told my wife that by choosing that day for our marriage, she probably saved my life.

On returning to the Squadron Al Deere must have thought that I would be worn out and in need of a rest as he gave me only light duties for the next few days. These included a day as duty officer, quite an honour, as I was still only a Sergeant. I flew on only one operation, that on the 27th, a trip that involved only fighters and was intended to tweak the Huns' tails. It obviously failed as, without bombers, the Luftwaffe showed no interest and saved their petrol.

During this month we had our first sighting of what we later learned was the Focke Wulf FW190. Sightings of a radial-engined machine had been reported as early as August but it was a well-kept German secret and we had no detailed knowledge of this machine. In the case of our squadron, in fact part of the Kenley Wing, our first sighting of the FW190 was when a large number of Spitfires, three or four Wings, made up of 12 or 16 squadrons, were involved in escorting a number of bombers. The FW190 appeared some distance in front of us flying at right angles to our particular Wing, travelling at very high speed. The pilot performed a series of quick rolls right and left. It was almost as if the Luftwaffe pilot was teasing us and metaphorically sticking up the proverbial two fingers, (he probably was), as there was no possibility of catching us. He ended the display with a perfectly executed climbing roll, immediately diving away at very high speed. Various attempts at identification were put forward; some said it was an early arrival of an American P47 Thunderbolt or even a Japanese Zero but after a few more sightings, it was found to be a new and very potent German fighter, something we learned to our cost over the ensuing year.

Summary for: September 1941   1 Spitfire   14-20
Unit: 602 Squadron
Date: 1/10/41
Signature: H.L. Thorne

In my logbook the following note appears in pencil; I do not know why!

Operational hours to date 44 hours 45 minutes
Score to date 1 E/A. (enemy aircraft) confirmed

Signed *J.D. Williams* F/Lt   *A.C. Deere* Sqdn Ldr
O/C A Flight   O/C 602 Sqdn

YEAR	1941	AIRCRAFT		Pilot or 1st Pilot	2nd Pilot, Pupil or Pass.	DUTY (Including Results and Remarks)	Flying Time		Passenger
MONTH	DATE	Type	No.				Dual	Solo	
October	1st	Spitfire	AB849	Self		Fighter sweep		1-35	
	2nd	Spitfire	P8791	Self		Circus		-55	
		Magister	R1915	Self		To White Waltham		-40	
	3rd	Magister	R1915	Self		White Waltham to base		-40	
		Spitfire	P8791	Self		High cover escort		1-30	
	6th	Spitfire	W3407	Self		Local flying		-30	
	7th	Spitfire	AD256	Self		Practice formation		-40	
		Spitfire	W3756	Self		Practice attacks		-55	
	10th	Magister	R1915	Self	LAC Dadge	To Little Rissington		1-00	
		Magister	R1915	Self		To Hullavington		-30	
		Magister	R1915	Self		Return to base		1-00	
	11th	Spitfire	W3407	Self		Practice formation		1-10	
	12th	Spitfire	W3407	Self		Operational sweep		1-30	
		Magister	T9873	Self	Some cadets	Joy rides for five cadets of the local ATC Squadron		-50	

	13th	Magister	R1915	Self		To White Waltham		-30	
	14th	Magister	R1915	Self		Return to base		-30	
	15th	Magister	R1915	Self	AC2	A 'flip' for one of our ground staff		-20	
		Magister	R1915	Self	S/Ldr Ward	Kenley to Tangmere		-30	
		Magister	R1915	Self		Tangmere to Merston		-10	
		Magister	R1915	Self		Merston to Kenley		-30	
		Magister	R1915	Self	AC2	Another 'flip' for a member of the ground staff		-20	
	17th	Spitfire	P8799	Self		Operational sweep, recalled		1-05	
		Spitfire	W3407	Self		Aerobatics		1-10	
	19th	Magister	R1915	Self		Fun flights for two ATC cadets		1-05	
	20th	Spitfire	AB848	Self		Camera gun practice		-40	
		Spitfire	W3756	Self		Camera gun practice		-25	
		Spitfire	AB848	Self		Camera gun practice		-3-	
	21st	Spitfire	P8799	Self		Fighter sweep		1-30	
		Spitfire	W3407	Self		Scramble to mid channel		1-35	
	22nd	Spitfire	W3641	Self		Practice formation		1-00	
	30th	Spitfire	W3899	Self		Lysander patrol		1-25	
	31st	Spitfire	W3641	Self		Roadstead to Dunquerque		1-15	

1 October: I was flying as Red 2, wingman to F/Lt J.D. (Johnny) Williams. We patrolled inland from Cap Gris Nez to Gravelines at 14 to 15,000 feet. We somewhat cautiously watched 6–plus ME 109s on a climbing approach from the south. Being in a favourable position, up sun and with a height advantage, we turned to meet them. Red 1 attacked the leading four of the 109s, selecting the leader who broke away in a steep dive to port. I followed him and opened fire; the e/a then went into a steeper dive with black and white smoke pouring out. I broke off and fired a short burst at a second e/a. As neither of the e/a's was seen to crash, I only claimed and was given, 1 probably destroyed. Sergeant Smith also claimed a 'probable'. Johnny came home with bullet holes in the wing and fuselage of his Spitfire. A lucky escape!

3 October: When escorting bombers, the supporting Wings would normally take up one of three positions: *Close escort* immediately above or around the bombers. *Escort cover* stepped up above the close escort or *High cover* could be 1,000 feet or more above the other participants. On a big 'show' more than one Wing could be stepped up to further heights in support of the operation. The operation on the 3rd was to escort six Blenheims to Dunquerque for an attack on enemy shipping. No engagement.

Extract from logbook for 1st to 3rd October 1941, signed by F/Lt Johnny Williams and S/Ldr Al Deere, showing an action in which F/Lt Williams returned with bullet holes in his wing and fuselage.

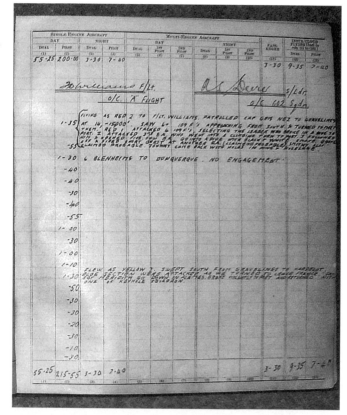

It was not always busy and dangerous. Members of the Squadron taking a well-earned rest. Len Thorne is second from right, 'Paddy' Finucane fourth from right. Date unknown.

10 October: A short visit to Hullavington to chat with my old instructors.

12 October: On this operation I flew as Yellow 3, sub-section leader on the port side of the leading section and slightly above it. We swept south from Gravelines to Hardelot, inland ten to fifteen miles from the French coast. Blue section, off to our right and slightly below us, were attacked by a group of 109s just as we made a starboard turn to leave France. The rest of us were immediately involved in several brief individual combats and for a few moments the sky seemed full of aircraft. In a momentary lull I saw Blue 4 off to my right spinning down, with the Spitfire completely engulfed in flames. I broke violently to port to avoid an attacker and became separated from the somewhat scattered squadron, so joined up with one of the 'Keyhole' (452 Australian) Squadron boys and got home safely. We later learned that Blue 4 was Sergeant Ted Meredith of B Flight and at that time he was believed to have perished in his flaming aircraft.

45 years later, in March 1987, I was chatting with the husband of one of my wife's friends. He noticed my RAF Association lapel badge and asked what I did in the RAF. Learning that I had been a fighter pilot, he told me of a friend who had also been a fighter pilot, named Ted Meredith and wondered whether I knew him. I said that I had known a Ted Meredith but it could not be the same chap, as I saw him shot down in flames. A quick phone call revealed that it was, indeed, the man I had known; not only was he alive and well but lived only eight miles away in Bromsgrove! Ted was a Freemason like me and we agreed to meet at the next meeting of his Lodge. A mutual friend tipped off a reporter of the local newspaper. The story not only appeared in the local papers but also made headlines in the *Daily Express*. A few days later we were interviewed by a team from the BBC. Instant fame! Ted and I remained friends until he really did die, in 1996.

15 October: My second trip on the 15th to Tangmere, was intended to be a visit to 41 Squadron but they had moved on. I did a quick hop over to Merston but again I was unlucky as they were airborne on a sweep.

The operations over France, Belgium and Holland were intended to carry the offensive to the Germans, to give some comfort to the occupied countries, as well as to tie up large numbers of the enemy forces. The various operations were given code names. *Rodeos* and *ramrods* were usually attacks against enemy shipping or specific land targets. A *fighter sweep* was a penetration into enemy-held territory with or without bombers. A *circus* involved a large number of fighter planes, as many as seven or eight Wings, each of three squadrons, the latter with strength of twelve aircraft, as cover for short-range bombers. A *Balbo*, named after the Italian general, would be even larger, including formations of light bombers. A *Rhubarb*, described earlier was a two-man operation over enemy-held territory looking for targets of opportunity.

17 October: Through September and October the Focke Wulfs continued to appear in ever increasing numbers and our losses increased at an alarming rate.

Worsening autumnal weather plus the heavier losses resulted in a curtailment of our operational activity. In November I flew only four operational trips and one of those was aborted by bad weather.

20 October: Camera gun practice was really mock dogfights between squadron members.

21 October: 'Fighter sweep.' I flew as Blue 3 with Sgt Quinn as my No. 2 (position now known as Wingman). The Squadron carried out a sweep – Hardelot–St. Omer–Boulogne. Just before leaving France, at about 15,000 ft, I became separated from the Squadron and went down to join up with 3 aircraft, on a westerly heading, thinking them to be Spitfires. They turned out to be 109s; the pilots had apparently not seen me. I attacked the lowest of the three, firing two bursts from the left quarter astern. I saw holes appear and my cannon shells bursting down left of the fuselage; a piece fell off the left wing. I broke away to port and came home (flat out). I claimed and was given one Me109 probably destroyed.

This sweep shows my progress in the squadron, being now considered sufficiently experienced to be a sub-section leader, the first occasion being a week earlier on the 12th. Initially my No. 2 would have been another NCO pilot but within a short time it was not unusual for a new officer to be in that position. I was considered to be a 'safe' pilot and most new boys, both NCOs and officers, made their initial sector experience flights with me.

My experience that day echoes a well-known RAF story: 'Having been separated from the rest of my squadron, I dived to join three Spitfires … Looking up from my dinghy five minutes later, I saw that they were Messerschmitt 109s.'

'Scramble.' Our section of four Spitfires was scrambled to intercept enemy aircraft over the Channel. We patrolled at 24,000 feet for 1 hour 35 minutes and saw vapour trails above to the east but were unable to intercept.

30 October: As well as sweeps, we also flew patrols over naval actions such as convoys and minesweeping. We sometimes flew as escort to little Walrus seaplanes and the fast surface AST (Air Sea Rescue) boats. On the 30th we escorted the Lysander, a special purpose aircraft initially designed for artillery spotting; however, by reason of its very short take-off and landing ability it was widely used, as on this occasion, for dropping or collecting agents into and from France.

31 October: This was a low-level attack on shipping in and near the harbour, with bombing successfully carried out by Hurribombers. In this operation we all joined in with cannon and machine-gun fire at some of the lighter ships and dockside installations. This was a most dangerous proceeding as German low-level anti-aircraft fire was murderous. Several of our aircraft were hit and the wing leader, Wing Commander Ernie Ryder, was shot down. He was an ace from the Battle of Britain and his was a grievous loss.

Summary for:- October 1941	1 Spitfire	19-15	
Unit:-	602 squadron	2 Magister	8-40
Date:-	1/11/1941		
Signature :-	H.L.Thorne		

Pencilled notes. Operational hours to date: 57 hours 45 minutes

Personal Score to date   1 ME. 109   Confirmed

                       1   Probable

                       1   Damaged

Signed *Norman C. Macqueen* F/Lt   *A.C. Deere* S/Ldr

O/C 'A' flight   O/C 602 Sqdn.

Above left: 602 Squadron. F/Sgt Les Scorer in the cockpit of his Spitfire.

Above right: Sgt Sanderson inspecting the cannon shell damage to his wing.

Left: Johnny Niven, Jimmy Garden, Sgt Smith, Len Thorne.

YEAR	1941	AIRCRAFT		Pilot or 1st Pilot	2nd Pilot, Pupil or Pass.	DUTY (Including Results and Remarks)	Flying Time		Passenger
MONTH	DATE	Type	No.				Dual	Solo	
November	1st	Magister	R1915	Self	F/O Edsall	To Hendon		-40	
		Magister	R1915	Self		To base		-40	
	2nd	Magister	R1915	Self		To Hendon		-25	
		Magister	R1915	Self	F/O Edsall	To base		-25	
						Grand total to date: 296 hours 40 minutes	3-30	7-40	
							55-25	230-05	4-40
	7th	Spitfire	P8791	Self		Hurribomber escort		1-35	
		Spitfire	P8791	Self		Practice formation		1-10	
	8th	Spitfire	P8791	Self		Operational sweep		1-45	
		Spitfire	P8791	Self		Manston to Kenley		-35	
	9th	Spitfire	AB848	Self		Squadron formation		-55	
		Spitfire	W3638	Self		Dummy sweep (ops)		-55	
	11th	Spitfire	AD515	Self		Sweep (wash out, bad weather)		-45	
	15th	Spitfire	W3898	Self		Local flying		-20	
		Spitfire	AD515	Self		Local flying		-20	
		Spitfire	W3898	Self		Local flying		-10	
	22nd	Spitfire	W3956	Self		Squadron formation		1-10	
		Spitfire	W3956	Self		Squadron (Pansy) formation		-40	
	26th	Spitfire	P8799	Self		Air and cannon test		1-10	

2 November: Doing a bit of ferrying. I seem to remember that on the outward flight we 'beat up' someone's girlfriend's house.

7 November: Flew as close escort to 6 Blenheims for the bombing of a distillery near Le Tréport. After the bombs had been dropped we all had a go at the distillery and nearby factory buildings and mill, with cannons and machine guns. On this occasion flak was light and we all got back safely but I wondered whether the French workers were so lucky.

8 November: Flew as top cover to 12 Blenheims attacking a factory near Lille. Having bombed successfully, we started our return but soon after making the turn, we were attacked by a large number of ME 109s that were supported by single pairs of Focke Wulfs. By then, having made the deep penetration almost to the Belgian border, our fuel state was critical, which made it difficult to fight back. I saw a Spitfire and a 109 go down in flames, both leaving trails of smoke. I made an emergency landing at Manston with about 2 gallons of fuel left. The rest of the squadron were scattered at other nearby airfields. I was surprised to find that all of our Wing returned home safely.

Immediately after being refuelled, those of us who could be contacted were ordered off to cover an air sea rescue 'Walrus' to pick up two aircrew who had run out of fuel and were 'in the drink'. They had both been picked up by the time we arrived so we returned to base.

9 November: I was flying as Yellow 3 with a new officer, P/O Max Charlesworth, as my number two. Nearing the French coast my engine briefly cut out but resumed after a few seconds but with reduced power. I thought it wise to return to base and turned for home closely followed by the rest of the squadron, which had no engagement. After the war Max achieved high office in, I believe, the Foreign or Colonial Office.

26 November:

Summary for:- November 1941		1 Spitfire	11-30
Unit:- 602 Sqdn.		2 Magister	2-10
Date:- 4/12/41		3	
Signature:- H.L. Thorne		4	
E. Edsal F/Lt	*A.C. Deere* S/Ldr		
O/C A Flight	O/C 602 squadron		

Promoted to Flight Sergeant

After the Dunkirk evacuation there was much bad feeling between certain parts of the Army and the Air Force. Even after eighteen months, it was still evident in some areas. They (the soldiers) felt that they had been let down by the RAF because they rarely saw our fighters over the beaches and did not appreciate that the RAF were doing their best to stop the Luftwaffe aircraft inland, before they reached the Dunkirk area. Sergeant Quinn, a young Irishman, while walking near Kenley, was one of several who were subjected to attacks from members of Army units based at nearby Caterham barracks. He was beaten up and was so badly injured that after some time in hospital he did not return to flying duties.

In the operations over enemy-held territory, if bombers were involved, it was the task of our fighters to protect them from the attacks of enemy fighters. Initially, Hurricanes flew as close escort but, as bomber speeds increased with the advent of aircraft like the American Boston, and more and more Spitfires came into service, the latter took over most close escort duties. Close escort was not a popular position, as having to fly at lower speeds to match the bombers we had to weave in order to maintain station, so we too became more vulnerable.

| YEAR | 1941 | AIRCRAFT | | Pilot or 1st Pilot | 2nd Pilot, Pupil or Pass. | DUTY (Including Results and Remarks) | Flying Time | | Passenger |
MONTH	DATE	Type	No.				Dual	Solo	
December	5th	Spitfire	AD515	Self		Scramble (false alarm)		-10	
		Spitfire	AD515	Self		Local flying		-45	
	7th	Spitfire	AD515	Self		To Shoreham		-20	
		Spitfire	AD515	Self		Air firing. Return to base		-5-	
		Spitfire	AD515	Self		To Leysdown for air to ground firing		-50	
	8th	Spitfire	P8723	Self		Scramble. Much too late, he'd gone		1-00	
	11th	Spitfire	AD515	Self		Practice formation		1-05	
		Magister	R1915	Self	Sgt Mitchell	To Shoreham		-30	
		Magister	R1915	Self		To base		-30	
	13th	Spitfire	AB849	Self		Cine gun practice		-55	
		Spitfire	W3956	Self		Squadron formation		-55	
		Spitfire	W3956	Self		Local flying		-55	
	15th	Spitfire	W3756	Self		Practice attacks		1-00	
	16th	Spitfire	W3956	Self		Aerobatics		-15	
	17th	Magister	R1915	Self	F/Lt Darling (nicknamed 'Mitzi'! I wonder why?)	To Llandowr		1-50	
		Magister	R1915	Self		To base. It was still cold		1-35	
	24th	Spitfire	W3756	Self		Practice formation		1-10	
		Spitfire	AD515	Self		Local flying		1-20	

	25th	Spitfire	AB848	Self		Local flying		1-00	
	26th	Spitfire	AD515	Self		'Beat up' some Beaufighters			
	28th	Spitfire	AD515	Self		Operational sweep			
	29th	Spitfire	W3956	Self		To Martlesham Heath			
		Spitfire	W3956	Self		Patrol over North Sea. Minesweeping operation			
						GRAND TOTAL TO DATE 329 HOURS 50 MINUTES	3-30	7-40	

8 December: This month I flew on only one operational sweep. The Luftwaffe took advantage of poor weather to start sending fighter-bombers, bomb-carrying ME109s and later, FW190s, at the start of what came to be known as the Baedeker raids. Towns, generally 70–80 miles from the coast, were picked apparently at random from a pre-war travel guide. In a way these were in retaliation for our *Rhubarbs* but on a much bigger scale. Usually a single bomb was dropped but sometimes targets were also attacked by machine gun and cannon fire. We spent many hours at 'readiness state' and I was scrambled on two occasions in an effort to intercept these raids. They really were hit and run, very few interceptions were successful, although the situation improved with practice.

17 December: A long trip to South Wales in a little trainer with open cockpits in mid-December. Brrr! Bitterly cold.

18 December: That night six of us fighter boys from 602 Squadron, 3 officers and 3 NCOs were invited to the Christmas dinner and dance of the East London Brewery Company. We were collected from Kenley by taxi and taken to the venue somewhere off the Old Kent Road. I spent most of the evening with a very pretty, very young lady. She was carefully watched over by her mum and dad! At the end of the evening we were invited upstairs to the Directors' boardroom for a nightcap and farewell drink. I have little recollection of being loaded into the taxi and returned to Kenley, each of us clutching a bottle of champagne. Some time in the night I awoke hanging on to the rocking bed; feeling thirsty, I drank the champagne and remembered nothing more until mid-day.

24 December: Estelle made the journey to Kenley by train early in the afternoon. Sgt Parker, the Link trainer instructor, had a house nearby and he and his wife had kindly offered us a bed for the night. We had been invited to a dance in the main building at Croydon Airport. With Sgt Des O'Connor and S/Ldr Reg Grant (C/O of 452 Sqdn), Estelle and I travelled the short distance to Croydon by train. Also in our carriage were three or four soldiers, all out for trouble; the usual complaint: 'Where were the Air Force planes at Dunkirk?' Reg silenced them with the remark that his brother was there and was shot down and killed. The following day I was back on duty and Estelle spent what she described as the most miserable Christmas Day of her life, in the train back to Slough, where she was still living with my sister.

25 December: I had said a rather sad goodbye to Estelle at the Parkers' that Christmas morning, leaving Sergeant Parker to drive her to Whiteleaf station. Before returning on duty at Kenley, the best I could do for Estelle was a few circles and a slow roll or two over what I thought was her train. Then back to earth to continue the Christmas Day activities. At lunchtime it was the custom (I believe in all the services) for the officers and senior NCOs to wait on the ground staff by serving their Christmas lunch. It was a good excuse for a booze-up.

29 December: Minesweeping. The weather was absolutely awful and throughout the patrol we saw no sign of ships. Despite the weather, we were kept at Martlesham in a full state of readiness until January 2nd. The duty note above tells only half the story. We were told that our operation was most important, as a major convoy was to pass through the Channel. The path to be taken by the ships was to be swept clear of mines. After the patrol on the 29th, in appalling weather, we were told that the convoy was postponed, pending an improvement but we were to remain at Martlesham ready for immediate action. On the morning of the 30th we were again ordered off but 'scrubbed' as no ships had appeared. We stayed grounded for another three days, fed up and frustrated.

602 was basically a Scottish squadron and something like 75% of the pilots were Scots. Back at Kenley parties and dances had been organised to celebrate Hogmanay and wives and girlfriends were there to join in the celebrations. All pleas to 'go back just for the night' fell on deaf ears but we were allowed transport into Ipswich that evening. The New Zealanders of 485 Squadron joined in the celebrations and we all got somewhat 'tanked up'. We were ordered out of the chosen pub at closing time and two very brave Special Constables arrived to enforce the order. They were kept in a revolving door until we were ready to leave! I have no memory of the return to Martlesham but found myself there the following morning.

At the crack of dawn, with the pilots of 485 Squadron, we were ordered to form up on the parade ground by an irate Station Commander. When the RAF standard was raised on the parade ground flagstaff it was found that some of the chaps had found, in the station theatre, a large green papier-mâché parrot and substituted it for the standard and there it flew proudly for all to see. The Station Commander was not amused. In addition, a formal complaint had been received from the Ipswich police, demanding that the ringleaders of the assault on two of his Specials should be handed over. This request, at the time, was ignored and the next day we all flew back to Kenley. The police agreed to quash any further action, on condition that they received a formal apology. Our two Squadron commanders, Al Deere and 'Hawkeye' Billy Wells, both highly decorated New Zealanders, flew over and their personal apologies were accepted. We heard nothing more about the convoy or the mine-sweeping operation, so I presume that some other squadrons provided the cover.

Summary for:- December 1941	1 Spitfire	16-55
Unit:- 602 Squadron	2 Magister	4-25
Date:- 2/1/42		
Signature:- H.L. Thorne		

Norman C. Macqueen F/Lt   *A.C. Deere* S/Ldr
O/C A Flight   O/C 602 Squadron
Popularly known as 'Queenie'

Through the autumn and winter months operational activity was greatly reduced but we filled in our time with other occupations. Pushed by Group Captain Beamish, the Station Commander, we made more regular visits to the Link trainer. Like most pilots, we heartily disliked this machine; the Link of those days moved jerkily and bore little resemblance to a real aeroplane. However, they certainly made an improvement to one's instrument flying, something that was really necessary in view of the frequent periods of bad weather. They were a far cry from the modern F16 simulator that I 'flew' many years later at Luke American Air Force base near Phoenix, Arizona, courtesy of the USAF. Our turn at Redhill in January and February 1942 saved us from further punishment.

It was fully expected that the Luftwaffe would resume its efforts to defeat the RAF in the spring of 1942 and that, as in Belgium, the German 'crack' parachute troops would spearhead an invasion. It was decided that all aircrew serving in the south of England should be taught the rudiments of unarmed combat. At Kenley our instructors were the tough NCOs from the Guards depot at nearby Caterham. They were great fellows who had been in the thick of the fighting in France. I think they let us down lightly but we all agreed that it was great fun while it lasted, despite a few bumps and bruises.

Another activity during the winter months was making frequent visits to the UVR (ultra violet ray) room. We used to strip down to our underpants and wear dark glasses. I seem to remember that sessions were restricted to 30 minutes. I also clearly remember the strong ozone smell. It was a great pity that the sessions were restricted to men only.

YEAR	1942	AIRCRAFT		Pilot or 1st Pilot	2nd Pilot, Pupil or Pass.	DUTY (Including Results and Remarks)	Flying Time		Passenger
MONTH	DATE	Type	No.				Dual	Solo	
January	2nd	Spitfire	W3956	Self		Return to Martlesham		-50	
	4th	Spitfire	P8799	Self		Formation and cine gun practice		1-30	
	12th	Spitfire	W3956	Self		Formation		-45	
	14th	Spitfire	AD515	Self		To Redhill		-20	
	26th	Spitfire	W3641	Self		To Redhill		-10	
	27th	Spitfire	W3756	Self		Practice formation		1-00	
	29th	Spitfire	BL288	Self		To Leysdown for gunnery practice, air to ground		1-15	
	30th	Spitfire	BL288	Self		Practice formation		-45	

14 January: The Kenley Wing comprised three squadrons: 602 City of Glasgow AAF (Auxiliary Air Force), originally all Scottish personnel, later mainly from Scotland but with chaps like me from other countries to fill the gaps; 452 Squadron, all Australians with the exception of one flight commander; and 485, all young men from New Zealand. Two squadrons were based at Kenley and the third at the small grass airfield at Redhill. The units were rotated and in January and February it was our turn at Redhill.

There were no living quarters at Redhill so, as at Kenley, the NCOs were in a commandeered house outside the airfield boundary. It was somewhat primitive with just toilet facilities. It was extremely cold during our stay. At the airfield there was a mess hut, with dining room, lounge area and a well-stocked bar. The latter was well patronised during the severe weather during our stay. Heavy snow made flying impossible although by united efforts we did manage to clear a runway.

Summary for:- January 1942   Spitfire   6-35
Unit:- 602 Squadron
Date:- 31/1/42
Signature:- H.L. Thorne

Total time on Spitfire   196 hours 10 minutes
Operational hours to date   68 hours 40 minutes

John B. Niven P/O. pp F/Lt   *B.P. Finucane* S/Ldr
For O/C A Flight   O/C 602 Squadron
Signed   *F.V. Beamish*. Group Captain
          O/C. RAF Station Kenley

Johnny Niven was one of the cadets with whom I went through the final few weeks of training. Some time in the autumn of 1941 we helped him to celebrate his 21st birthday in the Sergeants' Mess at Kenley. In what was alleged to be a Scottish custom, an empty pint pot was placed upon the bar counter. As a birthday present we were each expected to buy him a drink, all different, and empty it into the awaiting tankard. He had to drink it during the celebrations and the effect was catastrophic. He staggered outside, presumably for a breath of fresh air and started walking backwards towards the parade ground. It took two or three of us to overcome his objections and get him back to his billet. To our amazement he survived the experience without any apparent ill effect and reported for duty as usual the next morning.

He was the first of us 'new boys' to be commissioned and early in the spring of 1942 he was promoted to Flight Lieutenant and appointed flight commander of 'A' Flight. Later in the war, as a Squadron Leader, he was awarded a DFC but shortly afterwards was shot down and I believe was badly wounded. Many years after the war we met at the Hendon RAF Museum, when he recognised me across the width of a crowded restaurant. I gave him a lift back to Aylesbury where he was staying with friends. He invited Estelle and me to pay him a visit at his home in Inverness but sadly suffered a fatal heart attack before we could take up the offer.

Early in January another major change took place: our greatly respected commanding officer, my friend Squadron Leader Al Deere, was promoted to Wing Commander and departed to become leader of one of the other sector wings. He was replaced by Squadron Leader Brendan Paul Finucane, a dashing young Irishman, known to us all as 'Paddy'. He had joined 452 Squadron shortly after the Battle of Britain and eventually became one of their Flight Commanders. During 1941 he had built up a reputation as a crack shot and at that time was credited with having shot down over 20 Luftwaffe aircraft, nearly all in fighter-to-fighter combat. Although only 21 years of age, he had been awarded a DSO, DFC and bar. In his time at 602, up to mid-May when I completed my tour, he scored many more victories. His confirmed kills at that time stood at 31 and a half and I was honoured to share that other half. Away from Kenley he was modest and retiring although, by reason of his record, he was always in demand by the media. He was courting a lovely young woman who lived near Kingston-on-Thames and we sometimes travelled together on the Southern Railway when I paid a visit to Slough to see my wife. On such occasions, to spare my feelings, he always wore a buttoned-up raincoat to hide his medal ribbons. He and Johnny Niven were very much responsible for developing ways of overcoming, to some extent, our problems with the FW 190s. Paddy had a number of close calls but was never shot down by an enemy fighter.

Sadly, on 15th July 1942, having moved again to become wing leader at one of the other sector stations, he was brought down by ground fire when crossing the coast of France on a return trip. Paddy chose to attempt a landing in the Channel but his Spitfire nosed over and went straight down, like Group Captain F.V.Beamish; Paddy was never found.

During the first two weeks of February I was attached to a tank division of the Canadian Army to foster the co-operation that was essential to later operations. These fine young men, all of whom had volunteered to join in the fight against Nazi Germany, had not then seen any action. They treated us like gods and mollycoddled us through the manoeuvres on Salisbury Plain. The weather was fine but cold and while they slept in improvised hammocks, they gave us a warm spot alongside the engine of a Bren Carrier. We returned to Redhill loaded with Passing Cloud cigarettes and other goodies. Many of these men died in the fiasco at Dieppe later that year.

For two or three weeks of our stay at Redhill I was somewhat incapacitated by an infection and severe rash in a rather personal area. Treatment consisted of an application, night and morning, of a gentian violet preparation, which, while effective, was not a pretty sight. It was a relief that the medical staff at Redhill were male and not members of the WAAF. The rash was caused by poor laundry facilities and unclean underclothes. I stress this latter explanation!

Towards the end of February there were some operations and, after one in particular, I witnessed a spectacular escape. Sgt John Strudwick was badly shot up and his Spitfire severely damaged. He made several attempts to land and finally crashed. He was saved because he ploughed into a snow bank.

During the long, dark evenings of winter we received many invitations to attend events away from Kenley and Redhill. One of the Sergeant Pilots was a youngster named Paul Green, who had joined the Squadron during the autumn. Paul was a top class table tennis player and I was a fairly good exponent. On three occasions Paul and I were invited to venues in London to join in demonstration matches with the then world champions. Paul partnered Victor Barna, a Hungarian who held the world championship for many years, while I played alongside Richard Bergmann, a young Austrian who was the current world champion. This was for me a great honour and it was amazing how playing at this level lifted one's own capability.

We were often invited to London nightclubs and although not my cup of tea, I found it an experience which was quite enjoyable. I remember in particular the Artists' Club and Number 1 Piccadilly. I never saw the point of attending these places and paying inflated prices for drinks and service but as we seldom had to pay, it was worth joining in. More to my liking were the 24-hour passes for visits to Slough when Estelle and I met up with old friends for drinks at the local. My brother-in-law, Percy Climer, was a policeman and one of his duties was the stewardship of the South Bucks Police Recreation Club. I spent many happy hours there for games of snooker and darts. As a result I came to know many members of the regular police force, as well as quite a few Special Constables. They made me very welcome and tended to regard me as their own fighter pilot. It was through Percy that Estelle was engaged, nominally as secretary, to the Slough CID department. Though not officially a policewoman, she frequently assisted the 'tecs' in their dealings with female wrong-doers.

I got to know Mr. Tucker, the Superintendent, very well, especially after being reported for low flying! One low pass over Slough police station from North to

South took me over Windsor Castle and a sharp-eyed Windsorian caught my number. Fortunately, he reported it to the police and not to the RAF, so I got away with a tongue-in-cheek telling off from the Super.

On another evening I had a taste of fame. Then as now we maintained close links with the lads of the ATC (Air Training Corps) and often welcomed them at Kenley with introductory flights. As a result, two of us were asked to attend the headquarters of a South London squadron for a session with the press. The following morning and the same evening my picture appeared in the London papers giving the boys instruction about aero engines and combat manoeuvres. The captions over these pictures read 'Tips from an Expert' and described me as 'a British fighter pilot with several German notches to his credit.' As, at that time, I was credited with just one destroyed I came in for some ribbing from the rest of the Squadron. In fact it cost me a round of drinks in the mess.

YEAR	1942	AIRCRAFT		Pilot or 1st Pilot	2nd Pilot, Pupil or Pass.	DUTY (Including Results and Remarks)	Flying Time		Passenger
MONTH	DATE	Type	No.				Dual	Solo	
February	16th	Magister	R1915	Sgt Rolt		To Manston		-55	
		Spitfire	W3898	Self		Manston to Kenley		-40	
	18th	Spitfire	W3898	Self		To Leysdown for air firing		-30	
	20th	Spitfire	W3898	Self		Formation		1-10	
	23rd	Spitfire	AD536	Self		Practice ZZ landing		-55	
	24th	Magister	R1915	Self		To Martlesham via Kenley		1-25	
						GRAND TOTAL TO DATE 341 hours 45 minutes			
	24th	Magister	R1915	Self		From Martlesham Heath to Bircham Newton		-55	
		Magister	R1915	Self		Bircham Newton to Langham		-20	
		Magister	R1915	Self		Langham to White Waltham		1-05	
	25th	Magister	R1915	Self		White Waltham to Kenley		-30	
		Magister	R1915	Self		Kenley to Redhill		-10	
	28th	Spitfire	AD536	Self		An uneventful patrol		-50	
		Spitfire	AD536	Self		Circus		-10	
		Spitfire	AA942	Self		Practice formation		-20	

23 February: This was an early type of GCA (Ground Controlled Approach) to assist landing in bad weather conditions.

24 February: My elder brother, Leslie, 13 years my senior, also volunteered in late 1941 for service in the RAF. Having been closely involved in our father's garage repair and car hire service business at Waddesdon, Leslie was an experienced driver and mechanic. This would normally have seen him, by Murphy's Law, become a cook but miracles do happen and he served as a driver in the MT (Motor Transport) section. All his life Les had suffered from severe asthma and we couldn't believe it when, in February 1942, he was posted to India. All efforts to get the posting cancelled failed. So on this day, I obtained permission to fly to Bircham Newton in order to pay him a farewell visit. There I was informed that he was at nearby Langham and, having flown there, I was directed to the MT drivers' duty room. There were several aircraftsmen sitting around the room, all of whom stood to attention when I, a Pilot Officer, entered. Leslie was sitting on the far side, deeply engrossed in a magazine and when I walked over to stand before him, he still remained in his seat. So, very sharply, I shouted 'Thorne!' This achieved the required response; he sprang to attention, looked me straight in the eye and greeted me with 'You silly bugger!' There was a shocked silence from the other occupants until they realised that I was Leslie's younger brother. We were able to have a short chat, then he drove me out to my aeroplane for our farewell but refused the offer of a fun flight in the Maggie; he did not trust me not to subject him to a few aerobatics. We were not to meet again for four years, when he returned home in 1946.

28 February: This was, in fact, intended to provide cover to what was called a 'biting' operation returning from Le Havre. As part of the circus, shortly after take-off my hood jammed in the half open position and I was obliged to return to base. When the fault had been corrected it was too late to catch the other boys.

An Important Advancement in My Career

I was confirmed as the senior NCO pilot in 'A' Flight so no more flying as arse-end Charlie. I would continue as a sub-section leader but, more important, I could now deputise for a flight commander and lead a flight. Also, orders to the pilots of 'A' Flight were passed through me.

Summary for:- February 1942	Spitfire	4-25
Unit:- 602 Squadron	Magister	5-20
Date:- 1/3/42		
Signature:- H.L. Thorne		

Total time on Spitfire   200 hours 45minutes

Operational hours to date   69 hours 40 minutes

John B. Niven P/O pp F/Lt   *B.P. Finucane* S/Ldr
For O/C. A Flight   O/C 602 Squadron

[A written note]
LINK TRAINER FOR MONTH   *F.V. Beamish* G/Cpt.
                                   C/O of RAF Station Kenley

This was a sharp reminder from the station commander. Link trainer or else! This
was a dig from the boss; however, there was no entry to add for the Link trainer as I,
in common with the other pilots, had not done any. There was no Link at Redhill
and we could not be bothered to go back to Kenley – although we did go for
sessions in the UVR room!

Len Thorne giving
instruction in aero engines
to a member of Southwark
ATC in February 1942.

Southwark ATC listening
to a lecture on combat
manoeuvres given by
Len Thorne on the same
occasion.

F/Lt Roy 'Lulu' Lane, F/Lt Turley-George and F/Lt Desmond O'Connor. F/Lts Lane and Turley-George volunteered to be catapulted off merchant ships. This was considered to be a suicide job but both survived. Dessie O'Connor was killed in March 1942.

602 Squadron, March 1942. Sgt Paul Green, Sgt Sanderson (RAAF), S/Ldr Brendan 'Paddy' Finucane.

YEAR	1942	AIRCRAFT		Pilot or 1st Pilot	2nd Pilot, Pupil or Pass.	DUTY (Including Results and Remarks)	Flying Time		Passenger
MONTH	DATE	Type	No.				Dual	Solo	
March	1st	Spitfire	AD536	Self		Cloud flying and formation		-40	
		Spitfire	AD536	Self		Cloud flying and formation		1-00	
	3rd	Spitfire	AD536	Self		Sweep to Le Touquet and Calais		1-45	
	5th	Spitfire	AD536	Self		Redhill to Kenley		-20	

	8th	Spitfire	AD536	Self		Sweep to Le Touquet area		1-20	
		Spitfire	W3638	Self		Bomber escort to Abbeville		1-25	
	9th	Spitfire	AD536	Self		Air test		1-10	
	12th	Spitfire	P8799	Self		Convoy patrol		1-50	
	13th	Spitfire	W3898	Self		Drogue towing		-45	
		Spitfire	W3756	Self		Practice formation		-45	
		Spitfire	P8799	Self		Cricus to Hazebrouke		1-45	
	14th	Spitfire	AB794	Self		Circus to Le Havre		1-30	
	19th	Spitfire	P8799	Self		Formation and weaving practice		1-05	
	26th	Spitfire	BM186	Self		Air test and aerobatics		-45	
	27th	Spitfire	B7186	Self		Beat up Deal golf course		1-20	
		Spitfire	P8799	Self		Beat up Deal golf course		1-05	
		Spitfire	P8799	Self		Fighter sweep		-30	
	28th	Spitfire	BM142	Self		Cine gun and formation		1-00	
		Spitfire	BM187	Self		Fighter sweep		1-35	
		Spitfire	BM187	Self		Channel search for Group Captain F.V. Beamish		1-10	
	29th	Spitfire	BM156	Self		At first light we resumed the search for the Group Captain		2-00	
		Spitfire	BM142	Self		To Duxford		-45	
		Spitfire	BM142	Self		Army co-op beat up		1-20	

		Spitfire	BM142	Self		Return to Kenley		-40	
	31st					GRAND TOTAL TO DATE 373 hours 35 minutes	3-30	8-25	
							55-25	306-15	7-40

3 March: Although this was a very shallow penetration into enemy territory we remained in the area for some time, receiving a pretty fierce reception from flak, particularly from the Calais area, but no opposition from fighters. I was pleased that, two days later, we returned to the comforts of Kenley.

9 March: The rest of the Squadron did a sweep to Betune. My friend through most of my training time, particularly at Hullavington and Hawarden, Flight Sergeant Desmond (Dessie) O'Connor, failed to return and it was later confirmed that he was killed. Desmond was a quiet, likeable North-country lad and, although according to the author of *Lions Rampant*, the Squadron history, 'he was not outstanding' the gentleman should note that Dessie did the operations to the best of his ability and gave his life in the end. It was my first loss of a close friend and I missed him badly.

13 March: I am puzzled by this first entry as, to the best of my memory, no Spitfire was ever equipped with drogue-towing facilities. The entry should probably have read that we did air firing against a drogue target towed by another aircraft such as the Hawker Henley.

27 March: This was to test out, and give practice to, the ground defences against air attack (not the golfers). The starboard leg of my undercarriage folded up as I touched down for the landing but with full throttle I managed to get off again without any damage and went round again to make a safe landing.

On the return leg of the fighter sweep the air compressor of my aircraft failed, believed to be due to flak damage. I made an emergency landing at Kenley without flaps or brakes. Although I used the longer of the two runways, I finished up in the small, grassed area at the end of the runway, after 'ground looping' just short of the barbed wire barrier. There was surprisingly little damage to the Spitfire but I rescued the pitot head complete with its heater, which had been torn off and was just hanging on the electric wires. It lay in various places at home, among my bits of memorabilia, until around 2000 but found a more permanent resting place in the Wellesbourne Museum.

28 March: We swept south from the little fishing village of Hardelot to Le Tréport. Although we saw no enemy fighters, it was found after landing that Group Captain Beamish was missing. He and the Wing leader often joined in operations but rather as an independent pair; they obviously ran into trouble out of sight of the rest of us. He was seen by the Wing Commander to leave the French coast but soon afterwards disappeared, apparently into the Channel. After landing from the sweep we were immediately ordered off again to search the Channel area where he was believed to have gone in. We searched until it was too dark to have seen anything; in fact the last 45 minutes of this flight was entered in my logbook as night flying. Group Captain Beamish, although a strict disciplinarian, was always fair and was very popular with everyone at Kenley.

29 March: We continued to search for two hours until our fuel state was critical but sadly our efforts were in vain, the Group Captain was never found. Towards the end of the flight my electrical system went on the blink and I almost force-landed in a field when my petrol gauge read empty. At the last moment I realised that I was very close to Manston so I landed there without mishap.

The loss of Group Captain Beamish was particularly poignant to me as, a few days earlier, he had interviewed me and as a result would recommend that I be granted a commission.

Summary for:- March 1942   1 Spitfire   26-45
Unit:- 602 Squadron   -45
Date:- 31/3/42
Signature H.L. Thorne

Signed *James H. Lacey* F/Lt   *B.S. Finucane* S/Ldr
O/C A Flight 602 Sqdn   O/C 602 Sqdn

Total time on Spitfire 227 hrs 30 mins
Operational hours to date 84 hrs 20 mins

| YEAR | 1942 | AIRCRAFT | | Pilot or 1st Pilot | 2nd Pilot, Pupil or Pass. | DUTY (Including Results and Remarks) | Flying Time | | Passenger |
MONTH	DATE	Type	No.				Dual	Solo	
April	13th	Spitfire	BM187	Self		Local flying		1-05	
	14th	Spitfire	BM113	Self		Fighter sweep to Fécamps at 19,000ft		1-45	
		Spitfire	BM113	Self		Fighter sweep		1-30	
	15th	Spitfire	BM113	Self		Fighter sweep		1-20	
	16th	Spitfire	BM113	Self		Fighter sweep		1-10	
	17th	Spitfire	BM113	Self		Bomber escort		1-30	
		Magister	R1915	Self	LAC Crooks	To Martlesham Heath		1-00	
		Magister	R1915	Self		Return to Kenley		-45	

	25th	Spitfire	BM113	Self		Escort to air sea rescue	1-35	
		Spitfire	BM113	Self		Bomber escort, landed at Lympne	1-40	
		Spitfire	BM113	Self		Returned from Lympne to Kenley	-20	
	26th	Spitfire	BM113	Self		Bomber escort	1-35	
	27th	Spitfire	BM142	Self		Rodeo to St Omer	1-20	
		Spitfire	BM141	Self		Escorted bombers	1-5-	
	29th	Spitfire	BM142	Self		Ramrod 30 to St Omer	1-25	
		Spitfire	BM142	Self		Escort cover	1-20	
	30th	Spitfire	BM142	Self		Target support to Le Havre	1-30	
		Spitfire	BM142	Self		Rodeo over Cap Gris Nez	1-25	

13 April: When I returned to duty after 14 days leave, the CO was kind enough to give me an easy day to celebrate my 22nd birthday.

14 April: We patrolled at 19 to 20,000 feet, entering France at Fécamps in a curve inland to exit near Le Tréport. I was flying Yellow 3 and our flight started to chase seven enemy fighters but before it was possible to get into range, we were recalled to rejoin the Wing. It seems that the seven ME 109s were decoys for another group which was waiting up sun; they were unlucky this time. We returned with no other incident.

On the second sweep we patrolled at 24,000 feet from Desvres to Sangatte. I saw a single FW 190 passing over Yellow Cection and called a warning. When we turned to engage, it dived away before we could get within range. I was then attacked by two 190s but easily out-turned them. I took a quick squirt at another enemy aircraft which appeared behind the Squadron but saw no hits. I had to break off sharply and go into a steep climbing turn to avoid a Spitfire that was diving to attack the same enemy aircraft. In doing so I became separated from the squadron so dived to the 'deck' and returned alone.

16 April: Shortly after crossing the French coast into enemy territory, my No.2, P/O Max Charlesworth, lost a gun panel and we were obliged to return to base.

17 April: We provided escort cover to 6 Hurribombers, flying at 23,000 feet to Marquise. There was 10/10th cloud over the Channel that extended some way inland. After the Hurri boys had bombed we saw them clear of the target area then patrolled inland in a sweep to port that took us out over Dunquerque. At our height at this point we met a Spitfire wing, more or less head on, so had to climb to 27,000 feet to get out of their way. We saw only two enemy aircraft, low down over the coast, so came home.

25 April: This was, without doubt, the worst day of my RAF career and possibly the worst day of my life until I lost Estelle in 1997. It is the one on which I should have died or at least have been shot down. This would almost certainly have happened if the German pilot had been less impatient to add to his score.

A regular visitor to the Kenley Wing and particularly to 602 Squadron was Group Captain Hugh Corner, a doctor based at RAE (Royal Aircraft Establishment) Farnborough. He was researching the effect of operational stress in fighter pilots. He was also a qualified pilot and had flown with 602 on a number of occasions in order to gain first-hand experience.

He arrived on the morning of the 25th and flew with us on the air sea rescue escort patrol. He afterwards complained that it did not give any real experience of operations involving meeting the enemy. Later that day we were briefed on a deep penetration into France to bomb railway marshalling yards near Lille. Group Captain Corner persuaded the Wing leader and Paddy, the Squadron Commander, to allow him to take part. Paddy said, 'I will put you No.2 to Flight Sergeant Len Thorne; he is very experienced and you will be safe with him.' I was flying Red 3 in the centre section and theoretically protected by Blue and Yellow sections to our right and left. Before reaching the target area we carried out attacks on a pair of enemy fighters, then on a four and lastly on a single machine, at which I got in a long burst but did not see any strikes. Then, almost out of ammunition, we headed for home.

As we approached the French coast, the Group Captain and I were attacked by two FW 190s that came in a high-speed dive from the left rear. I saw the first burst of tracer passing over and under my starboard wing and immediately pulled into a tight climbing turn to port, calling to my No. 2 to break with me. I believe he was hard hit in the first burst of fire and failed to turn with me. I rejoined him, calling on other members of the Squadron to help and Paddy called, 'Close in on that Spitfire chaps and we will get him home.' Red 4 appeared to be still under control although he continued to fly straight on, losing height slightly, with a little smoke but no fire coming from the Spitfire. After a time he levelled out and continued to fly on across the Channel and the smoke stopped when he was about midway across. At this point two more or possibly the same pair of 190s attacked me again but their fire appeared to be too high over both my wings. I again pulled hard round and gave them the slip and closed on Red 4 in time to see him go into the sea. The Group Captain had baled out at something like 700 feet but his parachute did not properly open. I was able to see him clearly surrounded by the spreading area of yellow dye but he appeared to be dead. I circled his position but, very short of fuel, I had to leave and made an emergency landing at Lymne.

With Paddy and the Wing leader, I had to face a court of enquiry into the loss of Group Captain Corner and was completely exonerated from blame. There was severe criticism of the two senior officers for giving way to the Group Captain and allowing him to fly on what was known to be a hazardous operation. After the horse had bolted the stable door was closed and orders were issued to prevent a similar occurrence in the future. At the court of enquiry the President's comment was that I could not have avoided or prevented the tragedy. However, at the time and ever since, I have blamed myself and thought that I should have taken some action against the attacking German fighters.

My table tennis friend Sergeant Paul Green was also missing, later confirmed killed, on that fateful day. I was, indeed, extremely lucky to be the one that got away.

26 April: I was flying as Red 3 with one of the new boys as my No.2. We went in with the bombers, I believe they were the newly arrived Douglas Bostons, to Hazebroucke. As we left the French coast near Dunkirk, Red 1 (Paddy), attacked an enemy ME 109 which was in a climbing turn to starboard. I followed and as a result of maintaining a very steep turn, my speed dropped to 140mph. Although very near to stalling, I got a good burst into him. I claimed a 'damaged'. I rejoined Red 1 who attacked a second enemy aircraft, causing it to start smoking and go into a very steep, almost vertical dive. I followed it straight and, from dead astern with the enemy machine dead in my sights, I hit him with a long burst of cannon fire. After catching fire it went straight into the sea. I claimed and was given a half destroyed. Reading Doug Stokes' biography of Paddy some years later I learned that Paddy had withdrawn his claim so I was given one destroyed and one damaged.

27 April: On the first of the two operations above there was no engagement and no Huns were seen. The second was rather different. We escorted 12 Bostons on another deep penetration to Lille. Over the target the ME 109s appeared in force and went for the bombers. I managed to get a good burst at one of them. We faced repeated attacks all the way back to the coast. Only one bomber was lost, he dropped behind and force-landed in France.

29 April: This was another special day in my service career; we had patrolled from Calais to Dunkirk and back to Gravelines to cover the exit of a squadron of bombers from their bombing mission. Prior to taking off, King George VI had paid a visit to Kenley and I had the honour to be presented; after a brief conversation we shook hands and he wished me good luck. During the operation the King spent some time in the Operations room and actually spoke to us while we were over France. It was one of those episodes that one remembers forever.

Escort cover. We climbed to 27,000 feet from Hardelot to Cap Gris Nez; we saw many 109s but they did not attack our squadron and we could not engage.

30 April: I was flying Yellow 2, the first time I had flown as Paddy's No.2, the position known today as wingman. It was a position of great trust. When flying as No.4 or No.2, I had never lost my flight or section leader. We orbited 2 miles off Le Havre and the enemy were there in force. Red 1 attacked a FW 190 that was heading inland but broke off and started to orbit to starboard but suddenly pulled into a very tight climbing turn. I saw tracer coming past my aircraft and realised I was under attack from below by two 190s and that only Paddy's quick reaction had saved me from being hit. The second enemy machine overshot and I was able to give him a long burst with all armament. I had to dive almost vertically to get my sights on with considerable deflection. I saw strikes on the engine, the 190 went straight down, pouring black smoke and apparently out of control.

This was the biggest battle in which I had taken part, a forerunner of the Dieppe raid. I was very lucky not to be shot down and was certainly saved by Paddy's quick evasive action. I claimed 1 probably destroyed. The Squadron score that day was 1 destroyed (by Paddy), 3 probables and 1 damaged. I myself could not confirm Paddy's kill, being otherwise engaged, but Johnny Niven saw it crash.

Summary for:- April 1942   1 Spitfire   22–20
Unit:- 602 Squadron   2 Magister   1–45
Date:- 30/4/42
Signature :- H.L. Thorne

Signed *Johnny B. Niven* F/Lt   Signed *B.P. Finucane* S/Ldr
O/C A Flight   O/C 602 Squadron

Total time on Spitfire: 249–50 hours
Operational hours to date   105–45

| YEAR | 1942 | AIRCRAFT | | Pilot or 1st Pilot | 2nd Pilot, Pupil or Pass. | DUTY (Including Results and Remarks) | Flying Time | | Passenger |
MONTH	DATE	Type	No.				Dual	Solo	
May	1st	Spitfire	BM142	Self		Escort cover to Marquise		1-25	
	3rd	Spitfire	BM142	Self		Circus 145 to Desvres		1-20	
	4th	Spitfire	BM142	Self		Rodeo to Le Havre		-45	
	5th	Spitfire	BM142	Self		Rodeo to Le Havre		1-15	
		Spitfire	BM141	Self		Rodeo to St Omer		1-25	
						GRAND TOTAL TO DATE 403 hours 50 minutes	3-30	8-25	
							55-25	336-30	7-40

1 May: I attacked 4 Focke Wulf FW 190s, with my No.2, Yellow 4, in a short sharp dog fight; between us we managed to get in some good bursts of fire and claimed 1 probably destroyed and one damaged. As was usually the case, the enemy pilots dived away at high speed; we could not follow due to our escort duties.

5 May: For the first four days after May 5th there was a lull in operational activity, for me a very welcome break. After my narrow escapes towards the end of April, I was convinced that in my next operation my luck would run out and I would be the next for the chop. A pencilled note (not in my handwriting) on a strip of paper torn from a logbook:

Dawn readiness tomorrow
Flt. Sgt   Thorne   Leader
Sgts.   Meyer
               Strudwick
               Loud
               Sanderson
Any 'B' Flight Sergeant of 602
Transport from the sergeants' mess at 05.10 A.M.

Sergeant Lou Meyer was a young Dutchman who had made his way to England after the fall of France. I think this was the Sergeant John Strudwick who died 11th May 1945 in a mid-air collision between two Tiger Moths, while acting as a flying instructor at 7 EFTS Elmdon. Bill Loud, a butcher in civvy street, lived up to his calling and achieved great success against the Luftwaffe, ending the war as a Wing Commander. Sergeant Sanderson, an Australian, also survived the war to return to Australia.

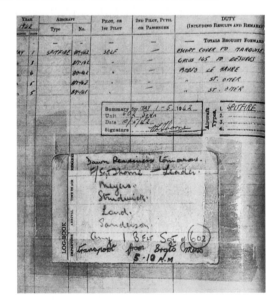

Early May, a note written by Paddy Finucane.

Summary for:- May 1st to the 5th   1 Spitfire   6–10
Unit:- 602 Squadron
Date:- 10/5/42
Signature:- H.L.Thorne

P.H.Major F/Lt   *E.A. Bocock* F/Lt For S/Ldr
For O/C A Flight   For O/C 602 squadron

Pencilled note:

Personal score 2 (or 3) Destroyed
                4 (or 3) Probably destroyed
                2 damaged

After April 25th, although I was not held responsible for the loss of Group Captain Corner, I felt then, and ever since, that I was in some way responsible, or there must have been something I could have done. My only consolation is that, despite being attacked myself, I rejoined and remained with him until after he had bailed out.

On the morning of May 10th we arrived at dispersal and were immediately ordered to the briefing room to be told of another deep penetration up to the Belgian border. Returning to dispersal, Johnny Niven said, 'I have put you to fly Red 3, is that OK?' My reply was somewhat sharp. 'If that's where you have put me, that is where I will fly.' I suppose that my tension was fairly obvious, for a few minutes later I was called by the Squadron Medical Officer, Dr. Hands. He said, 'You have had a rough time in the past few weeks. It is time you went on a rest from operations; you are excused duty immediately. Return to your billet, collect your kit and report to the orderly room where you will be given travel warrants and a posting notice.' Three other pilots who had also been on ops for nearly a year received similar instructions. I remember only two of their names, Sergeants Jimmie Garden of 'B' Flight and Gwilym Willis, like me in 'A' Flight, both of whom had been with me through training. Sergeant Willis went to the CO and said that he was all right and would like to remain with the Squadron. Permission was granted for him to do so; the very next day he was shot down and killed. A few days later the remainder of the squadron were taken out of 11 Group and posted to a station in the north of England for a well deserved rest.

At this point in my logbook a loose form had been stuck in between the pages; basically, it was as follows:

SUMMARY OF FLYING AND ASSESSMENT FOR YEAR COMMENCING JULY 1st. 1941

ASSESSMENT of ABILITY
(To be assessed as:- Exceptional, Above the Average, Average or Below the Average)

(i) AS A F PILOT   *Good Average*
ii) AS PILOT-NAVIGATOR/NAVIGATOR   *Good Average*

ANY POINTS IN FLYING OR AIRMANSHIP WHICH SHOULD BE WATCHED
Nil

DATE 10/5/42   SIGNATURE *E.R. Bocock* F/Lt For S/Ldr
OFFICER COMMANDING 602 (City of Glasgow) Sqdn A.A.F.

Normally a rest posting would be as an OTU or training school instructor; in exceptional cases it might be a short spell of non-flying duties. I was incredibly lucky in being posted to the AFDU, the Air Fighting Development Unit at Duxford, near Cambridge. I expected that my 'rest' would last for the usual six months but things did not turn out that way and I was never to return to Squadron membership.

George **VI,** *by the Grace of God,* OF GREAT BRITAIN, IRELAND AND THE BRITISH DOMINIONS BEYOND THE SEAS, KING, DEFENDER OF THE FAITH, EMPEROR OF INDIA, &c.

To Our Trusty and well beloved   **Herbert Leonard Thorne**   Greeting:

WE, *reposing especial Trust and Confidence in your Loyalty, Courage, and good Conduct, do by these Presents Constitute and Appoint you to be an Officer in Our* Royal Air Force Volunteer Reserve *from the* First *day of* May 1942. *You are therefore carefully and diligently to discharge your Duty as such in the Rank of* Pilot Officer *or in such higher Rank as We may from time to time hereafter be pleased to promote or appoint you to and you are at all times to exercise and well discipline in their Duties both the inferior Officers and Airmen serving under you and use your best endeavours to keep them in good Order and Discipline. And We do hereby Command them to Obey you as their superior Officer and you to observe and follow such Orders and Directions as from time to time you shall receive from Us, or any your superior Officer, according to the Rules and Discipline of War, in pursuance of the Trust hereby reposed in you.*

GIVEN at Our Court, at Saint James's
the Ninth day of June 1942 in the Sixth Year of Our Reign
By His Majesty's Command

Officer Commissioning certificate.

4

RAF DUXFORD AFDU (AIR FIGHTING DEVELOPMENT UNIT)

As I mentioned, a rest from operations usually lasted six months and for most chaps a spell in Training Command. The lucky ones went to OTUs (Operational Training Units) but most became instructors at EFTS (Elementary Training Schools, or SFTS (Service Flying Training Schools). The Empire training scheme was by then in full swing so many of the chaps went to Canada or South Africa and their positions became permanent. My old instructor, F/Lt Hall, was one of those posted to South Africa.

I was exceptionally lucky in being posted to the AFDU at Duxford. I arrived there on May 10th, still a Flight Sergeant and reported to the adjutant, Flt. Lt. Simms, always known as 'Simmy', to be told that my arrival there had to be a mistake as only Officer pilots were posted to the AFDU. I produced my posting papers and was passed on to the unit commanding officer, Wing Commander Campbell-Orde, who again informed me that there had to be a mistake. I said that, towards the end of April, I had had commission interviews, first with Group Captain F.V. Beamish, the Kenley station commander, followed by another with Air Vice Marshal Leigh Mallory, the officer in charge of fighter command. I suggested that my commission must have been approved but the information had not arrived at Kenley before I left. 'Simmy' was instructed to phone Air Ministry for confirmation and my suggestion proved to have been correct.

My commission was confirmed, Gazetted May 1st 1942. My rank now: Pilot Officer. At that time promotion from Flight Sergeant to Pilot Officer was something of a mixed blessing as it led to an actual reduction of income. As an NCO I was attached to the Sergeants' Mess and all food and accommodation was free but as an officer I received an initial uniform allowance of, I believe, £50, which was only enough to cover bare necessities; further purchases had to come out of my pocket. In addition, I moved into the Officers' Mess and had to pay mess bills so I was definitely worse off. This situation was put right by an immediate further promotion to Flying Officer for all of us who were promoted from Flight Sergeant or Warrant Officer rank.

YEAR	1942	AIRCRAFT		Pilot or 1st Pilot	2nd Pilot, Pupil or Pass.	DUTY (Including Results and Remarks)	Flying Time		Passenger
MONTH	DATE	Type	No.				Dual	Solo	
May	12th	Spitfire	(AF)R	Self		Fighter Affiliation, Co-operation with Sterlings at Marham		-20	
		Spitfire	R	Self		Co-op with Sterlings		1-10	
		Spitfire	R	Self		Return to Duxford		-20	
	13th	Spitfire	AD178	Self		Air test at 18,000ft		1-00	
	14th	Spitfire	R	Self		Target for cine gun		-25	
		Spitfire	Y	Self		Cine gun practice		-25	
	15th	Stinson Reliant	?	F/Lt Clive	Self	Circuits and bumps	-25		
		Stinson Reliant	?	Self	Sgt Kulczyk	A short flip around Duxford		-20	
		Spitfire	R	Self		Cine gun, improved type		-25	
		Defiant	?	Self	Sgt Reeve	Cine gun tests for rear gunner		-20	
		Spitfire	R	Self		To Waddington		-40	
		Spitfire	R	Self		Co-op with Lancasters		-40	
		Spitfire	Y	Self		Return to Duxford		-40	
		Spitfire	W	Self		To Seyerston		-30	
		Spitfire	Y	Self		Co-op with Lancasters		-25	
		Fairey Fulmar	?	Lieutenant ?	Self & Flt Sgt Brazendale	Return to Duxford			-25
	18th	Stinson Reliant	?	P/O Poole	Self	To White Waltham			-50
	26th	Spitfire	AB169	Self		Air and engine test		1-00	
	27th	Spitfire	AA983	Self		Inertia weight trial		-45	
		Spitfire	AB169	Self		Inertia weight trial		-55	

	Spitfire	AA983	Self		No weight and no IFF trial		-30	
	Spitfire	AB169	Self		Inertia weights, formation trial		-45	
	Spitfire	T	Self		To Langham		-35	
28th	Spitfire	T	Self		Return to Duxford		-30	
29th	Spitfire	T	Self		To Waddington		-30	
	Spitfire	T	Self		Co-op with Lancaster		-45	
	Spitfire	X	Self		Co-op with Manchester		-40	
30th	Spitfire	V	Self		To Scampton		-10	
	Spitfire	V	Self		Co-op with Lancaster		-20	
	Spitfire	V	Self		To Waddington		-10	
31st	Airspeed Oxford	?	F/Lt Murray	Self	Circuits and bumps	-55		
	Oxford	?	P/O Walker	Self & F/Lt Murray	To Duxford			-45
	Oxford	?	Self	F/Lt Murray & P/O Walker	To Waddington		-45	
					Grand Total: 421 hours 10 mins	3-30	8-25	
						56-45	352-30	5-35

14 May: It was usual in non-operational units, such as this and training schools, to refer to aircraft permanently on strength by letters rather than the registration numbers. Strictly speaking this only applied, in AFDU, to the machines used for fighter affiliation, transport or ferrying, as all other aircraft would normally have flown fully armed, ready to go into action if called upon. This will be apparent as these notes go on and later Marks of Spitfire, Mustangs, Hurricanes, etc. appear. In 1945 the situation was clarified when AFDU was given full Squadron status and became AFDS.

15 May: The first flight that day was my 'conversion course' on to a different single-engined aircraft, just a quick explanation of the controls, one landing demonstration by F/Lt Denis Clive, one circuit and landing for me without breaking anything and I was passed as qualified. Later, it was a look through the pilot's notes and perhaps a few words about any peculiarities and off I went. How different to today's requirements for Health and Safety!

The second flight was my first solo, with a passenger, on type. Tadeux 'Teddy' Kulczyk was a Polish junior officer, one of many Poles who had escaped from the Germans or the Russians when Poland was occupied. After his arrival in this country he, although a fully qualified pilot, was given retraining on Spitfires and joined AFDU while he awaited the formation of Polish fighter squadrons. During this period he met and married a very pretty English girl, Monica, from Somerset.

He and Monica had a room at the Duxford vicarage and, after I was given a 'sleeping out' pass and Estelle was permitted to join me, we came to know the Kulczyks very well and became good friends. Many years later we spent weekends with them at Sampford Peverell in Somerset. After the war ended Teddy returned briefly to Poland but, finding things difficult under Russian Communist dictatorship, he made a second escape and returned to England and joined Monica on the family farm in Somerset.

In the winter of 1942/43 Wing Commander Donald Finlay, an athlete of note, a pre-war member of the British Olympic team, was our commanding officer. A fanatic about physical fitness, he turned us out in the mornings for PT on the tarmac and sometimes, on cold and frosty mornings, for a 6-mile country run. This was not exactly popular with most of the pilots and on one such occasion, Teddy went sick but, sadly for him, appeared from behind a haystack armed with a 12 bore shotgun and carrying one or two dead rabbits. Donald carried on, pretending not to notice, but a week later Teddy was posted to one of the newly formed Polish Squadrons, I believe at Northolt.

My trip in the Defiant was with a very trusting rear gunner as this was my first solo flight in a 'Daffy'. It felt big, underpowered and heavy, but was easy to fly, handled rather like a Hurricane. It was intended for use as a night fighter but was not particularly successful. It was used in the Battle of Britain and for one day caught the Germans by surprise and had some success. It was short-lived; the Luftwaffe boys quickly realised that it had only rearward-firing guns in a powered gun turret. The next time it was used, the Squadron suffered horrific losses. It was, as far as I know, never used in daylight again.

I am a bit puzzled by this entry in my logbook about the Fairey Fulmar, a two-seater, pilot and observer/gunner; if we really were carried in a Fulmar one of the rear passengers would have been obliged to sit on the other's lap! I am inclined to think that my logbook, in this instance, was at fault and the aircraft was actually a Fairey Battle. The Fulmar was a Fleet Air Arm aircraft, a smaller and faster version of the Fairey Battle and used throughout the war as a fighter, whereas the Battle was a light bomber with a crew of three. At a casual glance they looked similar although, as I say, the Fulmar was much smaller.

I assume that Spitfire Y became unserviceable during our stay at Seyerston and Sgt Brazendale, our ground staff NCO, and I were ferried home by a pilot of our sister unit, NAFDU (Naval Air Fighting Development Unit).

18 May: P/O Poole had completed his spell at AFDU and shortly after the flight returned to his squadron. Three months later he was shot down and killed in the Dieppe raid, leaving behind his lovely young wife expecting their first baby, another of the war's tragedies.

27 May: These were my first flights as an experimental test pilot. Inertia weights were fixed to the control surfaces, elevators, ailerons and rudder, to make movement lighter or easier for the pilots. IFF was a small transmitter in the tail unit, the initials standing for 'Identification, Friend or Foe' that had to be switched on by the pilot immediately after take-off on every flight. As a check by the controller he, the pilot, would be asked to confirm 'my cock is crowing'. I never quite understood why this reply caused so much amusement. I believe that a similar device is still used today called a 'Transponder', which enables controllers worldwide to identify and locate every aircraft in the air in their sector.

29 May: The Avro Manchester was a twin-engine bomber to augment the heavy bomber force and replace the obsolete Whitley. It proved to be a failure, under-powered and unable to reach its planned operating ceiling with a full bomb load. It was redesigned with four of those magnificent Rolls-Royce Merlin engines and became the most successful bomber of the war – the Lancaster.

30 May: This was the night of the first 1000-bomber raid, the target, Cologne. Every unit in Bomber Command, including many OTUs, was involved. Likewise, to make up the number, even trainee aircrew members were roped in.

In our flight affiliation part of AFDU our Flight Commander, F/Lt (later Squadron Leader) Jock Murray, an intrepid pilot who had already completed two tours of bombing operations, volunteered to go, if an aircraft could be found for him. The Wing Commander at Waddington said they would see what could be done but it might be difficult to find a spare crew, particularly air gunners. Jock said, 'No problem, my three fighter pilots would love to join in and could be given a quick lesson in operating the gun turrets!'

A little later Jock was informed that the only possibility was a Halifax bomber that was undergoing routine servicing at nearby Scampton and, if the work could be finished in time, he could have it. To our great relief it was not ready in time for take-off, otherwise we might have been the only Spitfire pilots to have been on that raid. However, as willing(?) volunteers we were invited to attend the briefing and join the returned crews for their bacon and egg breakfast.

31 May: The AFDU operated a sub flight of three Spitfires to carry out co-operation/fighter affiliation, with Bomber Command units. They were usually flown by those pilots who were on short breaks at AFDU from operational duties, usually under the command of an experienced Squadron leader initially, during my stay F/Lt Murray DFC,DFM, soon to be promoted to S/Ldr. We were often detached for a week or more and took our own ground crews for servicing the Spitfires. These chaps were ferried, together with their tools and equipment with us, in a twin-engine aircraft, at this time a twin-engine Airspeed Oxford. As I had to take my turn flying the ferrying aircraft and had never flown a multi-engine machine, I had to be given a conversion 'course'. My conversion flight on to twins took a little longer than the previous one. Jock gave me a quick run through 'vital actions' before take-off, then demonstrated starting up procedure. This was interesting and took me back to the early days of motorcars, using a starting handle. To start each Oxford engine a starting handle was inserted in a hole in the side of each cowling then turned vigorously until the required revs were reached. The pilot then 'threw' in the starter and switched on the ignition; hopefully the engine started. If not, the whole procedure was re-run. Jock then took me through a take-off and landing and just told me what to do in case of one engine failure. That was it; he handed over to me for a couple of circuits and, being satisfied that I could do it without breaking anything, said, 'OK, you are passed out proficient on twins.' That was my only instruction on flying multi-engine machines. Later I flew the old Avro Anson, the powerful Douglas Boston, Percival Q6 and even handled a Lancaster. I reckon today's instructors would have a fit. As can be seen from my flight later that day, my colleagues had every confidence in my ability by allowing me to fly them, first to Duxford, then on to Waddington.

Summary for:- May 1942
Unit:- AFDU Duxford

1 Spitfire			14–35	
2 Stinson Reliant	–25		–20	
3 Defiant			–20	
4 Fulmar				–30
6 Oxford	–55		–45	–45

Date:- 3/6/1942
Signature:- *H.L. Thorne*

E. Smith S/Ldr
O/C Flying AFDU

My posting to Duxford was expected to last six months, after which I would return to either my old Squadron or as a replacement in another. I had already recorded 105 hours of operational flying with about 70 flights over enemy-held territory. During that first six months I was mainly regarded as a 'hack' pilot, first to do any odd flying called for, such as ferrying personnel or doing fighter affiliation with the bomber boys.

YEAR	1942	AIRCRAFT		Pilot or 1st Pilot	2nd Pilot, Pupil or Pass.	DUTY (Including Results and Remarks)	Flying Time		Passenger
MONTH	DATE	Type	No.				Dual	Solo	
June	1st	Spitfire	X	Self		Return to Duxford		-30	
		Spitfire	X	Self		Target aircraft for practice attacks		-15	
		Spitfire	X	Self		Cine gun exercises		-10	
	2nd	Skua	L2994	Self	LAC Ainslie	To Matlas		-50	
		Skua	L2994	Self	LAC Ainslie	Drogue towing		-30	
		Skua	L2994	Self	LAC Ainslie	Drogue towing		-10	
		Skua	L2994	Self	LAC Ainslie	Drogue towing		-30	
		Skua	L2994	Self	LAC Ainslie	Return to Duxford		-50	
	3rd	Spitfire	X	Self		Air test		-20	
		Spitfire	R	Self		To Waddington		-30	
	4th	Spitfire	R	Self		Air test		-20	
		Spitfire	V	Self		To Woodhall Spa		-25	
		Spitfire	V	Self		Co-op with Lancaster		-30	
		Lancaster	N	P/O ?	Crew & Self	Fire control			-50
		Spitfire	V	Self		To Waddington		-10	
	5th	Spitfire	V	Self		To Woodhall Spa		-10	
		Spitfire	V	Self		Co-op Lancasters, Landed at Scampton		-40	
		Spitfire	V	Self		Co-op Lancasters, Landed at Waddington		-25	
	7th	Spitfire	V	Self		To Bottesford		-10	
		Spitfire	V	Self		Co-op Lancasters		-50	
		Spitfire	V	Self		To Waddington		-10	
	8th	Spitfire	V	Self		To Desford		-20	

		Spitfire	V	Self		Back to Waddington		-20	
		Spitfire	V	Self		To Syerston		-15	
		Spitfire	V	Self		Co-op Lancasters		1-10	
		Spitfire	V	Self		To Waddington		-10	
	9th	Spitfire	V	Self		To Syerston		-10	
		Spitfire	V	Self		Co-op Lancasters		1-00	
		Spitfire	R	Self		To Waddington		-10	
	10th	Spitfire	R	Self		To Digby		-10	
		Spitfire	R	Self		To Waddington		-10	
		Spitfire	R	Self		To Duxford		-30	
		Oxford	AF	F/Lt Murray	Self	To Reading	-35		
	14th	Spitfire	CTE	Self		Air test		1-05	
	16th	Skua	L2994	Self	LAC Ainslie	To Ludham		1-00	
	17th	Spitfire	AB178	Self		Fuel consumption test		-25	
		Mustang	RMZ	Self		Familiarity on type. Air test		1-05	
		Spitfire	AB178	Self		Fuel consumption tests		-30	
	18th	Skua	L2994	Self	LAC Ainslie	To Ludham		-45	
		Skua	L2994	Self		To Duxford		-45	
	19th	Spitfire	T	Self		To Honnington		-15	
		Spitfire	T	Self		Co-op Wellingtons		1-10	
		Spitfire	T	Self		Co-op Wellingtons		1-10	
		Spitfire	T	Self		Return to Duxford		-15	
	20th	Spitfire	Y	Self		Ground attacks		-45	
		Spitfire	S	Self		Target for cine gun		-20	
	21st	Spitfire	Y	Self		Comparative speed runs v Seafire (landed at Stradishall)		1-20	

		Spitfire	R	Self		Escort to German of 1426 Flight		1-05	
	22nd	Spitfire	T	Self		To Boscombe Down			
		Spitfire	T	Self		Return to Duxford			
	23rd	Oxford	AF	F/Lt Rumble	Self	Further instruction in multi-engine aircraft			
	24th	Oxford	AF	Self	Sgt Reeve & crew	And the rest of the ground crew to Waddington			
		Oxford	AF	Self	Sgt Reeve & crew	Members of the ground crew to Duxford			
		Skua	L2994	Self	LAC Ainslie	Drogue towing. Landed at Ludham			
		Skua	L2994	Self	LAC Ainslie	Return to Duxford			
	25th	Spitfire	?	Self		Inertia weight trial			
		Spitfire	?	Self		Inertia weight trial			
		Oxford	AF	Self	F/O Poole	To White Waltham			
	28th	Oxford	AF	Self	LAC Watson & AC Smith	Local flying			
		Spitfire	AFT	Self		To Wyton via Oakington and Waterbeach		-25	
		Spitfire	AFT	Self		Co-op with Sterlings		1-00	
		Spitfire	AFT	Self		Return to Duxford		-2-	
	29th	Boston	AFZ	S/Ldr Smith	Self & F/O Poole	To Methwold		-25	
		Spitfire	AFW	Self		Return to Duxford		-20	
		Spitfire	AFW	Self		Co-op with Wellingtons		1-10	

	30th	Boulton Paul Defiant	V1121	Self	Sgt Reeve	Target for Spitfire	-35		
						GRAND TOTAL TO DATE 458 hours 45 minutes	3-30	8-25	
							58-30	388-20	7-15

1 June: Third flight. Two aircraft were involved in this type of trial, one acting as target, the other carrying out mock attacks, probably to test either an improved type of film or new camera.

2 June: No conversion course for the Skua. I do not remember any instructions at all, just get in and fly the thing. The Skua was a hopelessly obsolete aircraft that started out as a Fleet Air Arm ship-borne fighter but was quickly overshadowed and replaced by better machines. L 2994 arrived at Duxford, complete with LAC Ainslie who was trained in the use of drogue targets for air-firing practice. We flew to Matlas, somewhere on the east coast, and had the winch-towing equipment installed in the rear cockpit. In flight, the drogue, a canvas sleeve rather like a large windsock, could be streamed way out at the rear of the towing aircraft. It then became the target for the trainee fighter pilots. I was always concerned that they would hit the towing aircraft rather than the drogue but as we did not have a successful exercise, I never did find out whether it happened.

AFDU ground crew with Spitfire P7290, Mk 2.

Len Thorne in Spitfire P7290.   AFDU group at Wittering.

Tadeusz 'Teddy' Kulczyk and Len with Mustang 1, Duxford, 1942.

These exercises were carried out off the east coast, just off Lowestoft; they were all unsatisfactory. On two of the trips the drogue failed to stream and once almost got tangled into the tail-plane. On another effort, the fighter failed to turn up so although they say, 'If at first you don't succeed, try, try again,' three was enough, we gave up and went home. Further trials were postponed until June 18th.

4 June: When carrying out fighter affiliation exercises I was, on several occasions, invited to fly in a Lancaster. I was invited by the pilot to make this flight and it is entered in my logbook as 'passenger' but actually after becoming airborne, I took over the controls from the 2nd pilot's position to demonstrate corkscrewing. Although I did something similar on later flights it was always as 2nd pilot. What a delightful aeroplane the Lanc was to fly, as easy on the controls as any fighter.

8 June: First trip. An early morning flight to Desford to visit my old instructors and show off my prowess in a Spitfire. They were pleased to see one of their pupils who had successfully made it on to front-line fighters but green with envy, having to continue as instructors.

During this period we three fighter boys, P/O Walker, P/O Godefroy and I, together with Jock Murray, were officially 'detached'. This suited us very well as Waddington was one of the pre-war stations with an excellent officers' mess which had its own pig and poultry farm, so the food was first class. As we were only temporary visitors we paid no mess bills other than drinks at the bar. We generally had time on our hands and put it to good use in the games and snooker rooms. Jock, of course, knew many of the senior officers and arranged for us to spend time at the aircraft dispersals and attend the briefings when operations were taking place.

10 June: To Reading. Jock Murray had two sessions at AFDU during my service there and was promoted to Squadron Leader in the autumn of 1942. He was in command of the Fighter Affiliation flight and its operations. A tall, slim, raw-boned Scotsman, he started the war, like me, as an NCO pilot, being awarded a DFM for operations on Wellingtons. He was commissioned and went on to be awarded a DFC for another tour of operations, initially on Wimpies, later on Lancasters.

After his spell at AFDU, I believe that Jock went back on operations as one of the 'Pathfinders', flying both Lancasters and Mosquitos in that role, and received further awards. His wife sometimes travelled from their home in Scotland to attend ladies' nights and other social functions. I remember her as a handsome woman, as tall as Jock, and I could picture her leading a band of kilted Scotsmen to fight the Redcoats or members of another clan.

16 June: Another attempt at target towing; this time it was the weather that beat us, very low cloud and poor visibility over the sea.

17 June: Fuel consumption. For these tests the aircraft was fitted with a Kent flow-meter, installed by the manufacturers at Luton.

Mustang. This was my first solo on type, no special instructions other than take-off and final approach speed, then get in and fly it. This was a Mustang Mk 1, known to the American Air Force as the P51, which was powered by an Allison engine. Designed essentially for airfield defence, it was turned down by the RAF due to inadequate performance at high altitude.

18 June: Another wasted trip! We finally gave up and the Skua was returned to whence it came.

19 June: During this six-month period, the flights titled 'co-op' or 'co-operation' with various bombers should more correctly be called 'fighter affiliation'. They were intended to help the bomber boys cope with enemy fighter attacks, day or night. This mainly involved teaching them a manoeuvre called a 'corkscrew' to throw the attacker off his aim or merely to avoid being hit by his gunfire.

The trips were relatively short but very tiring. It would appear that we only did one or two exercises per day; this is not so, as only one fighter was involved each time and we fighter boys took it in turn to do the attacking, each in a different machine. On some occasions even Jock would join in; he loved to fly the Spitfires whenever he could.

21 June: The Seafire was the Fleet Air Arm equivalent to a Spitfire Mk 11, equipped for deck landings on an aircraft carrier, with an arrester hook instead of, or as well as, a tail wheel. In this instance, it would have been flown by a pilot of our sister unit, the NAFDU (Naval Air fighting Development Unit), commanded by Lieutenant Commander Brian Kendal.

The 1426 Flight was formed to fly any enemy aircraft that fell into Allied hands. Originally part of AFDU, they operated as an independent detached unit, although their administration was still looked after by the AFDU headquarters staff. Among others, they flew a Heinkel III, a Messerschmitt 110, a JU88, a Fieseler Storch and an ME 109E. Later, in 1943, a Focke Wulf 190 was also added to their strength. We escorted the Heinkel to Stradishall where we stayed overnight before flying on the next morning to Boscombe Down.

23 June: In addition to basic instructions, it was thought necessary for me to have further instruction into emergency procedures such as in the event of an engine failure, having to fly and land on one engine. F/Lt Rumble (always known as Tubby) was at that time the AFDU Flight Commander, a very experienced pilot with thousands of flying hours in his logbook.

24 June: I was wrong in my earlier comment, we had not yet seen the last of the Skua. Our efforts were rewarded – success at last!

Looking back I am surprised that the Skua winch operator was only a Leading Aircraftsman (LAC). Before the war and in the early months, many aircrew below pilot category were corporals or below. This unfair situation was corrected and later all members of aircrew were sergeants and above.

28 June: The first of the day was a fun flight for two of the lads. Funny; although I was inexperienced on twins, the members of the ground staff never questioned my capability. The flight to White Waltham on the 25th seems a bit peculiar; I assume that

I flew the Oxford there, then left the aircraft to hitch a lift to Slough for the weekend, leaving F/O Poole (usually known as Puddle) to make the return to Duxford.

After I had been at Duxford for two or three weeks, I was again summoned for a talk with the officer commanding AFDU, Wing Commander Campbell-Orde, for some reason always known as 'the General'. I was informed that he encouraged his married officers to 'live out' with their wives. I explained that even married women below a certain age had to do some form of war work and that my wife Estelle was the secretary to the CID department of Slough police force. He suggested that in order to get her released, I should take another week's leave and get her pregnant. I was quite willing to act on his suggestion and went off to Slough determined to do my best. In the event, I was not put to the test, as the officer in charge at Slough, Superintendent Tucker, was a friend of the family and Estelle was released without any difficulty, on condition that she obtained a job at Duxford. This did not happen as there was no suitable work nearby, so she merely left her name on the register and we fulfilled the Wingco's original suggestion before she was called upon.

For the first month we had a room at the Duxford village vicarage, a large rambling old house with lots of spare rooms. The vicar was the Rev. Dr. Braham, whose son was Wing Commander John Braham, at that time the top-scoring night fighter pilot. John's wife Joan and their baby son, Michael, also lived at the vicarage. Also in residence were our polish pilot, Tadeusz Kulczyk and his English wife, Monica. We all became good friends.

Two other temporary residents were the village schoolmistress and her daughter and the aristocratic Mrs. Hastings-Till. One morning the vicar announced that he hoped everyone would attend his church the coming Sunday and I remember Estelle's whispered comment that the day she attended a service he would fall out of his pulpit. Our quarters were not really ideal but at the time we were glad of them. We were delighted when F/O Peter Poole was posted back to his squadron and we were tipped off that their rooms at College Farm, also in Duxford village, were available if we wished to take them over. It was with great delight that we did so.

Our stay there lasted from the end of June until March 1943, when the 'Yanks' took over Duxford. College Farm was owned by Guy and Ynez Smith, a young couple much the same age as ourselves and who had also been married just the previous year. It was a working farm of some 600 acres and included much of the land to the south of the airfield. Guy's family farmed a large area to the south of Cambridge. Ynez's father was a director of the Bank of England. We paid the princely sum of £1 per week for our rooms – large bedroom, dressing room, sitting room, kitchen and scullery. As I was frequently away for several days at a time on fighter affiliation exercises, Ynez decided that it was not much fun for Estelle to cook meals just for herself, so she was invited to join Ynez and Guy at mealtimes. I believe there was a nominal extra charge for this but Ynez usually refused to take it. Ynez loved parties and encouraged us to invite other AFDU members and their ladies for evening meals.

Among some of the houseguests were Lieutenant Giles Guthrie and his beautiful wife, Rhona. Giles was a member of a private banking family and my opposite number in NAFDU. We met many years after the war, when he was the guest speaker at a Birmingham Chamber of Commerce luncheon. He recognised me across the room and immediately left his seat to come over for a chat; I felt very honoured.

Third flight. The Short Stirling was the third of the four-engine heavy bombers that came into service in 1941/2 and carried the war into the heart of Germany. It was not altogether a success and quite soon was almost entirely replaced by the Lancaster and Handley Page Halifax for the bombing role. It was used later in the war as a tug for troop-carrying gliders.

29 June: This was my first flight in an American Douglas Boston, a light twin-engine bomber, powered by two Wright Cyclone double row radial engines. It was a very powerful machine and with a cruising speed similar to a Spitfire, it was a welcome replacement for the Bristol Blenheim and made escort duty very much easier.

Summary for:- June 1942	1	Spitfire	23-55
Unit:- AFDU Duxford	2	Skua	7-40
Date:- 2/7/42	3	Lancaster	-50
Signature:- *L. Thorne*	4	Oxford	3-35
	5	Mustang	1-05
	6	Boston	-25
	7	Defiant	-35

E. Smith Sqdn Ldr
O/C Flying, AFDU Duxford

The Defiant, whilst something of a failure on operations, was easy to fly, handling rather like a Hurricane. Our ground staff chaps were always happy to come along for a flip; they could sit in the gun turret and play Biggles. Once again, this was only my second flight in a Defiant but the groundstaff boys seemed to have every confidence in my ability to take off and land safely.

YEAR	1942	AIRCRAFT		Pilot or 1st Pilot	2nd Pilot, Pupil or Pass.	DUTY (Including Results and Remarks)	Flying Time		Passenger
MONTH	DATE	Type	No.				Dual	Solo	
July	1st	Spitfire	T	Self		To Lakenheath		-15	
		Spitfire	T	Self		Co-op Stirlings		1-00	
		Spitfire	T	Self		Return to Duxford		-50	
	2nd	Defiant	V1121	Self	LAC Hatherley	Local flying		1-05	
		Defiant	V1121	Self	Sgt Reeve	Local flying. Sight test		1-10	

3rd	Defiant	V1121	Self	Sgt Reeve	Local flying. Sight test	-35	
	Spitfire	AB169	Self		Air test	-25	
4th	Spitfire	O	Self		Air test	-25	
	Spitfire	T	Self		To Scampton	-35	
	Spitfire	T	Self		Co-op with Lancasters	-50	
	Spitfire	T	Self		Co-op with Lancasters	-50	
	Spitfire	T	Self		Co-op with Lancasters	1-00	
	Spitfire	T	Self		Co-op with Lancasters	1-05	
7th	Spitfire	T	Self		Co-op with Lancasters	-45	
	Spitfire	T	Self		Co-op with Lancasters	-45	
	Spitfire	T	Self		Co-op with Lancasters	1-05	
8th	Spitfire	T	Self		To Woodhall Spa	-15	
	Spitfire	T	Self		Co-op with Lancasters	-55	
	Spitfire	T	Self		To Scampton	-15	
	Spitfire	V	Self		To Woodhall Spa	-10	
	Spitfire	V	Self		Co-op with Lancasters	-30	
	Spitfire	V	Self		Co-op with Lancasters	-40	
11th	Spitfire	V	Self		To Duxford	-35	
	Oxford	BG549	Self		To Scampton	-50	
	Oxford	BG549	Self	Cpl Barnes, LACs Watson & Andrioli	To Duxford	1-00	
	Oxford	BG549	Self		To Scampton	-45	
	Oxford	BG549	Self	3 passengers	To Duxford	-50	
12th	Spitfire	T	Self		To Kenley and Redhill	-45	
	Spitfire	T	Self		To Duxford	-45	
18th	Spitfire	T	Self		Aerobatics just for fun	1-20	
20th	Spitfire	T	Self		A local buzz around	-30	

	21st	Oxford	BG549	Self	3 passengers	Test camouflage of the airfield		-45	
		Oxford	BG549	Self	S/Ldr Haywood	To Derby (instructing)		-40	
		Oxford	BG549	Self	S/Ldr Haywood	Return to Duxford (instructing)		-40	
		Spitfire	W	Self		Target aircraft and sight test MOD		-50	
	23rd	Spitfire	T	Self		To Feltwell		-15	
		Spitfire	T	Self		Co-op with Wellington		1-00	
		Spitfire	T	Self		Co-op with Wellington		1-15	
		Spitfire	T	Self		Return to Duxford		-15	
		Spitfire	O	Self		Test hyrdomatic airscrew		-30	
		Spitfire	T	Self		To Oakington		-10	
		Spitfire	T	Self		Co-op Stirlings		1-05	
		Spitfire	T	Self		Co-op Stirlings		1-00	
	25th	Spitfire	T	Self		Return to Duxford		-10	
	26th	Spitfire	T	Self		To Wyton		-15	
		Spitfire	T	Self		Co-op with Stirlings and return to Duxford		-15	
		Spitfire	T	Self		Test new type 'Negative G' carburettor		1-10	
	27th	Oxford	BG549	Self	Sgt Kulczyk, F/Sgt Brazendale	To Heston		-35	
		Oxford	BG549	Self	F/Sgt Brazendale	To Duxford via Redhill		1-10	
	28th	Spitfire	T	Self		Interception of Typhoons		-50	
	29th	Oxford	BG549	Self	LACs Cuthbert & Rawlings	To Heston		-40	

		Oxford	BG549	Self	LACs Cuthbert & Rawlings and Sgt Kulczyk	To Farnborough		-20	
		Oxford	BG549	Self	As above	To Duxford		-45	
		Oxford	BG549	Self	S/Ldr	Dual instruction to S/Ldr		-40	
						GRAND TOTAL TO DATE 497hrs 45 mins	3-30	8-25	
							58-30	427-20	7-15

4 July: It may seem that on these fighter affiliation trips we had long spells just sitting around doing nothing. This was not the case; I do not remember ever being bored. We were allowed to attend the briefings for the bomber crews and would later watch them taking off, fully loaded with petrol, bombs and ammunition. Some mornings we would get up very early to watch the survivors coming home. Later we sometimes attended the de-briefings by the Intelligence Officers, and talked to the very tired crews. On days when there were no operations we could visit local places of interest; when at Waddington or Scampton, Lincoln was always a popular spot.

11 July: On one of these visits I met a most interesting officer, the station commander at Scampton, Group Captain Augustus Walker, generally known as 'Gus' Walker. In the course of operations, a Lancaster crashed on take-off with a full load of bombs on board. Gus led an attempt to rescue the crew. As he reached the stricken machine one of its bombs exploded, and he suffered severe injuries including the loss of an arm. He recovered and resumed his duties, remaining in the RAF after the war, attaining high rank and many decorations.

12 July: A visit to the old squadron (602), back at Kenley after a short rest up north, hardly any of the old lot left; the new boys appeared to be somewhat subdued. I did not repeat the visit.

21 July: Squadron Leader Haywood (always for some reason known as Scruffy) was attached to AFDU as a rest from operations. He was a member of High Society, married to a titled lady who, I believe, was the pre-war 'Health and Beauty Girl'. During his stay they lived in a caravan, parked in a pleasant meadow near a stream. One evening they invited Estelle and me for a meal, trout freshly caught from the stream. They were two lovely people and made us feel thoroughly at home, treating us, in every way, as equals.

As a rest from operations, officers up to the rank of Wing Commander were often posted to AFDU. Like me, up to the time of joining the unit, many had not flown multi-engined aircraft. As a result I sometimes found myself in the role of instructor and it was my great pleasure to instruct Squadron Leader Haywood, who proved an able pupil.

23 July: On some of the affiliation flights the Spitfires operated singly, either at varying times or over a different area. Usually not more than four bombers would take part in each sortie, taking it in turns to be the target aircraft. The fighter would carry out mock attacks on each in turn. In this way most of the bomber crews got their chance to practise taking evasive action, particularly by 'corkscrewing'.

29 July:

Summary for:- July 1942	Spitfire	26-30
Unit:- AFDU Duxford	Defiant	2-50
Date:- 3/8/42	Oxford	9-40
Signature:- H.L. Thorne		

H.S. Sewell Flt Lt
For O/C Flying AFDU

During this month Wing Commander Campbell-Orde and Squadron Leader Ted Smith were sent over to the US on a flag-waving publicity tour, to help the war effort. During their temporary absence, F/Lt H.S. (Bert) Sewell took over as acting O/C Flying, and in that capacity signed my logbook. F/Lt Sewell, known to us all as Susie, became my closest friend during our time together. He was the perfect example of a fighter pilot: young, handsome, debonair, popular. He played a mean game of snooker and had an inexhaustible store of songs and stories. Before the war I understood that he was a car salesman in Darlington and would certainly have fitted the bill. After the war I got in touch with him and found him settled down with his wife in a lovely village in the Darlington area. He was by then the headmaster of a junior school, very changed, not the Susie I remembered.

YEAR	1942	AIRCRAFT		Pilot or 1st Pilot	2nd Pilot, Pupil or Pass.	DUTY (Including Results and Remarks)	Flying Time		Passenger
MONTH	DATE	Type	No.				Dual	Solo	
August	4th	Spitfire	T	Self		To Dishforth		1-25	
	5th	Spitfire	T	Self		To Middleton-St.-George		-20	
		Spitfire	T	Self		Co-op with Halifaxes		-25	

		Boston	AFZ	S/Ldr Swales	Self	To Dishforth			-20
	6th	Boston	AFZ	S/Ldr Swales	Self	To Middleton-St.-George			-25
		Spitfire	T	Self		Air test	-20		
		Spitfire	T	Self		Co-op with Halifaxes	-40		
		Spitfire	T	Self		To Dishforth	-25		
	7th	Spitfire	T	Self		To Middleton-St.-George	-25		
		Spitfire	T	Self		To Dishforth	-25		
	9th	Spitfire	T	Self		To Duxford	1-00		
	19th	Magister	R1915	Self	S/Ldr Watkins	Ferrying to Hucknall	1-00		
		Magister	R1915	Self	S/Ldr Watkins	Return to Duxford	1-00		
	20th	Spitfire	T	Self		To Mildenhall	-20		
		Spitfire	T	Self		Co-op with Wimpies (Wellingtons)	1-00		
		Spitfire	T	Self		Co-op with Wimpies	-50		
		Spitfire	T	Self		Return to Duxford	-15		
	21st	Spitfire	T	Self		To Upwood	-15		
		Spitfire	T	Self		Co-op Blenheims	1-00		
		Spitfire	T	Self		Co-op Blenheims	-45		
		Spitfire	T	Self		Co-op Blenheims	-40		
		Spitfire	T	Self		Co-op Blenheims	-45		
		Spitfire	T	Self		Return to Duxford	-20		
	22nd	Spitfire	W	Self		To Oakington	-10		
		Spitfire	W	Self		Co-op Stirlings and return	1-00		
	23rd	Spitfire	T	Self		Weather test	-10		
		Spitfire	T	Self		To Lakenheath	-20		
		Spitfire	T	Self		Co-op Stirlings	-50		
		Spitfire	T	Self		Return to Duxford	-20		

24th	Spitfire	T	Self		To Lakenheath		-20	
	Spitfire	T	Self		Co-op Stirlings		-40	
	Spitfire	T	Self		Return to Duxford		-20	
	Spitfire	T	Self		To Colerne		-50	
	Spitfire Mk V	Q	Self		Return to Duxford		-50	
26th	Spitfire Mk IX	BF273	Self		Air test to 25,000ft		-50	
	Spitfire	V	Self		Co-op with 'Wimpies'		1-05	
27th	Spitfire	BF273	Self		To Cranfield		-20	
	Stinson Reliant	?	P/O Walker	Self & P/O Mause	To Duxford		-25	
28th	Spitfire	S	Self		To Lakenheath		-40	
	Spitfire	S	Self		Co-op Stirlings. Landed back at Duxford		-40	
29th	Wellington	?	F/Sgt ?	Self & crew	Co-op by 'Teddy and Scotty'			1-30
	Airacobra	AH574	Self		Air test		-35	
30th	Spitfire	AD318	Self		Air and engine test		-50	
31st	Spitfire	T	Self		To Upwood		-20	
	Spitfire	T	Self		Co-op Blenheims		-45	
	Spitfire	T	Self		Co-op Blenheims		-45	
	Spitfire	T	Self		Co-op Blenheims		1-15	
	Spitfire	T	Self		Return to Duxford		-20	
					GRAND TOTAL TO DATE 527 hours 55 minutes	3-30	8-25	
						58-30	457-30	9-30

6 August: First flight. Flying as a passenger in a Douglas Boston was an interesting experience. Our machine was the light bomber/night fighter version, with a crew of three, each isolated from the others: the pilot, who also did the navigation, a mid upper gun position and a bomb aimer position in the nose. By choice I usually flew in the latter position, lying prone and watching the runway hurtling past on take-off and landing; the ground looked very close at these times.

19 August: Hucknall was an airfield near Nottingham, the headquarters and production unit of Rolls-Royce Aero Engine division.

24 August: The flight to Colerne made a change; after weeks going north and east I enjoyed the trip to Colerne near Bath, on a lovely day, over familiar territory. The co-op too, was a new one with Mosquitos. The Mosquito had an all-wooden fuselage and wings, two Merlin engines, and was very fast. It became known as 'the Wooden Wonder'. The PRU (Photographic Reconnaissance Unit) version was faster than most contemporary fighters and needed no armament, relying on its speed for protection. On arrival at Colerne, the Mossies were already airborne so we completed the exercise before landing, then enjoyed a very pleasant lunch before returning to Duxford.

26 August: This was my first flight in a Spitfire Mk IX. After nearly a year of domination by the Focke Wulf FW190s, the RAF was able to re-establish its superiority. Strangely, the Spitfire Mk IX was intended as a temporary measure, being a Mk V modified to take the larger and more powerful Merlin 60 series engine. With its 2-speed, 2-stage supercharger it was faster and could operate at greater heights than its predecessor. Its handling was superb and most pilots agreed that it was the best of all the Spitfires.

The Mk VIII was still on the drawing board, with a completely redesigned airframe to take the bigger engine and would not be ready for action until many Mk IXs were already in action. By the end of 1942, two American companies, Packard and Ford, were manufacturing Merlin 60 series engines, mainly for their own needs in the Mustang (P51) aircraft but also for the increasing British demands for the Spitfire and Lancaster. Spitfires powered by the American engine were known as Mk XVIs; this version also had American .5mm machine guns instead of the Hispano 20mm cannons.

27 August: The first Mk IXs, like the Mk Vs, had the original flat-sided sliding cockpit canopy. I believe that the flight to Cranfield was to have a blister hood with bulging sides fitted to improve visibility, especially to the rear.

29 August: To assist the Wellington crew I took over the controls soon after take-off to demonstrate the action of 'corkscrewing'. This constituted my first solo in that type of aircraft.

That day also saw my first solo in a Bell Airacobra and my first experience of a tricycle undercarriage (i.e. a nose instead of a tail wheel). The Airacobra was a unique aircraft in that the power plant was installed in the rear fuselage behind the pilot and drove a propeller by a shaft that passed through the cockpit under the pilot's seat.

I always had visions of the potential damage to one's private undercarriage if the shaft fractured, although I never heard that such an accident ever occurred. The installation allowed a cannon to fire through the propeller boss, which would add considerably to its accuracy. This machine, the Mk I version, was powered by an American Allison engine and was turned down by the RAF because of poor performance at altitude. Some were used in the North Africa and Italian campaigns and others to very good effect in Russia.

31 August:

Summary for:- August 1942	1 Spitfire 24-55
Unit:- AFDU Duxford	2 Boston -45
Date:- 1/9/42	3 Magister 2-00
Signature:- H.L. Thorne	4 Stinson -25
	5 Wellington 1-30
	6 Airacobra -35

Signed: *D. Clive* Fl Lt
O/C Flying AFDU

F/Lt H.S. Sewell (Susie) was posted back to his squadron round about this date and newly promoted. F/Lt Denis Clive took over as flight commander. Denis was a fine figure of a man, over six feet tall and broad with it; he had a real fighter pilot's moustache. He told us of his pre-war career as a film star and, when Estelle and I went to a cinema in Cambridge to see a film, we were amused to spot him in a minor part, the stars being Jessie Matthews and Alistair Sim. He and his wife Jane also had rooms in Duxford village and Estelle sometimes joined Jane and the other wives for morning coffee.

YEAR	1942	AIRCRAFT		Pilot or 1st Pilot	2nd Pilot, Pupil or Pass.	DUTY (Including Results and Remarks)	Flying Time		Passenger
MONTH	DATE	Type	No.				Dual	Solo	
September	2nd	Defiant	V1121	Self	P/O Ireland	To Nottingham		-45	
		Defiant	V1121	Self		To Duxford		-45	
	3rd	Spitfire	W	Self		To Tempsford		-15	
		Spitfire	W	Self		To Chelveston		-15	
		Spitfire	W	Self		To Duxford		-20	
	6th	Spitfire	W	Self		To Dishforth		1-00	
		Spitfire	W	Self		To Topcliffe		-15	
		Spitfire	W	Self		Co-op Wellingtons		1-20	

		Spitfire	W	Self		To Dishforth		-15	
	7th	Spitfire	W	Self		To Topcliffe		-15	
		Spitfire	W	Self		Co-op Wimpy		1-15	
		Spitfire	W	Self		To Dishforth		-15	
	8th	Spitfire	W	Self		Co-op Wimpy		1-20	
						GRAND TOTAL TO DATE 536 hours 10 minutes	3-30	8-25	
							58-30	465-45	8-00
		Spitfire	V	Self		Co-op Wimpy		1-00	
	9th	Spitfire	V	Self		Co-op Wimpy		1-10	
		Spitfire	V	Self		Co-op Wimpy		1-00	
	10th	Spitfire	V	Self		To Skipton		-15	
		Spitfire	V	Self		Co-op Wimpy		1-30	
		Spitfire	W	Self		Co-op Wimpy		-40	
		Spitfire	W	Self		Co-op Wimpy		-40	
		Spitfire	W	Self		Co-op Wimpy. Landed at Dishforth		-35	
	11th	Spitfire	W	Self		To Skipton		-10	
		Spitfire	W	Self		Co-op Wimpy		1-10	
		Spitfire	W	Self		Co-op Wimpy		-40	
		Spitfire	W	Self		Co-op Wimpy		-45	
		Spitfire	W	Self		Co-op Wimpy		-30	
		Spitfire	W	Self		To Dishforth		-10	
		Spitfire	W	Self		To Duxford		1-00	
	12th	Spitfire	O	Self		Sighting test then on to Lakenheath		-20	
		Spitfire	O	Self		Co-op Stirlings		1-00	
		Spitfire	O	Self		To Duxford		-20	

	13th	Spitfire	W	Self		Co-op Wimpy		1-05	
	14th	Spitfire	AD318	Self		Speed trial		-20	
	15th	Spitfire	S	Self		Co-op Wimpy		1-05	
	16th	Hurricane	AFU	Self		To White Waltham		-40	
		Hurricane	AFU	Self		White Waltham to Northolt		-15	
		Hurricane	AFU	Self		To Duxford		-40	
	17th	Oxford	BG549	Self	Messrs Hall, Lovelock & Austin	A fun flight for members of the Observer Corps		1-30	
	20th	Spitfire	Y	Self		Air test		-20	
	21st	Spitfire	W	Self		Co-op Wimpy		1-05	
	22nd	Spitfire	R	Self		To Waterbeach		-15	
		Spitfire	R	Self		Co-op Stirlings		-40	
		Spitfire	R	Self		To Duxford		-15	
	23rd	Spitfire	W	Self		To Thurleigh for co-op with B-17s (Flying Fortresses)		1-15	
	24th	Spitfire	T	Self		Co-op Fortresses		-55	
		Stinson Reliant	?	S/Ldr J.A.F. MacLachlan	Self & P/O Godefroy	To Langley			-30
		Stinson Reliant	?	P/O Godefroy	Self	To Duxford		-30	
	27th	Spitfire	T	Self		To Bourne		-10	
		Spitfire	T	Self		Co-op Stirlings		1-00	
		Spitfire	T	Self		To Duxford		-10	
	29th	Spitfire	T	Self		To Upwood		-15	
		Spitfire	T	Self		Co-op Blenheims		-50	
		Spitfire	T	Self		Co-op Blenheims		-45	
		Spitfire	T	Self		Co-op Blenheims and return to Duxford		1-05	

2 September: I had hoped that I had seen the last of the Defiant (known as the Daffy) but had to fly it back to base. Luckily, it was my final flight in one. It was not my favourite aeroplane and my sympathies went out to those brave chaps who had to fly one during its brief operational career.

11 September: From the 5th to the 11th was a week of detachment and the commanding officers of the Wellington Squadrons made us really earn our corn. Remembering that there were three of us in the affiliation flight, all of whom would have taken part at all times, this was a week of intensive activity. I was very relieved to get back to Duxford, as the 11th was Estelle's birthday and she would have been very fed up if I had not returned in time to celebrate it.

13 September: We must have missed this one up at Skipton and he followed us home.

15 September: Another one we missed at Skipton!

16 September: This was our first wedding anniversary. I was not given the day off but some easy cross-country and some fun flying in an old Hurricane, including a 'show off' to White Waltham and a very quick visit to the Climer family at Slough. I made sure that I got back to Duxford in good time and was let off duty early. Assuming that I needed rest, the CO gave me light duties the next day.

17 September: I gave them a trip over the Thames valley. Actually it was a very gentle cross-country at only 2,000 feet, taking in Marlow on the Thames, Bicester and Banbury, then back to base. My three passengers varied in age but no one was airsick and all assured me that it was a very pleasant experience.

23 September: My logbook does not say but I assume that the Fortresses were the early arrivals of the USAAC (United States Army Air Corps), getting ready for their daylight raids on Germany. This was not my first meeting with a 'Fort'; earlier in the year a single machine landed at Duxford. The pilot was completely lost and asking for directions back to his base, apparently having no idea of how to call up on radar.

24 September: These exercises were interceptions followed by mock attacks on the American machines to get the crews used to seeing fighters come in and, hopefully, let them know what a Spitfire looked like.

Squadron Leader James MacLachlan was one of the real heroes; he was involved in the defence of Malta and won many decorations. He was shot down while flying a Hurricane and badly wounded, losing his left arm just below the elbow. He was fitted with an artificial limb, which had a false hand with various attachments to enable him to grip controls. He recovered from his wounds, overcame the difficulties and was quickly back flying fighters. His story is told in his biography *One Armed*

Mac. In early 1944 he and F/Lt Geoff Page, flying two P51 Mustangs, executed a low-level operation right across France to the German border area, where the Luftwaffe had operational training bases. In a series of completely surprise attacks they shot down, between them, seven enemy aircraft. Six weeks later they attempted to repeat the operation but were intercepted and James was shot down by ground fire and died in a German hospital. He is buried in Pont l'Évêque, Normandy.

29 September: When, in early 1941, the RAF started an offensive in daylight over the enemy-held territories in Western Europe, the Bristol Blenheim was the only light bomber that could be used. It was not really ideal, with a comparatively low speed and small bomb load. As soon as the American Douglas Boston, also called the Havoc, became available it largely took over the daylight role. The Blenheim continued to be used in some theatres and a modified version, the Beaufort, was successful, particularly in the Mediterranean area, as a torpedo bomber. Even more successful was the Beaufighter. Used as a night fighter, with airborne radar, in conjunction with the Mosquito it became the terror of the Luftwaffe. Armed with four 20mm cannon mounted in the nose, its firepower was devastating. Later, in the far eastern theatre, it was used against the Japanese and because of its sudden and relatively quiet approach, it became known as 'Whispering Death'.

Summary for:- September 1942	1 Spitfire 32-20
Unit:- AFDU Duxford	2 Defiant 1-30
Date:- 1/10/42	3 Hurricane 1-35
Signature:- H.L. Thorne	4 Oxford 1-30
	5 Stinson -30

D. Clive F/Lt
O/C Flying AFDU

YEAR	1942	AIRCRAFT		Pilot or 1st Pilot	2nd Pilot, Pupil or Pass.	DUTY	Flying Time		Passenger
MONTH	DATE	Type	No.			Flying Time (Including Results and Remarks)	Dual	Solo	
October	1st	Spitfire	X	Self		To Warboys and return		1-00	
	2nd	Spitfire	X	Self		To Oakington		-15	
		Spitfire	X	Self		Co-op Stirlings		1-30	
		Spitfire	X	Self		Return to base		-15	
	6th	Spitfire	T	Self		To Stradishall		-15	
		Spitfire	T	Self		Co-op Stirlings		-50	
		Spitfire	T	Self		Co-op and return		-50	
	8th	Spitfire	W	Self		To Stradishall		-15	

		Spitfire	W	Self		Co-op Stirlings	1-15
		Spitfire	W	Self		Return to base	-20
9th		Spitfire	X	Self		To Warboys	-25
		Spitfire	X	Self		Co-op Wimpys	-45
		Spitfire	X	Self		Co-op Wimpys	-45
		Spitfire	X	Self		Return to base	-20
10th		Spitfire	W	Self		To Stradishall	-15
		Spitfire	W	Self		Co-op Stirlings	-50
		Spitfire	W	Self		Return to base	-15
11th		Spitfire	W	Self		To Mildenhall	-15
		Spitfire	W	Self		Co-op Wimpys	1-00
		Spitfire	W	Self		To Stradishall	-15
		Spitfire	W	Self		Co-op Wimpys and return to base	-30
12th		Spitfire	AD318	Self		Speed trials at 20,000 and 25,000 feet	-40
		Spitfire	Y	Self		Demonstration attacks	-25
13th		Stinson Reliant	?	S/Ldr MacLachlan		To Tangmere	-50
		Stinson Reliant	?	S/Ldr MacLachlan		To Burtonwood	1-45
		Stinson Reliant	?	Self	2 passengers	Burtonwood to base	1-20
		Stinson Reliant	?	S/Ldr Haywood	Self	To Langley	-40
15th		Spitfire	R	Self		To Syerston	-50
		Spitfire	R	Self		To Langar	-15
		Spitfire	R	Self		Co-op Lancaster	-45
		Spitfire	R	Self		Co-op Lancaster. Landed and refuelled at Lichfield	-45
16th		Oxford	BG549	P/O Walker	Self	To Syerston	-15
17th		Oxford	BG549	P/O Walker	Self	To Langar	-15
		Oxford	BG549	P/O Walker	Self	To Duxford	1-05
		Spitfire	W	Self		To Syerston	1-00
		Spitfire	W	Self		Return to base	-40
18th		Spitfire	G	Self		Co-op Wimpy	-30
31st		Stinson Reliant	?	Self	AC Sirello	To Boscombe Down	1-10

		Stinson Reliant	?	Self	P/O Godefroy, AC Sirello	To Farnborough		-30	
		Stinson Reliant	?	Self	P.O Godefroy, AC Sirello	To base		1-00	
						GRAND TOTAL TO DATE 592 hours 20 minutes	3-30	8-25	
							60-00	520-25	8-30

6 October: Although only my own flights are recorded in my logbook, our flights to the many Bomber Command airfields would usually be the three Spits in formation, the senior pilot (F/O Walker) leading. Just to show off we usually performed a 'Fleur de Lys' breakaway before landing.

10 October: Carrying out fighter affiliation day after day when the weather permitted may sound boring but I do not remember ever feeling that way. The joy we felt when flying a Spitfire was a sensation that has never faded. The same is true when flying those other wonderful machines such as the Mustang, and even, later on, the Focke Wulf FW 190.

11 October: This would have been a special treat for anyone interested in horse racing as the airfield was in the centre of what is now the racecourse.

12 October: It may seem strange to be carrying out speed runs on a Spitfire Mk Vb as the type had been in operational service for about two years. But most aircraft were constantly improved and modified during their service life to keep abreast – or if possible – get a step ahead of the enemy. In the case of the Spitfire the most notable improvements were to the cockpit canopy, clipped wings, more powerful engines and different propellers. All had to be tested under operational conditions and approved before being generally introduced.

13 October: It was always a pleasure to fly with S/Ldr MacLachlan and he could usually be relied upon to produce something out of the ordinary. On the flight, a P51 Mustang with American markings decided to 'beat up' our little Stinson by a series of dummy attacks. Having had his fun the pilot dropped his flaps and undercarriage to slow down and flew too close on our port side. Mac unscrewed his false arm and waved first the stump, then the false arm out of the cabin window. A very shaken Mustang pilot peeled off and we saw him no more.

On the final flight of the day 'Scruffy' Haywood acted as my taxi driver and dropped me off at Langley, the home of the Hawker Aircraft production factory and the nearest airfield to Slough. This enabled me to spend a night with Estelle and the

Climer family. Estelle, all 5 feet of her, was very popular with the detectives of the CID department who had nicknamed her 'Tiny'. We were always invited to social occasions such as dances at the local pubs.

Summary for:- October 1942	1 Spitfire	18-10
Unit:- AFDU Duxford	2 Stinson	7-15
Date:- 4/11/42	3 Oxford (2nd pilot)	1-35
Signature:- H.L. Thorne		

E. Smith S/Ldr
O/C. Flying AFDU Duxford

1 November: Promoted to Flying Officer.

YEAR	1942	AIRCRAFT		Pilot or 1st Pilot	2nd Pilot, Pupil or Pass.	DUTY (Including Results and Remarks)	Flying Time		Passenger
MONTH	DATE	Type	No.				Dual	Solo	
November	4th	Spitfire	P	Self		Camera trial		-35	
	6th	Spitfire	X	Self		To Dishforth		1-00	
	7th	Spitfire	X	Self		Weather test		-20	
		Spitfire	X	Self		Co-op Wimpy		1-00	
		Spitfire	X	Self		Co-op Wimpy		-35	
	8th	Spitfire	X	Self		Co-op Wimpy		-30	
		Spitfire	X	Self		To Leeming Bar		-10	
		Spitfire	X	Self		Co-op Halifax		1-10	
		Spitfire	X	Self		Co-op Halifax		1-15	
		Spitfire	X	Self		Return to Dishforth		-10	
	9th	Spitfire	X	Self		To Catterick		-15	
		Spitfire	X	Self		To Walsingham		-20	
		Spitfire	X	Self		To Leeming		-30	
		Spitfire	X	Self		Co-op Halifax		1-10	
		Spitfire	X	Self		Co-op Halifax		-40	
		Spitfire	X	Self		Return to Dishforth		-10	

	10th	Spitfire	Y	Self		Return to Dishforth		1-00	
		Spitfire	B	Self		Air test		-30	
		Spitfire	B	Self		Aborted flight		-50	
	11th	Oxford	BG549	Self	P/O Walker	Crashed taking off			
	11th	Spitfire	R	Self		Delivery to Cranfield		-20	
	11th	Stinson Reliant	?	F/Lt Clive	Self	To Duxford			-20
	13th	Stinson Reliant	?	Wingco Campbell-Orde	Self	To Henlow		-20	
		Stinson Reliant	?	F/Lt Clive	Self	To Duxford		-20	
		Stinson Reliant	?	F/Lt Clive	Self	Air test		-20	
	17th	Stinson Reliant	?	Self	P/O Walker	To Dishforth		1-30	
		Stinson Reliant	?	Self		To Catterick		-20	
		Stinson Reliant	?	Self		To Dishforth		-20	
		Stinson Reliant	?	Self		To Duxford		1-20	
	20th	Spitfire	B	Self		To Bourne		-15	
		Spitfire	B	Self		Co-op Stirling		1-00	
		Spitfire	B	Self		Return to base		-15	
	26th	Spitfire	B	Self		To Fullbeck (landed at Wellingor)		-40	
		Oxford	BG549	S/Ldr Swales	Self	To base		-50	
	27th	Spitfire	U	Self		Air test		-15	
		Spitfire IX	BS 552	Self		Speed runs at 1,000 feet		-40	
	28th	Spitifre IX	BS 543	Self		Speed trials at 1,000 feet		-55	
	30th	Spitfire	P	Self		Range judging and dog fight		-40	
		Spitfire	P	Self		'Speedy bomber' trial		-40	

		Stinson	?	Self	AC McCormick	To Molesworth		-20	
		Stinson	?	Self	S/Ldr Hobhouse	Return to base		-20	
						GRAND TOTAL TO DATE 616 hours 15 minutes	3-30	8-25	
							60.00	544-20	8-50

8 November: When carrying out fighter affiliation at distant airfields we became temporary members of the Officers' Mess, in this case Dishforth in North Yorkshire, a pre-war permanent station. Financially this was good for us, as when on temporary detachment we paid no mess bills other than for drinks.

9 November: Catterick was still the home base of 41 Squadron so this would have been a quick visit to see old friends.

The Halifax was the third of the new breed of four-engined bombers, similar to the Lancaster in appearance, apart from the square tails and Bristol radial engines. It never quite reached the achievements of the Lancaster in bomb-carrying capacity and performance, although some Halifax crews would disagree. Losses in action were also heavier than those of the Lanc. Nevertheless, the Halifax made a useful contribution to the bombing campaign. Later in the war they were used as glider tugs.

10 November: The final flight was aborted after we set out for Dishforth. As we flew farther north, the weather conditions worsened and we were forced back to base. As the bad weather persisted, fighter affiliation exercises were discontinued, apart from one sortie against some Stirlings.

16 November: I have no recollections of this crash; it must have been a very minor one as I continued flying as usual. I also note that BG549 was flying again ten days later, on November 26th. After a pilot was proficient on a type he was always credited with pilot time even if he was not actually flying the aircraft. It is more than possible that in this instance P/O Walker was the pilot.

26 November: Squadron Leader Swales (always known as Blondie) courted and married one of the Duxford WAAF officers. Blondie remained at AFDU for some months after taking over from Jock Murray. I never knew either of those officers by their actual Christian names, always Jock or Blondie. After the war Blondie flew helicopters as a civilian and was kidnapped by members of the IRA and forced, at knife point, to land in the courtyard of the Maze Prison in Ireland. Three of the prisoners boarded the helicopter and made a successful escape but were later recaptured.

28 November: The Spitfire Mk 1X went into service in the late summer of 1942 in the HF (high flying) version. This type's 2-speed, 2-stage, supercharger was set to give best performance at heights up to 40,000 feet. The LF (low flying) version followed to give its best performance at 18 and 25,000 feet. These two types covered the performance with speeds superior to the Focke Wulf FW 190 at almost every altitude.

30 November: The Germans had started to use ME 109s and FW 190s for hit and run bombing raids, initially on towns in the coastal areas. These came to be known as the Baedeker raids. This was the first trial of the Spit for use as a fighter-bomber.

Summary for:- November 1942	1 Spitfire	17–55
Unit:- AFDU Duxford	2 Stinson	5–10
Date:- 1/12/42	3 Oxford	–55
Signature:- H.L. Thorne		

E. Smith Sqdn Ldr
O/C Flying AFDU Duxford

| YEAR | 1942 | AIRCRAFT | | Pilot or 1st Pilot | 2nd Pilot, Pupil or Pass. | DUTY (Including Results and Remarks) | Flying Time | | Passenger |
MONTH	DATE	Type	No.				Dual	Solo	
December	1st	Spitfire	S	Self		Delivery to Cranfield		-15	
		Oxford	BG549	F/Lt Sewell	Self	To Hucknall		-45	
		Oxford	BG549	F/Lt Sewell	Self	To base		-45	
	4th	Spitfire	K	Self		Air test and dog fight		-40	
		Spitfire	P	Self		Home guard beat up		-45	
		Spitfire	K	Self		Air test with modified ailerons		-50	
		Stinson	?	Self	3 passengers	To Foulsham		-35	
	7th	Stinson	?	Self	2 passengers	To Martlesham Heath		-35	
		Stinson	?	Self	2 passengers	To base		-40	
	8th	Spitfire	P	Self		Circuit and landing		-15	
		Mustang	618	Self		Sliding hood test			

9th	Spitfire	BS543	Self		Speed trials		-45	
	Spitfire	P	Self		Camera gun trials, air to ground		-45	
11th	Spitfire	P	Self		Air test		-25	
12th	Spitfire	P	Self		Camera air to air		-40	
	Spitfire	P	Self		Camera and gun fire into the sea		-45	
16th	Spitfire	L	Self		Aileron air test		-20	
28th	Spitfire	A	Self		Aileron air test to 30,000ft		1-00	
	Spitfire	P	Self		Aileron air test to 30,000ft		-55	
30th	Spitfire XII	EN223	Self		Air test climbs to 10,000ft		-35	
31st	Stinson	?	Self		To Snailwell		-2-	
	Stinson	?	Self		To base		-2-	
					GRAND TOTAL TO DATE 629 hours 50 minute s	3-30	8-25	
						60-00	557-55	8-50

1 December: Hucknall was the Rolls-Royce engine production factory and development department with an airfield nearby. Following the trials in June of the P51 Mustang Mk 1 and its unfavourable reception due to poor performance at altitude, Mr. Ronnie Harker, the Rolls-Royce chief test pilot, was invited to Duxford to add his opinion to that of AFDU. The story we believed at that time was that Wing Commander Campbell-Orde had said, 'Take the Mustang back to Hucknall and fit a Merlin 60 series engine similar to that installed in the Mk1X Spitfire.' Whoever had the idea, it was tried out, the Mustang was transformed and the war-winning fighter aircraft was born. The Americans graciously accepted the change and agreed to fit future Mustangs with the Merlin power plant. As Rolls-Royce could not meet the additional demands for Merlins, two American companies were licensed to produce Merlins, not only for the Mustang but also for one version of the Spitfire, the Mk XV1, which also had US .5mm. machine guns.

4 December: The Foulsham trip was probably air experience for members of Cambridge Home Guard following the 'beat up' the previous day. I wonder whether one of them fell out, as there were only two of them on the next flight!

Above: LAC Leslie Thorne.

Left: Christmas card received by Len Thorne from his elder brother, Leslie, serving in India.

Left: Air-to-air filming. Spitfire Mk VI, as a Mk Vb but with experimental pressurised cabin and cabin blower fitted.

8 December: The original Mustang had an 'up and over' canopy (like the ME 109); it had to be closed for take-off and could not be opened in flight. Its framing also interfered with visibility. Mustang 618 was probably a Mk111 powered by a Merlin 61 and was intended for service with both the RAF and the USAAF. To improve all-round visibility an experimental Spitfire (and Hurricane) type sliding hood was fitted. The new type of canopy was an immediate success and proved to

Summary of flying and assessment, June–December 1942.

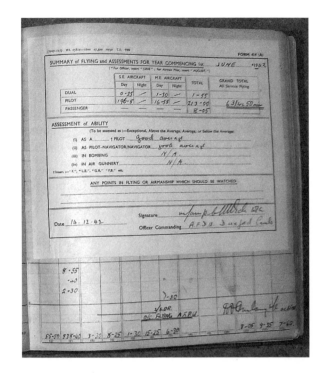

be very popular with the pilots. In the next two years there were several variations to the shape of the canopy, mainly the teardrop and the bubble.

11 December: Every RAF aircraft had to be given a daily inspection (DI0) and the results recorded on Form 700. The various members of the Ground Fitter E (engines) and Fitter A (airframes, electrician, instruments and armaments) signed their appropriate section, countersigned by the NCO in charge and finally by the pilot before flight. Any work between flights, such as repair, correction or maintenance was always the subject of an air test.

30 December: The Mk XII was the first Spitfire to be powered by a Rolls-Royce Griffon engine of 2050 HP to become operational. It was a basic Mk VIII, strengthened for the Griffon engine. Two major differences to earlier Spits were factory-made square wingtips to improve the rate of roll and the engine revolved anti-clockwise. The greatly increased power resulted in much more torque, which had to be carefully controlled on take-off and landing. At heights below 10,000 feet the Mk XII was much faster and almost the complete answer to the FW 190. The exception was the rate of roll which was, even with clipped wings, not quite as good as the Focke Wulf.

31 December: On this page of my logbook there is a printed form showing the summary for the second half of this year, commencing June 1942, similar in layout to that appearing on an earlier page. It confirms that my grand total of all service flying hours to date is 631 hours 50 minutes, dated Dec.14th and signed by Campbell-Orde, Wing Commander, Officer Commanding AFDU Duxford.

Summary for:- December 1942	1 Spitfire	8-55
Unit:- AFDU Duxford	2 Mustang	-40
Date:- 1/1/43	3 Stinson	2-30
Signature:- H.L.Thorne	4 Oxford	1-30

Signed *E. Smith*   *D.O. Finlay* Wing Commander
O/C Flying AFDU   O/C AFDU Duxford

5

DEVELOPMENT FLIGHT AFDU, RAF DUXFORD

Throughout 1942 the output of aircraft from the United Kingdom, Canada and Australia had steadily increased and by the end of the year the stream had become a flood. American aircraft for both the RAF and US forces, including fighters and light and heavy bombers, appeared in ever-increasing numbers. Every machine had to be tested off the production line or on arrival in the country. Routine test pilots were in short supply so, to safeguard my position at AFDU, I was invited to become one of the permanent staff test pilots. My time as a 'hack' pilot was over and although I still did fighter affiliation occasionally, more and more I was included in the on-going test programmes.

YEAR	1943	AIRCRAFT		Pilot or 1st Pilot	2nd Pilot, Pupil or Pass.	DUTY (Including Results and Remarks)	Flying Time		Passenger
MONTH	DATE	Type	No.				Dual	Solo	
January	1st	Spitfire	AFN	Self		Cloud formation and cine gun target		-20	
	2nd	Spitfire	U	Self		Cine gun		-10	
		Spitfire	U	Self		Cine gun at 5,000ft		-35	
		Spitfire	U	Self		Cine gun air to ground		-50	
		Spitfire	U	Self		Cine gun at 2,000ft on B26		-30	
	3rd	Spitfire	U	Self		Cine gun at 30,000ft on Mustang		1-30	
		Spitfire	U	Self		Cine gun, air to sea and at 15,000ft on Spit. IX		1-30	

	4th	Spitfire	U	Self		Cine gun retake at 30,000ft on Mustang		-45	
	8th	Spitfire	U	Self		Cine gun retake air to ground		-25	
		Spitfire	P	Self		Cine gun at 15,000ft with aileron and ASI comparative test		-35	
		Spitfire IX	EN225	Self		Aileron test		-30	
	9th	Spitfire Vb	U	Self		Target for 'Susie' at 15,000ft		-45	
		Spitfire Vb	U	Self		Cine gun air to sea		1-10	
	13th	Spitfire XII	EN223	Self		Trial to ascertain operational ceiling		-50	
		Spitfire XII	EN223	Self		Speed runs at 2, 3, 6 and 10,000ft		-55	
	14th	Gloucester Gladiator	K8040	Self		To Little Rissington		-50	
		Stinson	?	Self		Return to base		-50	
	15th	Spitfire XII	EN223	Self		Dog fight against 'Susie' in a Spit. IX at 20,000ft		1-00	
		Spitfire XII	EN223	Self		Low Flying		-30	
		Spitfire Vb	P	Self		Comparative trials versus U		-40	
	17th	Spitfire XII	EN223	Self		Climbing trials to 27,000ft		-45	
		Spitfire Vb	P	Self		Comparative trials versus U		-50	
	25th	Spitfire Vb	U	Self		Interception practice		1-05	
	26th	Spitfire Vb	U	Self		To Foulsham		-30	
		Spitfire Vb	U	Self		To base		-20	
	27th	Spitfire IX	Q	Self		Test new type harness release		-25	

		Master Mk III	?	Self		Circuits and bumps. Dual		-45	
		Master Mk III	?	Self		Circuits and bumps. Dual		-45	
	28th	Spitfire Vb	Q	Self		Test new harness release		-20	
		P51 Mustang	442	Self		Air test		-20	
		Spitfire Vb	U	Self		Target for 'Scotty'		-20	
	29th	Spitfire IX	BS552	Self		Comparative rate of roll versus Mustang at 20,000ft		-45	
		Spitfire Vb	H	Self		Air test		-20	
		Spitfire Vb	P	Self		Camera gun on cloud		-15	
	30th	Spitfire Vb	P	Self		Beat up Mustangs of 169 Squadron		-40	
		Spitfire Vb	Q	Self		Test harness and gun sight		1-05	
						GRAND TOTAL TO DATE: 654 hours 30 mins	3-30	8-25	
							60-00	582-35	8-50

2 January: Fourth flight. This would have been co-operation with the USAAF. The B26, called the Mitchell by the RAF, was a powerful and fast twin-engine medium bomber, now appearing in increasing numbers in Europe. It was a squadron of these machines that took off from an American aircraft carrier to achieve a major propaganda coup by bombing Tokyo.

4 January: With every 1,000 feet of altitude the air temperature drops by 1.5 degrees, so that at 30,000 feet the air temperature was 45°F below that at ground level. For example, on a cold January day with the temp at ground level 2°F, at 30,000 feet it would have been 43 degrees below zero. Freezing up of ancillary equipment such as camera guns was a potential problem.

8 January: The ailerons, which control turning, are on the rear edge of each wing. In each aileron is a small panel known as a trimming tab; either metal or fabric-covered. They can be adjusted to balance the ailerons or to lighten the load for the pilot and are a help with control of the Spitfire's turning circle.

13 January: The operational ceiling of a fighter aircraft was the height that a fighter could achieve with sufficient control to be a fighting unit. In the case of a Spitfire XII, this was approximately 35,000 feet. The absolute ceiling is the height that an aircraft can reach before losing control and literally falling out of the sky.

The thrill of a full throttle speed run cannot be described! The roar of the engine and the feeling of power in one's hands has to be experienced. I was increasingly involved in the test programme of the Mk XII. This would involve flying to operational heights, time taken to reach them, turning circles, rates of roll and of course, speed runs at various height intervals. The Mk XII had a top speed at its best height of nearly 450mph.

14 January: This was truly a heartbreaking flight taking one of the last of the lovely old biplane fighters on its final journey. They were the original defenders (Faith, Hope and Charity) of Malta and did sterling work in the brief Norwegian campaign, flying off the surface of a frozen lake. It was my first and only flight in a Gladiator, to Little Rissington where, with others, it would be broken up.

15 January: 'Susie', F/Lt Sewell won the contest!

In the fenlands of Norfolk, Cambridgeshire and Lincolnshire there were designated areas where low flying was permitted. A pilot had to be particularly wary of electricity pylons and cables and, although the odd farmer could get a bit stroppy if we frightened his pregnant cows, more usually they accepted the need for training with good grace. It was only when flying near to the ground that the speed of our fighters was fully appreciated. In a Mk XII, with the throttle set for maximum cruising, speeds well over 300 mph were easily achieved. What a thrill, great fun and (nearly) all legal.

27 January: We frequently had visitors from Bomber Command for conversion to single-engine fighters so I added instructor to my other AFDU duties. Most of these officers were very experienced pilots who had clocked up many hours flying multi-engined aircraft, so their conversion was really an academic exercise. The Miles Master Mk III was powered by an American Pratt and Whitney Wasp radial engine. Consequently the Mk III sounded like, and was frequently taken for, an American Harvard trainer.

28 January: P/O Scott was a new member of AFDU. On rest from operations, he was a very lively young Australian, barely 5 feet tall. He was a great joker and at the New Year's party in the Duxford Officers Mess a very large cardboard carton that had been made up specially was wheeled into the ante room. With bangs and flashes at the midnight hour, out popped Scotty. He and my wife, Estelle, being about the same height, made a good pair and Scotty made it his business to take care of her, she at that time being some six months pregnant.

29 January:Third flight. Some of the cloud formations that winter were spectacular, so on this occasion I was 'scrambled' to record them on film before they broke up.

Summary for:- January 1943		Spitfire	21-10
Unit:- AFDU Duxford		Gladiator	–50
Date:- 31/1/43		Stinson	–50
Signature:- H.L. Thorne		Master MkIII	1-30
		Mustang	–20

MONTLY TOTAL 24 hours 40 minutes

E. Smith S/Ldr
O/C Flying AFDU

YEAR	1943	AIRCRAFT		Pilot or 1st Pilot	2nd Pilot, Pupil or Pass.	DUTY (Including Results and Remarks)	Flying Time		Passenger
MONTH	DATE	Type	No.				Dual	Solo	
February	1st	Mustang X	AL963	Self		Experience on type		-45	
		Spitfire	P	Self		Target for cine gun		-25	
		Mustang X	AL963	Self		Quarter attacks testing swing		-45	
	2nd	Spitfire Vb	P	Self		Co-op with Mustangs of 169 Squadron		-45	
		Spitfire	P	Self		Co-op with Mustangs of 169 Squadron		-25	
	3rd	Tiger Moth	?	Self	F/Lt Stubbs	Instruction in aerobatics		-45	
		Spitfire Vb	O	Self		Follow my leader with F/Lt Stubbs who earlier made his first solo in a Spitfire		1-00	
	5th	Spitfire XII	EN223	Self		Power failed on take-off		-05	
	6th	Spitfire XII	EN223	Self		Fuel consumption trial		1-00	
	7th	Spitfire XII	EN223	Self		Fuel consumption test		-50	

		Tiger Moth	AF1	Self		Searchlight co-op		1-00	
		Tiger Moth	AF1	Self		Searchlight co-op		-25	
	10th	Spitfire XII	EN223	Self		Fuel consumption trial		-40	
	13th	Spitfire Vb	AF9	Self		ASI calibration		-30	
		Stinson	?	Self	Unit Padre S/Ldr Fountain, F/O Collins (Unit Engineer Off.)	To Hunsden		-20	
		Stinson	?	Self	F/O Collins	Return to base		-25	
		Stinson	?	Self		To Bovington		-40	
		Stinson	?	Self		To base		-35	
	14th	Spitfire Vb	AF6	Self		Camera gun, air to air		-15	
		Spitfire Vb	AF6	Self		Camera gun, air to ground		-25	
		Spitfire Vb	AF6	Self		Camera gun, air to ground		-25	
		Spitfire Vb	AF6	Self		Camera gun, air to air		-35	
	15th	Stinson	?	Self	Sgt Hill & Mr Charles	To Bovington		-30	
		Stinson	?	Self	F/Lt Clive & Cpt Dyar	To Duxford		-20	
		Stinson	?	Self	Cpt Dyar	To Wittering		-45	
		Stinson	?	Self		To base		-25	
	16th	Spitfire XII	EN230	Self		Zoom climbs		-35	
		Mustang X	AL963	Self		Camera gun test films		-25	
		Spitfire	AB169	Self		Hooded camera test		-20	
		Spitfire	AB169	Self		Hooded camera test		-15	
	17th	Spitfire XII	EN230	Self		Zoom climbs		-35	
		Spitfire XII	EN230	Self		Zoom climbs		-40	
	18th	Spitfire XII	EN230	Self		Zoom Climbs		-40	
		Spitfire Vb	AF6	Self		Co-op Stirlings		-30	
	19th	Spitfire IX	BS552	Self		Cine gun tests and target		-30	

		Spitfire Vb	AF8	Self		Stall tests		-35	
		Spitfire IX	BS552	Self		Cine gun target		-15	
		Mustang X	AL963	Self		Cine gun film test		-20	
		Mustang IA	442	Self		Cine gun film test		-20	
	24th	Spitfire Vb	AF8	Self		Stall tests		-25	
		Spitfire Vb	AF6	Self		Stall tests		-25	
		Mustang 1A	442	Self		Cine gun test films		-20	
	25th	Spitfire Vb	AD204	Self		Stall tests		-20	
		Spitfire Vb	AF8	Self		Cine gun, air to air		-20	
		Spitfire Vb	AF8	Self		Cine gun, air to ground		-20	
		Spitfire Vb	AF8	Self		Cine gun, air to ground		-20	
		Thunderbolt P47	16198	Self		Experience on type		-30	
	26th	Thunderbolt	16198	Self		Air firing at 30,000ft		-55	
		Mustang 1A	442	Self		Cine gun test films		-20	
		Spitfire XII	EN230	Self		Target for cine gun filming		-25	
		Mustang X	963	Self		To Hucknall		-30	
		Mustang X	121	Self		Hucknall to Bovington		-45	
		Oxford	BG549	F/O Scott	Self	Bovington to Henlow		-30	
		Oxford	BG549	F/O Scott	Self, P/O Solak	Henlow to base		-20	
	27th	Spitfire XII	EN223	Self		Stall tests		-30	
		Spitfire XII	EN223	Self		To Foulsham		-25	
		Spitfire XII	EN223	Self		Affiliation with B25s		-30	
		Spitfire XII	EN223	Self		Affiliation with B25s		-40	
		Spitfire XII	EN223	Self		To base		-30	
						GRAND TOTAL TO DATE 684 hours 50 minutes	3-30	8-25	
							60-00	612-55	8-50

Len with Mustang P51b in Duxford, 1943.

1 February: Another first flight on type. The Mk X was similar in many respects to the Mk III but with a tear drop canopy. All Mustangs were a delight to fly but the Mk X was outstanding for all flying, particularly cross-country, with its wonderful all-round visibility.

2 February: 169 Squadron was one of the first RAF units to be equipped with the Mustang P51 fighter. The Mustang's longer range meant that daylight raids with fighter cover could be extended to all of Belgium, Holland and most of northern France, up to the Rhine. Later in the year, with long-range drop tanks, Mustangs were able to escort the USAAF daylight raids right into the heart of Germany.

3 February: I enjoyed instructing F/Lt Stubbs; he was a good pupil and very enthusiastic about flying a Spitfire. He went on to command the Fighter Affiliation Flight.

5 February: I used up one of my nine lives when power failed just as I was about to become airborne but, luckily, I had enough room to abort the take-off and come to a stop well short of the airfield boundary. As far as I remember this was my only total engine failure in over 1,500 flights with Merlin or Griffon engines. It must have been a very minor fault as I flew EN 223 again the next day.

7 February: This entailed flying over the site in circles at varying altitudes up to about 5,000 feet. In a Tiger Moth with an open cockpit, in February, it was not much fun and very, very cold, definitely 'brass monkey' weather. It was noticeable that none of the ground staff rushed to occupy the second cockpit.

10 February: Fuel consumption was always a matter of importance, especially in an aircraft like the Spitfire that was designed as a purely defensive fighter. With the bigger, more powerful Griffon engine, consumption for the MkXII would have been roughly 5 % worse than in a Mk IX.

13 February: The ASI (Air Speed Indicator) was worked by a pressure device called the pitot tube mounted on a stem below the wing so that air pressure through it would vary with forward speed. The information obtained was passed to the dashboard instrument.

The Hunsden trip was a joyride for two of the unit's officers who did not often get the chance of a flight, S/Ldr Fountain, the C. of E. Chaplain and F/O Collins (known as Lottie), the AFDU Engineering Officer during our stay at Duxford.

14 February: For air-to-air camera work there would have been another aircraft acting as target. For air-to-ground work we would usually have aimed at a target in The Wash but in view of the short duration of the flight the target was probably at nearby Colley Weston airfield.

15 February: More joy rides. Sergeant Hill was one of the ground staff on aircraft maintenance, Mr Charles one of the technical experts attached to the unit; popularly known as Boffins. F/Lt Clive, was our flight commander and Cpt. Dyer was the C/O of the searchlight unit.

16 February: Zoom climbs were better than anything at a fair. This test started flying at nought feet, straight and level, then opening up to maximum cruising throttle setting, waiting until speed settled down at something over 300mph, then pulling up into a 45/50 degree climb, recording times to 5,10 and 20,000 feet. This procedure had to be repeated a number of times to get an average result. Lovely!

17 February: The zoom climbs were a repeat of previous test runs but with different starting throttle settings.

For the second test the aircraft was flown at full throttle to a speed of over 400mph, then pulled up into the steepest possible climb. Phew! By now I was involved in the full test programme for the Spitfire XII, so at last I could call myself a real test pilot.

19 February: I never really cared for stall tests; they entailed putting the aircraft into a climb, closing the throttle and waiting for the speed to drop off. In a Spitfire the nose would suddenly drop and the aircraft start a dive from which it was easy to recover. At the point of stall, if you kicked on hard rudder one way or the other, the machine would go into a spin. A Spitfire behaved well and was easy to recover but in some types the stall could be violent and recovery difficult; some aircraft would go into a spin and be reluctant to come out. So as I say, I did not enjoy stalling: it was not pleasant to leave your stomach up there when you were down here.

24 February: Stall tests again, definitely not recommended for the morning after a boozy night out! The move to Duxford caused difficulty for travelling home either to Waddesdon and Brill (Poletrees Farm) or to Redditch. My brother-in-law, Percy Climer, owned a 1936 Austin 10 Ruby saloon car he had laid up for the duration, due to petrol restrictions. He offered it to me for the price he had paid, the princely sum of £35. I gladly accepted his kind offer and that solved the problem of travelling home on leave as well as local journeys around Duxford. It was a most reliable vehicle, not very fast, about 55 mph was top speed but it would cruise happily at about 40 mph and seemed capable of going on forever.

Some time in the early summer of 1943 I was offered a Vauxhall 14 by an airman who was posted abroad. It seemed a good move so I bought the Vauxhall. My faithful Ruby was sold to one of our other pilots, a New Zealander, F/O Bill Burge, with whom I reestablished contact postwar. He kept the old Austin until the war ended and he returned to New Zealand. He later moved to Australia. The Vauxhall proved to be a disaster and caused me nothing but trouble. I was very glad to see the back of it early in 1944, after AFDU moved to Tangmere.

25 February: AD204 had been named the Andoverian, having been paid for and given by the people of Andover to the Air Force.

It started its service life at Ibsley, Hampshire with 118 Squadron in September 1941 and had a long, interesting history, surviving the war. The book *Johnnie Spitfire* by H.T.N. Ling (1980) tells the story.

26 February: The P47 Thunderbolt, because of its shape and size, was nicknamed the 'Jug'.

It was a most impressive aeroplane and with its heavy armament of 8.5 machine guns and its longer range, did sterling work in the USAAF, escorting the B17s on their daylight raids into Germany. It was easy and pleasant to fly; number 16189 arrived at Duxford under the charge of an American Top Sergeant, who was nearly as big as the aeroplane and seemed to regard it as his own personal property. Alone, he covered all aspects of servicing. As far as I know, the P47 was not adopted by the RAF.

On this day I made seven flights in five different types or marks of aircraft, three of which were American, one a Spitfire and finally two trips in a twin-engine Oxford.

27 February: AFDU's first co-operation with American pilots and aircraft. We found it necessary to use the Spitfire Mk XII in order to match the speed of the B25 Mitchells. (The B25 was known in the RAF as the Mitchell.) It was my first all-day stay at an American base over lunchtime: grilled pork chops with 'Jello' and peanut butter all on the same plate, followed by lashings of ice cream. Lovely! The jello and peanut butter were new to me; I liked the jello, which made a nice change from apple sauce, but had reservations about the peanut butter.

Summary for: February 1943
Unit: AFDU. Duxford
Date: 1/3/43
Signature: H.l. Thorne

1 Spitfire Vb	8-10	
2 Spitfire IX	-45	
3 Spitfire XII	8-15	
4 Mustang IA	-40	
5 Mustang X	3-50	
6 Thunder bolt	1-25	
7 Stinson	4-00	
8 Tiger Moth	2-25	
9 Oxford	-50	(2nd pilot)

Monthly total: 30 hours 20 minutes

E. Smith Squadron leader
O/C. Flying AFDU

YEAR	1943	AIRCRAFT		Pilot or 1st Pilot	2nd Pilot, Pupil or Pass.	DUTY (Including Results and Remarks)	Flying Time		Passenger
MONTH	DATE	Type	No.				Dual	Solo	
March	1st	Mustang 1A	442	Self		Speed trials		-30	
	3rd	Spitfire Vb	P	Self		To Ridgewell		-15	
		Spitfire Vb	P	Self		To base		-15	
	4th	Tiger Moth	AF1	Self		To Cranfield		-30	
		Tiger Moth	AF1	Self		To base		-40	
		Spitfire Vb	169	Self		Air test		-30	
	5th	Mustang 1A	442	Self		Speed trials		-35	
		Master Mk III	8839	Self		Local flying		-40	
	6th	Spitfire XII	EN223	Self		Escort to an enemy aircraft of 1426 Flight		1-00	
		Master	8839	Self	F/Lt Anderson	Circuits and bumps		-25	
	7th	Mustang 1A	FZ442	Self		Speed runs		-30	
	8th	Spitfire Vb	4064	Self		Cine camera and guns		-35	
		Spitfire Vb	4064	Self		Flight cancelled		00	

		Spitfire XII	AF2	Self		Air test	-15	
	9th	Tiger Moth	AF1	Self	LAC Sigrist	Searchlight calibration	1-15	
	10th	Mosquito	666	W/Co Finlay	Self	Air test		-30
	11th	Master III	8839	Self	F/Lt Cook	Circuits and bumps	-10	
		Master III	8839	Self	F/Lt Cook	Circuits and bumps	-5	
	12th	Master III	8839	Self	S/Ldr Aldis	Circuits and bumps	-35	
		Spitfire Vb	P	Self		Air test	-10	
		Master III	8839	Self	S/Ldr	Circuits and bumps	-15	
		Master III	8839	Self	S/Ldr	Circuits and bumps	-20	
		Master III	8839	Self	S/Ldr	Circuits and bumps	-10	
		Spitfire Vb	4064	Self		Air test	-10	
		Avro Anson	?	S/Ldr Smith	Self	Experience on type	-25	
	23rd	Spitfire XII	EN223	Self		To Wittering	-15	

5 March: When the original Mk I Mustang went through its speed trials in this country, the top speed was recorded as 380mph at 1,000ft. In one of my test flights in Mustang X FZ107 (in early 1944) at the same height, I recorded 448mph. This made it the fastest operational aircraft in the world at that time. In a later flight I achieved an indicated speed of 455mph at ground level.

The Master III was similar to the Mk I, which I flew for my SFTS training at Hullavington except that it was powered by an American Pratt and Whitney Wasp. The same engine was used in the US Harvard trainer, consequently the Master Mk III sounded like, and was often mistaken for, a Harvard.

6 March: 1426 Flight was a unit within AFDU but operated as a detached, independent unit, based at nearby Colley Weston airfield. They flew, to my knowledge, a number of German machines including a Heinkel III, a Messerschmitt 110, a Henshall 126, an ME109 and a JU 88. Some time later they also acquired a Focke Wulf FW 190 A3. If their flight plan took them into the sensitive area of the southeast of England, it was necessary to provide a Spitfire escort. On this flight it was the Heinkel III that we escorted to somewhere in 11 Group.

10 March: Although I made several flights in a Mosquito, I have always regretted that I did not actually fly it solo. On this flight, the wing commander allowed me to take the controls, but as I did not carry out the take-off and landing, I could only claim this and subsequent flights as 2nd pilot. A great pity as the Mossie was such a lovely and successful aircraft.

11 March: This short flight was caused by a fault in the aircraft, which was corrected and off we went again.

12 March: S/Ldr Aldis was obviously quite expert and as he did not need any more instruction was sent straight off solo.

In the Avro Anson, this time it was me who was under instruction. A quick whip round and a couple of landings and S/Ldr Ted Smith passed me proficient to take the 'Annie' solo. Some of my older readers may remember motor cars with starting handles (and a few broken wrists). The Anson was a pre-war wood and canvas aeroplane, used by Coastal Command for reconnaissance and for twin-engine training at SFTS. The engines were started by inserting a starting handle in the appropriate hole at the side of the engine cowling and with a few turns to get the prop revolving, hopefully, to start the engine. The undercarriage was retracted and lowered by a hand-winding wheel on the floor behind the pilot and I remember that it took quite a few turns to get the wheels up or down.

6

DEVELOPMENT FLIGHT AFDU, RAF WITTERING

It had become obvious that Duxford had become badly overcrowded. Several USAAF squadrons including P47 (Thunderbolts), P38 (Lightnings) and P51 (Mustangs) with all their support units had moved in. It was decided that AFDU and NAFDU would be moved 30–35 miles north, to Wittering, near Stamford in Lincolnshire, while 1426 Enemy Aircraft Flight would be moved to Colley Weston, at the western end of the Wittering complex. The move started around 20th March and, apart from some machines undergoing maintenance in the hangars, was complete by the end of the month.

YEAR	1943	AIRCRAFT		Pilot or 1st Pilot	2nd Pilot, Pupil or Pass.	DUTY (Including Results and Remarks)	Flying Time		Passenger
MONTH	DATE	Type	No.				Dual	Solo	
March	23rd	Boston	?	F/Lt Clive	Self	To Duxford			-15
	24th	Mustang 1A	442	Self		To Wittering		-25	
		Boston	?	S/Ldr Murray	Self	To Duxford via Grandsen Lodge			-25
		Mustang X	107	Self		To Wittering		-25	
		Boston	?	F/Lt Clive	Self	To Duxford via Gransden Lodge			-25
	27th	Spitfire Vb	AFX	Self		To Duxford		-15	
		Spitfire Vb	AFX	Self		Co-op Lancaster		-45	
		Spitfire Vb	AFX	Self		To Wittering		-25	
	28th	Spitfire Vb	AFX	Self		To Duxford		-20	
		Spitfire Vb	AFX	Self		Co-op Lancaster		1-10	

		Spitfire Vb	AFX	Self		To Wittering		-40	
	29th	Spitfire Vb	AFX	Self		To Duxford		-20	
		Spitfire Vb	AFX	Self		Co-op Lancaster		-50	
		Spitfire Vb	AFX	Self		To Wittering		-15	
		Spitfire Vb	AFE	Self		To Colley Weston		-10	
	30th	Mustang 1A	442	Self		To Duxford		-20	
		Mustang 1A	442	Self		Co-op Lancaster		1-00	
		Mustang 1A	442	Self		To Wittering		-20	
	31st	Mustang 1A	442	Self		To Duxford		-20	
		Mustang 1A	442	Self		Co-op Lancaster		1-20	
		Mustang 1A	442	Self		To Wittering		-45	
						GRAND TOTAL TO DATE 705 hours 25 minutes	3-30	8-25	
							60-0	633-30	10.25

31 March:

Summary for:- March 1943	
Unit:- AFDU Wittering	
Date:- 2/3/43	
Signature:- H.L. Thorne	

1 Spitfire II & V		7-05
2 Spitfire XII		1-30
3 Mustang IA & X		6-30
4 Master III		2-40
5 Tiger Moth		2-25
6 Anson		-25
7 Boston	} Passenger	1-05
8 Mosquito		-30

Total for month: 20 hours 35 minutes

Signed: *J.H. Hallowes* S/Ldr
O/C Flying AFDU

Squadron Leader Jim Hallowes was one of the aces who shot down many enemy aircraft in the Battle of Britain. He started off as a Sergeant Pilot in the battles over France and was awarded a DFM. Returning to England, he took part in the July and

August battles and was awarded a bar to his DFM. Subsequently, he was commissioned and given rapid promotion when, as a Squadron Leader, he was awarded a DFC. When the war ended he was credited with 22 enemy aircraft destroyed. During his brief spell as O/C Flying at AFDU we found him a quiet unassuming man, one of the nicest with whom I served.

During this month we completed the move to Wittering with almost all personnel and aircraft there by the 23rd. Prior to that date, with many regrets, we gave notice to Guy and Ynez of the move. Our eight months at College Farm had considerably widened our education. Living there was very close to the high society of which we could previously only dream. Guy and his family were part of the landed gentry of Cambridge and Lincolnshire and Ynez, through her father, moved freely in London society.

Estelle was pregnant in October 1942. I had carried out the Wing Commander's order! It had taken a little longer than expected but in time to spare Estelle from having to take on some form of war work. So Estelle and I had to move to other accommodation near to the airfield at Wittering. We had not been able to find anything suitable before the move and, despite the expense, had to stay for two or three weeks at the George Hotel in the middle of Stamford. We were beginning to get a bit desperate when we were lucky in being given the name of Mr Fred Walker, a retired bank manager.

With his wife, Dolly, Fred lived at Chain Cottage, in the village of Easton-on-the-Hill, about two miles south of Stamford and just outside Colley Weston, Wittering's satellite airfield. For us, this was an ideal situation. Chain Cottage was an old L-shaped place with outbuildings and a large, well-kept walled garden. For a cosy little sitting room, a kitchen and work room on the ground floor, with a bedroom and use of a bathroom, we paid the princely sum of £1.00 per week. Estelle was by then seven months pregnant and the Walkers, both in their seventies, had doubts about the addition of a newborn baby to their household but agreed to give it a whirl. In the event, they came to be very happy about it and Fred in particular made a fuss of baby Gill as if she was his own granddaughter. We spent two very happy years with Fred and Dolly, until March 1945.

| YEAR | 1943 | AIRCRAFT | | Pilot or 1st Pilot | 2nd Pilot, Pupil or Pass. | DUTY (Including Results and Remarks) | Flying Time | | Passenger |
MONTH	DATE	Type	No.				Dual	Solo	
April	1st	Spitfire Vb	X	Self		To Duxford		-20	
		Spitfire Vb	X	Self		Co-op Lancaster and return		1-20	
	3rd	Mustang X	107	Self		Army co-operation		1-20	
		Spitfire XII	EN223	Self		Army co-operation		-55	
		Spitfire XII	EN223	Self		Army co-operation		-25	

Date	Type	No.	1st Pilot	2nd Pilot	Duty		Time		Time
	Spitfire Vb	4064	Self		Angle of dive test		-25		
4th	Spitfire Vb	X	Self		Colley-Weston to Wittering		-10		
5th	Spitfire XII	EN230	Self		Scramble		-50		
6th	Spitfire XII	EN230	Self		Duxford to Wittering		-25		
	Boston	?	S/Ldr Murray	Self	To Duxford				-20
8th	Spitfire IX	860	Self		Local flying		-15		
9th	Typhoon	622	Self		To Duxford		-25		
	Typhoon	622	Self		To base at Wittering		-25		
10th	Typhoon	622	Self		Handling		-45		
11th	Typhoon	622	Self		Handling		1-10		
	Typhoon	622	Self		Dog fighting v. Mosquito		-35		
12th	Mosquito	666	F/O Corser	Self	Speed runs				1-00
13th	Heston Phoenix	?	Self		To Foulsham		-45		
	Phoenix	?	Self	F/O Corser	To Duxford		-55		
	Phoenix	?	Self	F/O Corser	To base		-40		
14th	Spitfire Vb	AD318	Self		To Feltwell		-25		
	Spitfire Vb	AD318	Self		To Wittering		-35		
17th	Spitfire IX	JK860	Self		To Duxford. Fuel consumption test at 14,000ft		1-00		
	Spitfire IX	JK860	Self		To base and repeat the above test		1-00		
	Spitfire IX	JK860	Self		Consumption test at 17,000ft		1-20		
18th	Spitfire IX	AF10	Self		Operational scramble to 25,000ft		-40		
	Spitfire IX	AF10	Self		Air test		1-05		
	Spitfire IX	JK860	Self		Consumption test		1-05		
20th	Spitfire IX	JK860	Self		Operational scramble to 28,000feet. Landed at Coltishall		1-05		

		Spitfire IX	JK860	Self		Operation. I was scrambled direct from Coltishall but had to abort as my oxygen bottle had not been replaced.		-40	
		Spitfire IX	JK860	Self		To Ibsley at 35,000 feet		-45	
		Spitfire IX	JK860	Self		To base at 35,000 feet		-50	
	22nd	Spitfire Vc	AF6	Self		Harness test		-20	
	24th	Spitfire Vc	AF6	Self		To Duxford		-25	
		Spitfire Vc	AF6	Self		Camera work		-20	
		Spitfire XII	EN230	Self		Camera work		-25	
		Spitfire XII	EN230	Self		Camera work		-25	
		Mosquito	666	F/O Corser	Self	To base			-30
	26th	Oxford	BG549	Self	F/Lt Sewell	To Martlesham Heath		-45	
		Oxford	BG549	Self	F/Lt Sewell	To base		1-00	
	28th	Heston Phoenix	?	Self	F/Lt Simms	To Duxford		-35	
		H. Phoenix	?	Self	F/Lt Simms	To base		-45	
						GRAND TOTAL TO DATE 733 hours 10 minutes	3-30	8-25	
							60-00	661-15	12-15

4 April: A bit of a leg pull here: Colley Weston and Wittering were one and the same, the latter to the east alongside the A1 main road and the former to the west about three miles away. Seeing the need for an emergency runway the Commanding Officer at Wittering cleared the land between the two airfields, creating an enormous 'dumbbell' some three and half miles long. It was mainly used by bombers in trouble, particularly the American B17 Flying Fortresses that had been damaged in the daylight raids of 1943–45.

5 April: At AFDU the operation machines, Spitfires, Mustangs etc. carried out their tasks fully armed and ready for action. I was about to take–off for a normal test flight when an enemy PRU JU86 was detected over the east coast. I was immediately ordered by control to attempt an interception but, seeing me climbing to intercept, the enemy pilot dived to pick up speed and went home.

9 April: My first flight in a Hawker Typhoon (known as the 'Tiffie'). The Typhoon was the successor to the Hurricane but was a very different aircraft. It was much larger and heavier, powered by a Napier Sabre liquid-cooled engine of over 2,000 HP. At lower levels it was faster than most of its contemporaries but not ideal for close dog-fighting. Heavily armed with four 20mm cannons and later one of the first to carry RPs (Rocket Projectiles), it was able to take considerable punishment and came into its own as a tank buster.

12 April: On this flight I acted as observer taking down the instrument readings, leaving F/O Corser free to do the flying but, as stated earlier, I still regret that I did not fly a Mossie as first pilot.

13 April: I got a treat for my 23rd birthday, to fly a new type, the little Phoenix four-seat high-wing passenger plane.

As can be seen, for a few weeks we had frequent trips to Duxford to collect aircraft and maintenance personnel who were not able to move with the main group. We were sorry to lose the Americans, we enjoyed some of their mess treats and made many friends. Estelle and I had made one good friend in particular. One of the Squadron IOs (Intelligence Officers) was Captain Fergie Prince. He was a frequent visitor to College Farm, usually with a box of goodies for Estelle. In the main we got on well with those chaps, except on one or two occasions.

The Red Lion hotel at Whittlesford was a favourite watering hole but it took some time for the 'Yanks' to get used to our licensing laws. One dark night in the late winter, the landlord called last orders at the usual time. One of the American pilots, a little chap, all of 5 foot nothing, was loath to drink up and had to be persuaded by his friends to leave. Out in the car park he showed his displeasure by drawing his revolver and firing several shots into the hotel wall. The civilian police were informed but failed to arrive before the Americans had returned to camp. The following morning a strong complaint was made by the police who demanded the name of the guilty officer. The American C/O called for the guilty party to own up and when he failed to do so all American flying personnel were confined to camp until further notice. Somewhat upset, some of his 'friends' took the law into their own hands; that evening they caught him in the mess ante-room and stripped him naked. Before they could take further action, the youngster, enraged, stepped back, tripped on the large open fireplace and sat backwards on to the fire that burned therein. He suffered burns to his nether regions and spent some weeks in hospital. We never saw him again, so I assume he was posted back home in disgrace.

There was also some trouble over gambling in the mess, caused by some RAF officers being foolish enough to get involved in high stakes poker. The American boys could, in the main, afford their losses but the Brits could not. The British C/O wisely put all gambling in the mess out of bounds to RAF personnel.

17 April: As these tests were done at medium altitude, I assume that 860 was an LF (Low Flying) version of the Mk IX, when the two-stage supercharger would have cut in at 12 and 18,000 feet.

18 April: Another crack at a PRU JU86. These Luftwaffe machines had specially tuned engines for high-altitude flight. I saw it far away to the south, but it was the boys from North Weald who shot it down. I like to think he was watching me and failed to see them climbing up to the south into the sun.

20 April: As early as this, the Germans were expecting a repeat of the Dieppe raid and possibly a full-scale invasion attempt. Their PRU aircraft came over most days, flying at heights above 35,000 feet but they usually turned for home as soon as they saw RAF fighters climbing up to intercept. They would go into a shallow dive to pick up speed and were most difficult to catch. So this was another one that got away despite my battle climb at full throttle. As AFDU included the latest version of Spitfires and Mustangs, in the hope of one day achieving success, the unit maintained at all times a flight of two Spitfire Mk IXs, a Mustang X and later, a Spitfire Mk XIV. The latter aircraft, with its superb climbing speed, had a real chance of catching one of the JU88s.

24 April: The Spitfire Vc had a slightly different wing, to take two 20mm cannons on each side. The installation was never really successful and was not liked by the pilots. Despite this, many Spitfires came out of the factories with the 'C' wing but the extra cannons were not fitted and the stub apertures were blanked off.

28 April: F/Lt Simms (Simmie) was the Unit Adjutant and joined AFDU when it was first formed, as a civilian Civil Service clerk. He was commissioned into the service and remained as the adjutant until soon after the war ended, when he returned to the Civil Service. We became great friends and remained in contact for many years. Our final meeting took place when I paid a visit to the RAF Maintenance Unit at Hartlebury, where he was stationed. Shortly after, he was posted elsewhere and sadly we lost contact.

Summary for:- April 1943	1 Spitfire Vb and Vc	4-20
Unit:- AFDU Duxford	2 Spitfire IX	9-45
Date:- 4/5/43	3 Spitfire XII	3-25
Signature: H.L. Thorne	4 Mustang X	1-20
	5 Typhoon	3-30
	6 Heston Phoenix	3-40
	7 Oxford	1-45
	8 Boston	-20
	9 Mosquito	1-30

TOTAL FOR MONTH: 27 hours 45 minutes

Signed *J.H. Hallowes* Squadron Leader
O/C Flying AFDU

YEAR	1943	AIRCRAFT		Pilot or 1st Pilot	2nd Pilot, Pupil or Pass.	DUTY (Including Results and Remarks)	Flying Time		Passenger
MONTH	DATE	Type	No.				Dual	Solo	
May	3rd	Phoenix	?	S/Ldr MacLachlan	Self	To Snailwell		-35	
		Phoenix	?	Self		To base		-35	
		Phoenix	?	S/Ldr Hallowes	Self	To Hixon		-45	
		Phoenix	?	S/Ldr Hallowes	Self	To base		-40	
	4th	Spitfire Vb	AF6	Self		Target for cine gun		-20	
		Spitfire Vb	AF6	Self		Testing modified gun-sight		-35	
		Spitfire IX	BS552	Self		Handling with bomb racks fitted		1-05	
	5th	Typhoon	622	Self		Experience on type		-10	
		Typhoon	622	Self		Air experience		1-00	
		Spitfire IX	BS552	Self		Straight and level speed runs		-45	
	7th	Spitfire Vb	AD318	Self		Bombing runs		1-15	
		Spitfire IX	BS552	Self		Light-series bomb racks		-15	
		Typhoon	622	Self		Handling		-50	
	10th	Mustang X	AM203	Self		Test handling		1-05	
		Spitfire IX	BS552	Self		Glide bombing 5 to 3,000ft		-40	
		Spitfire IX	BS552	Self		Handling with a 250lb bomb		-50	
	12th	Spitfire Vc	AEF	Self		Handling, light-series racks		-30	
		Spitfire Vc	AEF	Self		Glide bombing, low level		-30	

	13th	Phoenix	?	Self		To North Luffenham		-20	
		Phoenix	?	Self		To base		-20	
		Spitfire IX	BS552	Self		Bombing, 7,000 to 4,000 feet		-55	
	14th	Spitfire IIb	AFU	Self		To Woolfox		-10	
		Spitfire IIb	AFU	Self		Affiliation with Wimpy		1-25	
		Spitfire IIb	AFU	Self		Co-op and return to base		-35	
		Spitfire Vb	AEP	Self		Bombing, 7,000 to 4,000 feet		-30	
		Spitfire Vb	AEP	Self		Bombing, 9,000 to 6,000 feet		-30	
	15th	Spitfire Vb	AEP	Self		Bombing, 9,000 to 6,000 feet		-25	
		Spitfire IX	AF10	Self		Operational scramble		-10	
		Spitfire Vb	AEP	Self		Bombing		-30	
		Spitfire Vb	AEP	Self		Bombing		-30	
	18th					Father of one			
	20th	Tiger Moth	AF1	Self	F/Lt Brown	Local		-30	
	21st	Spitfire Vb	AEP	Self		Bombing		-20	
		Boston	?	W/Co Smith	Self	To Worthy Down			-30
		Spitfire XII	EN222	Self		To base		1-00	
		Spitfire Vb	AEP	Self		Bombing		-20	
	22nd	Spitfire Vb	AF6	Self		Local		-25	
		Phoenix	?	F/O Corser	Self	To Digby		-30	
		Phoenix	?	F/O Corser	Self & F/Lt Luing	To base		-40	
	23rd	Mustang X	AM203	Self		Co-op with Mosquito		-35	
		Spitfire Vb	AF6	Self		Speed runs		-25	

	24th	Spitfire Vb	AF6	Self		Bombing in formation		-30	
		Spitfire XII	AF2	Self		Formation bombing		-25	
	25th	Phoenix	?	Self	F/Lt Joce	To Manby		-50	
		Phoenix	?	F/Lt Sewell	Self, Luing and Calder	Viewing new bombing range		-25	
		Spitfire XII	AF2	Self		Live bombing with 250 lb. bombs		-20	
		Spitfire Vb	AEP	Self		Live bombing with 250 lb. bombs		-25	
		Spitfire Vb	AEP	Self		Live bombing with 250 lb. bombs		-30	
		Spitfire XII	AF2	Self		Live bombing with 250 lb. bombs		-25	
		Spitfire XII	AF2	Self		Live bombing with 250 lb. bombs		-10	
		Phoenix	?	Self	Sgt Green	Watch 'Susie' bombing		-15	
		Phoenix	?	Self	F/Lt Joce	To base		-40	
	26th	Spitfire Vb	AF6	Self		Comparative dives versus a Mk IX		-45	
		Spitfire IX	AF10	Self		Low-level bombing		-25	
	27th	Spitfire Vb	AEP	Self		Bombing		-20	
		Spitfire Vb	AF6	Self		To Duxford		-20	
		Spitfire Vb	AF6	Self		Cine gun		-20	
		Spitfire IX	AF10	Self		Cine gun		-20	
		Spitfire IX	AF10	Self		To base		-20	
	28th	Spitfire IX	AF10	Self		Air test		-35	

		Mustang X	AM203	Self		To Duxford		-20	
		Mustang X	AM203	Self		To base		-20	
	29th	Spitfire XII	EN222	Self		Experience testing .511 reduction gear		-30	
		Typhoon	622	Self		Dive bombing		-45	
	30th	Spitfire Vb	AEP	Self		To Digby		-15	
		Tiger Moth	AF1	F/Lt Sewell	Self	To base		-25	
		Spitfire XII	EN223	Self		Dummy attacks on Mosquito		-35	
		Spitfire Vb	AUJ	Self		Test curved windscreen		-15	
		Spitfire XII	EN222	Self		Target for the curved windscreen		-15	
	31st	Spitfire XII	EN222	Self		Aileron test		-55	
		Spitfire XII	EN222	Self		Aileron test		1-00	
		Spitfire Vb	AF8	Self		Air test		-20	
						GRAND TOTAL TO DATE 770 hours 55 minutes	3-30	8-25	
							60-00	699-00	12-45

5 May: When the Typhoon first went into Squadron service it suffered from engine trouble due, I believe, to air locks in the fuel system. On the first flight, when the engine coughed after take-off, I decided that a quick emergency landing was called for. We deliberately flew the Typhoon under varying conditions, in an attempt to reproduce the engine cutting that was worrying the squadron pilots. Needless to say, on these flights we stayed close to the airfield so that if one of us succeeded in producing an engine cut, a 'dead stick' landing could be made. It did not happen to me but one of the other pilots managed to get an engine cut at 6,000 feet over the airfield and successfully made a forced landing.

7 May: Spitfire Vb. This was the start of our experiments to develop methods of using fighters as bombers.

14 May: In these early days of using fighters for bombing, we were trying to develop techniques for accuracy as well as the best method. The safety of the pilot had to be considered, bearing in mind the murderous accuracy of German low-level flak.

15 May: At first bombing was a novelty but after a time I came to hate it; but our work was necessary. We first had to ascertain exactly what the Spitfire could carry, starting off with a single 250 lb. bomb, then one under each wing. Getting more ambitious, a single 500 lb. bomb was successfully carried under the centre section and finally the 500 pounder, plus a 250 lb. under each wing.

After November 1942, when General Montgomery, leading the 8th Army, drove the Germans out of North Africa following the battle of El Alamein, enemy fighter opposition was almost eliminated. From then on almost all Allied fighters were used more and more for ground attack.

This operational scramble was meant to be an attempt to intercept one of the high-flying JU 86s. These aircraft had been developed by the Germans for PRU operations; they had pressure cabins and although somewhat slow, could accelerate quickly in a dive, so were very difficult to catch. Shortly after take-off, I discovered that I had lost my radio and could not receive instructions from control. I had no alternative but to return to base and land. It was found that the radio connection had not been fully tightened and vibration caused it to fall off. It was one of two occasions when I had to put a ground staff member on a charge. In this instance the fitter (radio) was charged with carelessness and severely admonished, which went on his records. I was particularly upset as I had been scrambled early and stood a real chance of achieving an interception and adding to my score.

18 May: On 16th May I was given four days leave to take Estelle back to her family home in Redditch as our baby was due any day. On the morning of the 18th she was given a routine examination by her midwife, Mrs Gwen Jefferies, who switched to panic stations saying, 'No way can she have this baby; she is too small!' She called in the doctor, who agreed. Estelle was given an emergency admission to the Smallwood Hospital in Redditch, seen by Sir Beckwith Whitehouse, an eminent surgeon and immediately prepared for a caesarean section operation. The operation was successfully performed that evening, so Gill was born and, as is recorded in my logbook, I became a 'father of one'.

At that time caesarean operations were still fairly rare and very much an emergency situation. Things did not go well for Estelle. There were no antibiotics and penicillin was not readily available for civilians. She remained in Smallwood Hospital, seriously ill, for three weeks, followed by a further week in bed at her mother's home in Redditch, which was not a good place to be as the house was cold and inclined to be damp. Despite protests from her mother, I took Estelle and baby Gill to Poletrees Farm where, for the next two weeks, they were cared for by my sister Gwen and my mother. The baby had to be bottle-fed and I often wondered whether the same bottle was used to feed the motherless lambs! It was nearly two months before Estelle came back to me at Easton.

Meanwhile, bearing in mind the Walkers' doubts about a new baby in the house, I had been scouring the neighbourhood for alternative accommodation. I had eventually found rooms some eight or ten miles from the airfield and informed Mr and Mrs Walker accordingly. They were taken aback and explained that their comments were only a passing concern; they really liked having Estelle and me and were sure there would be no baby problems. Good! So we stayed on at Chain Cottage. The new cot was installed on Estelle's side of the bed. Baby Gill was always as good as gold; she and the Walkers took to one another on sight.

21 May: To Worthy Down. This was a well-earned promotion to Wing Commander for Squadron Leader Smith, though we said a sad farewell to Wing Commander Campbell-Orde.

25 May: F/Lt (later Squadron Leader) Joce was the Unit Armaments Officer, having taken over from Squadron Leader John Hobhouse (the Hon. John Hobhouse). Squadron Leader Joce was a short, thickset man, usually known as 'Sawn off'.

These bombing tests were from straight and level flight; although very inaccurate, it was wrongly believed to be safer for the pilot. In a later flight, S/Ldr Tom Wade and I proved that there was no danger in releasing a bomb in a steep dive. There was more satisfaction in dropping live bombs and seeing the explosion on impact. Nine flights today. Is this a record? I believe it was for me, but we shall see!

28 May: It is obvious that we were still spending a lot of time at Duxford. The AFDU maintenance section continued to function for some time in No. 2 hangar, which also housed some of the offices. The boffins technical section, which was shared by NAFDU, were still there. Many years later in the making of the film *The Battle of Britain*, No. 2 hangar was made the main target of the Luftwaffe bombing and was completely destroyed; only the outline foundations can still be seen.

29 May: Dive bombing in a Tiffie was not, in my opinion, very much fun; the aircraft picked up speed quickly in a dive and there were a number of fatal accidents in training and on operations through leaving the pull-out too late.

30 May: During the next few weeks, while Estelle was in hospital back in Redditch, I moved back into the Duxford Officers' Mess and spent a lot of time with 'Susie'. He was good company, played a good game of snooker and usually beat me. His stock of service songs and stories was unbelievable. He had a number of female friends in the locality and on one occasion attempted to lead me into temptation. I rashly agreed to make up a foursome when we were invited for the evening at one lady's house, somewhere over towards Peterborough. I spent the evening in the lounge writing a letter to Estelle.

The unit maintenance staff had learned about our expected happy event, so one day the Flight Sergeant Fitter (A), the A stands for 'Airframes', who was a skilled carpenter, invited me into his section for a chat. He asked whether we had a cot for the expected new baby. I said no, we were intending to buy a 'utility'. He said he would make one for us and the maintenance staff would like to give it as a present. Of course I jumped at the offer, as utility furniture was pretty poor stuff. The new handcrafted cot was magnificent and was duly installed at Chain Cottage. It was beautifully made; even the metal fittings were hand-made in the station workshops. When, in 1945, the unit moved to Tangmere and we took up residence in the seaside village of Bracklesham Bay, it moved with us. When Gill had outgrown it, the cot went into storage to be brought out when Penny arrived in 1948. We eventually gave it to one of the office girls at Black and Luff, the Birmingham company of which I was a Director, in 1957 or '58. I like to think that somewhere in her family it is still in use. In a letter I found among Estelle's memorabilia and dated June 1st 1943 I had written: 'F/Sergeant Bennett is getting on nicely with the new cot for the baby; he is a damn good chap and is making a splendid job of it.'

Summary for:- May 1943	1 Spitfire II & Vb	13-15
Unit:- AFDU Duxford	2 Spitfire IX	6-20
Date:- 2/6/43	3 Spitfire XII	5-35
Signature:- H.L. Thorne	4 Typhoon	2-45
	5 Mustang X	2-20
	6 Tiger Moth	-55
	7 Heston Phoenix	6-35
	8 Boston	-30

Total for the month: 37 hours 45 minutes

Signed *J.L. Hallowe*
O/C Flying AFDU

YEAR	1943	AIRCRAFT		Pilot or 1st Pilot	2nd Pilot, Pupil or Pass.	DUTY (Including Results and Remarks)	Flying Time		Passenger
MONTH	DATE	Type	No.				Dual	Solo	
June	1st	Phoenix	?	Self	F/Lt Joce	To Manby		-35	
		Spitfire XII	EN223	Self		Bombing		-35	
		Spitfire IX	AF10	Self		Bombing		-45	
		Spitfire IX	AF10	Self		Bombing		-40	
		Phoenix	?	Self	F/Sgt Rudman, F/Lt Joce	To base		-50	
	2nd	Typhoon	DN622	Self		Low-level bombing		-35	

	4th	Typhoon	DN622	Self		Low-level bombing		-30	
		Spitfire Vb	AUJ	Self		Test curved windscreen		-40	
		Spitfire XII	EN222	Self		Aileron test		-15	
		Spitfire XII	EN223	Self		Engine cutting test		-30	
		Tiger Moth	AF1	Self		To Westcott		1-00	
	5th	Tiger Moth	AF1	Self		Westcott to Hockley Heath		1-15	
	7th	Tiger Moth	AF1	Self		To base		-50	
		Mustang 1A	FD442	Self		Camouflage test		-50	
	10th	Spitfire XII	EN223	Self		Engine cutting at Positive G		-25	
	11th	Spitfire XII	EN223	Self		Air test		-15	
	12th	Spitfire Vb	AU-J	Self		Air firing		-55	
		Typhoon	DN290	Self		To Manby		-35	
		Typhoon	DN290	Self		Bombing		-50	
		Typhoon	DN622	Self		Bombing		-45	
		Typhoon	DN622	Self		To base		-40	
	15th	Hurricane IV	KX581	Self		Low flying VP attacks		-55	
	16th	Hurricane IV	KX581	Self		Low flying VP attacks		-50	
		Hurricane IV	KX581	Self		Low flying live VP practice		-45	
		Spitfire Vb	AF6	Self		Night flying test		-15	
		Spitfire Vb	AF6	Self		Local		-10	
	17th	Mustang	AM107	Self		Speed runs		-40	
	19th	Spitfire Vb	AU-J	Self		Air test		-10	
		Spitfire XII	EN222	Self		Low flying attacks on a Mosquito		-35	
		Spitfire Vb	AF6	Self		Night flying test		-35	
		Spitfire Vb	AF6	Self		Local flying		-40	
	20th	Spitfire Vb	AF9	Self		Air test		-25	
		Spitfire Vb	AF8	Self		To Lichfield		-25	
		Spitfire Vb	AF8	Self		To Castle Bromwich		-10	
	22nd	Spitfire Vb	AF8	Self		To base		-25	

		Typhoon	EK290	Self		High speed dive bombing	-55	
		Spitfire IX	AF10	Self		Engine test	-25	
	23rd	Typhoon	EK290	Self		High speed dive bombing	-40	
	24th	Spitfire IX	AF10	Self		Army co-operation	1-40	
	25th	Spitfire Vb	AF8	Self		Cine gun	-30	
		Spitfire Vb	AF8	Self		Target	-30	
	26th	Spitfire XII	EN222	Self		Acting as target	-20	
	27th	Heston Phoenix	2891	Self		To Church Fenton	1-05	
		Phoenix	2891	Self		To base	1-05	
						GRAND TOTAL TO DATE 798 hours 15 minutes	3-30	9-15
							60-00	725-30	12-45

1 June: Manby was a localised area north of The Wash used initially for bombing trials. There were no facilities for marking the fall of bombs; results were judged by observers in the aircraft or on the ground.

4 June: Flying straight and level or in a shallow dive right down to ground level was very exciting in a Tiffie, which had a fair turn of speed, but the result was very inaccurate bombing.

Apparently on some Spitfire XIIs with the new Griffon engine there had been one or two cases of the engine cutting out or missing a beat. We tried to reproduce the fault by flying at varying altitudes and making sudden throttle movements but our tests never showed up the trouble. The Griffon had a harsher beat than the Merlin so we deduced that pilots who were used to the latter were taking time to get used to the change.

Westcott was a Wellington OTU at the foot of Waddesdon Hill, Buckinghamshire, only a mile or so from the village itself and actually inside the boundaries of Westcott village. It was the nearest airfield to Poletrees Farm, the home of my sister Gwen and her husband Joe; my mother also lived at the farm. It was only 6 or 7 miles away, so very convenient for me to pay them a call. After scrounging a lift from the airfield to see them, Joe would take me back to the airfield, a real adventure for Joe, as I managed to fix a one hour visitor's pass so that he could take me right up to the little Tiger Moth. On future visits that I made in more advanced aircraft like a Spitfire or a Mustang, it was an even greater treat, as those types attracted a lot of attention and some envy from the staff at Westcott.

5 June: There was one small blister hangar at Hockley Heath in which I parked the Tiger Moth overnight, properly picketed and tied down safely. As the Tiger had to be started by hand, I had to teach one of the temporary staff to swing the propeller. On the occasions when I stayed overnight, I had to do my own DI (Daily Inspection) and sign the form 700. It was all totally against procedure and regulations but, surprisingly, I was never caught or questioned. In arranging for Estelle and the baby to move on to Poletrees, I made myself most unpopular with her mother and sister; they obviously thought she would stay home for some time or possibly permanently. It was Estelle's own wish to move back to Chain Cottage as soon as possible but until she was fully recovered, to stay at Poletrees.

10 June: One of the disadvantages of the Spitfire and Hurricane was that, with the ordinary carburettor, if positive G was applied by pushing the control column forward, the engine stopped. Various modifications helped but it was not until the Bendix-Stromberg carburettor was introduced that the problem was solved.

16 June: I cannot remember what VP attacks were; perhaps VP was an earlier name. The Hurricane was possibly the first to try out the RPs. These flights were my first experience of what came to be known as Rocket Projectiles, or RPs. To carry and fire the RPs, the aircraft had four parallel rails under each wing and these were the forerunners of most modern systems.

The night flight was short and sweet; although I had so little experience of night flying, I quite enjoyed it.

17 June: This flight marked my first duty as a test pilot in a complete programme for the testing of an aircraft. It was to go through the detailed trials of the Mustang III, powered by the British Rolls-Royce Merlin 60 Series engine. It was the full production version with .5mm Colt machine-gun armament instead of 20mm cannons. In addition, it had a sliding canopy after the style of Spitfires and Hurricanes.

19 June: I cannot remember the reason for the 'local flying', unless it was to see if the searchlight boys were awake and on the ball. At this time of the year, this would have been a 1 or 2 o'clock in the morning stunt in order to find real darkness.

20 June: The first flight was presumably to pay a quick visit to my brother Leslie's wife and family. Their house was on the boundary of Lichfield airfield, a 'Wimpie' OTU. I then went on to Castle Bromwich, where the majority of Spitfires were produced, and landed at the factory airstrip. It was a difficult landing right alongside one of the main factory buildings but was the nearest place for an overnight visit to Redditch. The visit was to make final arrangements for Estelle's return to Easton on the Hill after she and baby Gill had recuperated at Gwen's farm.

22 June: As I said before, the Tiffie built up speed very quickly, in a steep dive often reaching a speed of 550 mph or more. Great care was needed in the recovery, in order to avoid a high speed stall which, if near the ground, could prove fatal.

25 June: It has to be remembered that most cine camera gun exercises involved two aircraft; we took it in turns to act as target.

27 June: At last I have recorded a registration number for the Phoenix; strange that it was not recorded earlier.

Summary for :- June 1943		
Unit :- AFDU Duxford		
Date :- 8/7/43		
Signature :- H.L. Thorne		

1. Spitfire XII		2-40
2. Spitfire IX		2-40
3. Spitfire Vb	NF	-50
Spitfire Vb		5-00
4. Typhoon		5-30
5. Mustang III		1-30
6. Hurricane IV		2-30
7. Tiger Moth		3-05
8. Heston Phoenix		3-35

TOTAL FOR THE MONTH 27 hours 20 minutes

J.L. Hallowes   S/Ldr
O/C Flying AFDU

I was now given ten days' leave to travel to Poletrees Farm to collect Estelle and baby Gill. My sister, Gwen, whose only child was a boy, John, would have loved to keep the little girl. Her love for Gill showed throughout her life. Gill, and later our younger daughter Penny, spent many happy school holidays at Poletrees, revelling in farm life.

YEAR	1943	AIRCRAFT		Pilot or 1st Pilot	2nd Pilot, Pupil or Pass.	DUTY (Including Results and Remarks)	Flying Time		Passenger
MONTH	DATE	Type	No.				Dual	Solo	
July	9th	Spitfire VIII	JF664	Self		Air test		-35	
	11th	Spitfire Vb	AF6	Self		Local flying		-20	
		Spitfire Vb	AF8	Self		More local flying		-30	
		Spitfire VIII	JF664	Self		Formation climb with 'Susie' to 35,000ft		-40	

	12th	Spitfire VIII	JF664	Self		To North Weald		-30	
		Spitfire VIII	JF664	Self		Comparative trials		1-00	
	13th	Spitfire VIII	JF664	Self		Climbs to 35,000ft		-50	
	14th	Spitfire Vb	AF8	Self		To North Weald		-30	
		Spitfire IX	AHT	Self		Comparative trials at 40,000ft		1-00	
		Spitfire VIII	JF664	Self		To base		-30	
	15th	Spitfire VIII	JF664	Self		Speed runs		-50	
		Spitfire VIII	JF664	Self		Rate of roll		-30	
	16th	Mosquito	666	F/Lt Fender		To Pershore			-30
		Spitfire Vb	AF6	Self		To base		-45	
	17th	Spitfire VIII	JF664	Self		To Northcotes		-30	
		Hurricane	581	Self		Bombing		-40	
		Spitfire VIII	JF664	Self		To base		-20	
		Lockheed Hudson	635	F/Lt Sewell	Self	Bombing			-45
	18th	Spitfire VIII	JF664	Self		Escort Focke Wulf FW 190		-20	
		Spitfire XII	EN222	Self		Handling at low level		-35	
	20th	Spitfire XII	AB191	Self		Weather test		-10	
	21st	Mustang	AM107	Self		Local flying		-20	
	22nd	Typhoon	EK290	Self		To Langley		-45	
		Mosquito	666	F/Lt Sewell	Self	To base		-45	
	23rd	Spitfire IX	BS552	Self		Air test		-10	
		Grumman Martlet	?	Self		Air experience		-45	
		Spitfire IX	BS552	Self		Air test		-15	
		Spitfire XII	EN222	Self		Escort FW 190		-30	
	25th	Spitfire Vb	AB191	Self		Aileron test		-10	
		Spitfire IX	BS552	Self		Rate of roll tests		-20	
	26th	Spitfire VIII	JF664	Self		To Boscombe Down		-40	

		Spitfire VIII	JF664	Self		To base		-45	
		Spitfire VIII	JF664	Self		Comparative trials v. Spitfire XIV		-45	
		Spitfire XIV	JF317	Self		Comparative trials v. Spitfire Mk VIII		-20	
		Spitfire XIV	JF317	Self		Comparative trials v. Spitfire VIII		-20	
		Spitfire XIV	JF317	Self		Climb to 40,000ft		1-05	
	28th	Spitfire XIV	JF317	Self		To 30,000ft		1-05	
		Spitfire VIII	JF664	Self		To 30,000ft		-50	
	29th	Oxford	BG549	Self		To Ford		1-35	
		Oxford	BG549	S/Ldr Dyson	Self	To base		1-10	
	30th	Spitfire XIV	JF317	Self		To Boscombe Down		-45	
		Mosquito	HJ666	F/Lt Sewell	Self	Crashed at White Waltham. Write-off			-15
		Percival Q6	?	Self	Lt Kendal	To base		-50	
		Phoenix	?	Self	F/Lt Joce	To Fowlmere and return		1-15	
		Oxford	BG549	Self		Air test		-15	
	31st	Spitfire VIII	JF664	Self		To Boscombe Down		-50	
		Spitfire VIII	JF664	Self		Boscombe to White Waltham		-15	
		Spitfire VIII	JF664	Self		White Waltham via Langley		-10	
		Spitfire VIII	JF664	Self		To base		-35	
						GRAND TOTAL TO DATE 826 hours 35 minutes	3-30	9-15	
							60-00	753-50	15-00

9 July: This was one of the first Mk VIIIs to come off the production line and was a complete redesign of the Mk V, powered by the Merlin 61 engine and with a modified canopy. Like the Mk VII, VI, IX and XVI, it had a four-blade airscrew. It was similar to the Mk IX in its flying characteristics and just as pleasant to handle.

11 July: The comparative flights on the 11th and 12th were against a Spitfire Mk IX flown by Susie, and at North Weald by pilots of the Squadrons. In due course they would probably receive Mk VIIIs and wanted to see how they compared with their Mk IXs.

13 July: Timed climbs to various heights and handling at high altitude.

14 July: I am puzzled by the flight to North Weald as I flew there in a Spitfire Vb but returned to Wittering in a Mk VIII. It is possible that Susie and I flew down in formation in the two different types and changed aircraft for the return journey. Otherwise fairies or gremlins must have been at work! It was a privilege to fly with the Squadron boys who were flying operations over France and Belgium almost every day. They had also been scrambled several times to intercept the Luftwaffe's high-flying PRU aircraft. My flight on the 14th to 40,000 feet was my highest so far.

15 July: The roll tests on the 15th would have been timed to ascertain the rate of roll; this was most important when compared with the Focke Wulf FW 190.

16 July: Pershore was the nearest airfield to the RRE (Radar Research Establishment), based in the pre-war girls' school at Malvern. Aircraft being used for experimental work and needing a special radio or radar fitting were flown there for modification.

17 July: I did it again: flew in to Northcotes in a Spit VIII, changed to a Hurricane for bomb dropping, then back to the Spit VIII for the return to Wittering.

The Hudson was a twin-engine American machine, originally a pre-war civilian airliner known as the Ventura and adapted for use as a wartime light bomber. It was also used for maritime reconnaissance. In this instance Susie was trying his hand at orthodox bombing while I acted as his observer.

18 July: Susie and I, each in a Spitfire, met up with the Focke Wulf FW190 that was being flown from Farnborough to AFDU for comparative tests against various Allied fighters. It was the first 190 to fall into our hands, the pilot having got confused after a bombing attack on Portland Bill; he had flown north instead of south. Instead of crossing the English Channel, he flew over the Bristol Channel and landed at Pembrey in South Wales. After brief tests at Wittering the aircraft was returned to Farnborough for technical evaluation.

Handling at low level was a favourite occupation, usually over the East Anglian fenlands or 'drains', an authorised low flying area. In a Spitfire XII, at speeds well over 500 mph and at heights below 50 feet, the sensation of speed was fantastic. It didn't half frighten the cows and sheep (and some of the natives) but they all got used to it. All such flights were supposed to be authorised but we all cheated when no one was looking.

22 July: Langley, Bucks, was two miles from Slough, and very convenient for a quick visit to sister Doris and family. I flew the Typhoon for modification and adjustment to the fuel system. Langley, with its adjoining airfield, was the site of the Hawker Aircraft factory where the Typhoons were produced. Susie, flying the Mosquito, followed me in and I made the return to Wittering flying as his navigator.

23 July: My first flight in an aircraft of the Fleet Air Arm, the Grumman Martlet, American-made radial-engine FAA fighter. It was widely used by the American navy and the British Fleet Air Arm. The first of a family that included the Hellcat, it took quite a beating from the Japanese Zeros and was rapidly replaced by better machines. I flew it with permission from our sister unit, NAFDU.

About this time the RAF had the good fortune to have two 190s drop into their hands. The first that I mentioned previously, after its tests at Farnborough, went to 1426 Enemy Aircraft Flight at Colley Weston and the other, PM679, came to AFDU. I will have more to say about this machine at the beginning of August.

26 July: This was our first experience with the Spitfire Mk XIV, the high-flying version with the Griffon engine. The main differences were the bigger and more powerful engine with 2035 HP and a 5-blade airscrew. Particular care had to be taken to control torque on take-off and landing, bearing in mind that the Griffon engine revolved anti-clockwise. These trials were for general handling, climbing performance, diving, turning circles, rate of roll etc.

The fourth flight of the day was my first flight in the Spit. Mk XIV, after landing and changing aircraft. There was a noticeable difference in power and handling techniques. The next two were timed climbs to pre-arranged heights, up to what was found to be the operational ceiling of that particular aircraft. On one such climb I actually topped 45,000 feet; this, of course would have been the absolute, not the operational ceiling. We had no cockpit heating then and it was extremely cold. Spitfires, except for the Mk VI and VII, had no pressure cabins; consequently it was very tiring at the higher altitudes, so we did not stay up there very many minutes.

30 July: Squadron Leader Dyson took over from Squadron Leader Smith. He was ex-Indian Air Force. After Ted Smith, I found S/L Dyson difficult to get on with; he tended to treat us like members of the Colonial Service in the Raj had treated their Indian servants. It was a relief that he did not stay very long with us.

Susie and I flew many exercises together and, on this occasion, he had flown from Wittering to pick me up from Boscombe Down, intending to carry on with fuel consumption runs. I acted as observer, recording the Kent Flowmeter readings. At 5,000 feet, over the Thames valley, the port engine failed and we were cleared for an emergency landing at the nearest airfield. This was White Waltham, a smallish airfield near Maidenhead. We made a precautionary approach in a shallow descent, using a fair amount of power from the good engine. As we crossed the boundary hedge our final approach was baulked by three airmen on bicycles. Susie automatically opened up the starboard engine to full power, to go round again but that engine, too, cut out. The Mossie stalled at about 200 feet and we crashed badly, more or less in the centre of the landing area. As we careered across the grass we shed first both engines, then the rear fuselage and finally both wings. We were very lucky that the cockpit and nose section remained intact.

To the surprise of the crash wagon crew, we stepped out of the wreck with only a few bumps and bruises, very minor injuries to show for our experience. It was normal procedure following a crash, if possible, to fly again as soon as possible. Susie, however, suffered severely from shock and refused the offer to fly back to Wittering at the controls of the Percival Q6 that had come to collect us. I accepted the offer and flew it back. This was a new type to me and I was closely watched by Lieutenant Hugh Kendal of NAFDU, who had offered to collect us. I suffered no ill effects from the crash. A few days later, much to my sorrow, Susie was taken off flying and posted away for a rest.

This was an eventful day; while I made only five flights, they were all in different types of aircraft. First a Spitfire Mk XIV, then the Mosquito, badly damaged in our crash and a write-off, followed by a return to base in the Percival Q6, another type to add to my logbook; finally the little Phoenix and the Airspeed Oxford. Another record? I wonder!

31 July: In the course of my duties, I made several flights to Boscombe Down. Boscombe, on Salisbury Plain, was the base for another of our sister units, the A and AEE. Their function was the initial flying of all new or modified aircraft and the preparation and production of 'Pilot's Notes'. These booklets were always available to pilots when flying a new type of machine.

Summary for :- July 1943	1 Spitfire V	2-25
Unit:- AFDU Duxford	2 Spitfire VIII	11-55
Date:- 2/8/43	3 Spitfire IX	1-45
Signature:- H.L. Thorne	4 Spitfire XII	1-05
	5 Spitfire XIV	3-35
	6 Hurricane	-40
	7 Mustang III	-20

8	Typhoon	-45
9	Oxford	3-00
10	Heston Phoenix	1-15
11	Martlet	-45
12	Percival Q6	-50
13	Mosquito	1-30
14	Lockheed Hudson	-45

Total for the month 28 hours 20 minutes

Signed *N.C.H. Dyson* S/Ldr
O/C Flying AFDU

7

ENTER THE FOCKE WULF 190

Flight Lieutenant H.S. Sewell, Susie, had been made responsible for the comparative testing of the Focke Wulf FW190 against various Allied fighters, mainly the latest Spitfires and the P51 Mustang. When these were complete the Air Ministry ordered the 190 to be flown to the most important RAF fighter stations, followed by fighter OTUs, PRU stations and some light bomber bases. It was essential to give our pilots confidence when they went into combat against the radial-engined, much-feared German machine. Although the AFDU Wing Commander and the squadron Leader O/C Flying made one or two flights Susie did, or was intended to do, most of the work.

The account of how this aircraft, reregistered PM679, fell into our hands is intriguing. Because the Germans had no suitable heavy bombers, the only way they could strike at England was to use the ME109 and the FW190 as fighter bombers. These were used for hit and run attacks in the Baedeker raids. On 23rd May three 190s made a night attack in northwest London but got lost when they turned for France. They crossed the Thames estuary at its widest point and thought they had crossed the Channel. Seeing an airfield (it turned out to be Manston, Kent) with the landing lights on and a twin-engine aircraft landing, they followed it into the circuit. They wrongly identified the machine as a JU88 when, in fact, it was a Mosquito, for which the airfield lights had been switched on. The first Focke Wulf landed safely and taxied in to the control tower. The pilot got out and started to order his machine to be refuelled before realising his mistake. Meanwhile the second 190 had landed but as he came to a stop, realised his mistake and attempted to take off downwind. He was prevented from doing so by being shot up by the crew of a Beaverette armoured car, the pilot being wounded and the aircraft badly damaged. The third German fighter was on his final approach when the airfield controller realised that something peculiar was happening and turned off the landing lights. As a result the 190 crashed short of the runway and I believe the pilot died.

As a result of our Mosquito crash and Susie's rest from flying I, being the next senior, was delegated to take over the 190 programme. I was promoted to Flight Lieutenant and appointed Flight Commander of AFDU. Even more important, my pay was increased to 22/6d per day (£1.12½p).

| YEAR | 1943 | AIRCRAFT | | Pilot or 1st Pilot | 2nd Pilot, Pupil or Pass. | DUTY (Including Results and Remarks) | Flying Time | | Passenger |
MONTH	DATE	Type	No.				Dual	Solo	
August	1st	Avro Anson	?	Self	2 'Erks'	Air test		-30	
	3rd	FW 190	PM679	Self		Air experience		-30	
	6th	Oxford	BG549	F/Lt Sewell	Self	To Newmarket		-40	
		Oxford	BG549	F/Lt Sewell	Self	To Hornchurch		-30	
		Oxford	BG549	F/Lt Sewell	Self	To White Waltham		-15	
		Oxford	BG549	F/Lt Sewell	Self	To Langley		-15	
		Oxford	BG549	Self		To base		1-00	
	7th	Hurricane	KX581	Self		Compass test		1-05	
	8th	Spitfire Vb	AF8	Self		Compass test		-45	
	9th	Phoenix	2891	Self	F/O Borham	To White Waltham		1-00	
		Phoenix	2891	Self	F/O Borham	To Langley		-15	
		Typhoon	EK290	Self		To base		-35	
	10th	Spitfire VIII	JF299	Self		To test new shape canopy known as the 'Tear Drop'		-35	
	12th	FW 190	PM679	Self		Advanced handling		-25	
		Mustang X	AM203	Self		Gun sight trial		-25	
		Mustang III	AM107	Self		Gun sight trial		-55	
	13th	FW 190	PM679	Self		Handling. Gun-post beat up		-25	
	15th	FW 190	PM679	Self		To North Weald		-40	
		FW 190	PM679	Self		Dog fight versus Spitfire Mk IX		-30	
		FW 190	PM679	Self		Dog fights versus Spitfire Mk IX		-30	

		FW 190	PM679	Self		Dog fights versus Mosquitos	-40	
	16th	FW 190	PM679	Self		To Biggin Hill	-30	
	17th	FW 190	PM679	Self		Dog fights v. the Biggin Squadron's Spitfires. Landed at Northolt	-45	
		FW 190	PM679	Self		Dog fight v. Spitfire IXs. Landed 21.00 hrs on flarepath	-25	
	18th	FW 190	PM679	Self		To Hornchurch	-30	
		FW 190	PM679	Self		Dog fight v. Spitfire IXs	-25	
	19th	FW 190	PM679	Self		To Kenley	-20	
		FW 190	PM679	Self		Dog fights and beat up	-30	
	20th	FW 190	PM679	Self		To Tangmere	-30	
		FW 190	PM679	Self		Dog fights and beat up	-35	
	21st	FW 190	PM679	Self		To Ibsley	-30	
		Oxford	V6791	Self		To Westcott via Tangmere	1-10	
		Oxford	V6791	Self		To Ibsley	1-10	
	22nd	FW 190	PM679	Self		To Exeter	-40	
		FW 190	PM679	Self		Beat-up	-30	
		FW 190	PM679	Self		Dog fights and beat-up	-30	
	23rd	FW 190	PM679	Self		To Portreath	-40	
	24th	FW 190	PM679	Self		To Colerne	-45	
		FW 190	PM679	Self		To Wittering	-50	
	29th	Oxford	V6791	Self		BAT (Blind approach trainng)	1-10	
	30th	Mustang III	AM107	Self		Air test	-10	
		Oxford	V6791	F/Lt Meredith	Self	BAT	1-00	
		Oxford	V6791	W/O ?	Self	BAT	1-00	
	31st	Spitfire Vb	AF8	Self		Cine film	-45	

		Spitfire Vb	AF8	Self		Cine film		-35	
		Spitfire Vb	AF8	Self		Cine film		-30	
						GRAND TOTAL TO DATE: 855 hours 35 mins	3-30	9-15	
							60-00	782-50	15-00

1 August: My first flight in an Anson, another pre-war, wood and fabric, twin-engine aircraft. There was no question of my being given any instruction or a conversion course; I was just told to get in and fly it. The two members of ground staff must have had supreme confidence in my ability as they came along for the ride.

3 August: The German pilot, Uffz Heinz Ehrhardt, when landing at Manston, had not been kind enough to bring with him a set of Pilot's Notes for the FW190. I was dependent on the few instructions Susie had given me prior to being posted away. As many things were different, I spent three days studying the 190, the movement of the controls and particularly checking the radio and oxygen systems before making my first flight. This delay caused a severe brush with Squadron Leader Dyson, who was under pressure from Air Ministry to get going on the programme, in particular the visits to our fighter bases in the south of England. In the event, and being extremely careful, I made my maiden flight with no problems at all.

6 August: These flights were to attend the court of enquiry into our Mosquito crash.

Sadly, that day I had to leave Susie to take up the first part of his move to non-flying duties; it was with great regret and a real sense of loss that I waved goodbye.

15 August: This was the start of a ten-day tour of fighter stations in the southeast part of Britain, from which most of the attacks on the Germans in France and Belgium were launched. It was my first demonstration of the 190's capabilities in mock combat. I merely threw the 190 around, particularly demonstrating its wonderful rolling performance, while the Spitfire pilots took turns to attack. I hardly had time to draw breath before they had me up for a repeat performance. It was the same when I was on the ground; all the boys wanted to examine the 190 at close quarters and have their turn to sit in the cockpit.

17 August: I continued to play with them the next morning before going on to land at Biggin Hill. This was one of the most famous Battle of Britain airfields and this was my first visit there.

The Polish Wing of three Squadrons was based at Northolt. Well known for their undying hatred of the Germans, they were all eager to have a go at the 190. I just hoped they would all remember that it was just an exercise and not for real.

The Polish chaps kept me going until it was dark, so I performed a night landing, with some trepidation but no trouble. On one of these mock combats one of the Spits developed engine trouble and peeled off streaming black smoke. I had a momentary fear that the Poles would think I had shot it down and, being notoriously trigger happy, take a shot at me. Their Group Captain was flying with them and kept them under control.

18 August: When flying the Focke Wulf I always had a Spitfire escort, usually two aircraft. At Hornchurch, as I arrived in the circuit, the resident Squadron was returning from a sweep. The Squadron Leader, seeing a FW190 in the circuit, gave me a bad moment when he started an attack, only stopping at the last minute when he saw that my wheels and flaps were down. A clean pair of pants was required! After that, when flying in 11-Group airspace (the S.E. corner of England), I had a 4-Spit escort.

19 August: The FW190, with its high wing loading, had a landing touch-down speed of 100/110 mph, compared to a Spit's 80/85 mph, and usually a longer landing run. It was left to my discretion whether I went into airfields such as Kenley with a short runway. As most of my operational flying was from Kenley, I felt that I had to make the attempt and, in the event, had no trouble.

At Kenley, my old station with 602 Squadron, I could not resist doing an aerobatic beat-up at low level as part of my demonstration. Show off! I wonder whether any of my WAAF friends were there to see it.

20 August: Having spent some time in the Tangmere sector whilst serving with 41 Squadron, I treated them to a display of low aerobatics as well. The FW190 had a phenomenal rate of roll and my party trick was to dive from 1,000 feet, pull back the stick to almost vertical, apply full throttle and perform a series of climbing rolls, left then right, until the speed dropped to near stall. 8½ rolls was my record and onlookers were always impressed.

I spent that night in the Tangmere Officers' Mess and witnessed one of the war's tragedies: late evening, we heard a large aircraft, which turned out to be a four-engined Halifax, circling the airfield in an attempt to land but obviously in trouble, with two engines badly damaged. The pilot made two abortive attempts to land, managing to stagger round again. At the third try he touched the runway, swung violently to port, stalled and pancaked on to two of the hangars. What we did not know was that a tannoy message had gone out ordering all personnel to evacuate the airfield as the Halifax still had an unexploded 4,000 lb. bomb on board. The Officers' Mess tannoy system had failed and we had not heard the message, so we streamed to the scene of the crash, where the Halifax and two hangars were burning furiously. Only the tail-gunner was still alive, trapped in the turret; we could do nothing to help as he burned to death. Meanwhile, a young corporal of the crash crew had enlisted our help and two Spitfires were pushed clear and saved. Two others and five Typhoons were destroyed.

The crew of the Halifax all perished in the blaze. The following morning they could only be found by rows of buttons and belt buckles. That young corporal showed great bravery and should have received a medal. The information about the bomb proved to be false.

21 August: I sneaked a trip to Westcott for a quick visit to Mother, Gwen and family at Poletrees.

22 August: These 'beat-ups', low-level dives on the airfield, were authorised to show off the fantastic rate of roll of the 190. Thrills galore!

23 August: Portreath was a very small grass airfield, sloping up from the cliffs on the north coast of Cornwall, an approach from the sea to the upward-sloping field. To make matters worse, I had been fired on by members of a coastal defence ack-ack battery who had apparently not been warned of a visiting enemy aircraft. As usual (*Deo Volente*) they missed. Despite the problems I decided to have a go and landed safely.

24 August: The short flight to Colerne included displays at both airfields and demonstrating the 190 to resident Mosquito squadrons.

The return ended two weeks on detachment with intensive flying activity. Wherever I went, the Focke Wulf aroused great interest, so I was kept busy even when on the ground. Everyone wanted to sit in the cockpit and have his (or her) questions answered. At one airfield, the station commander, a Group Captain who shall remain nameless, asked me to show him the taps so that he could fly the FW. I explained that I had no authority to allow anyone else to fly the machine as it was, at that time, the only airworthy version in Allied hands. He did not take kindly to a refusal from a mere Flight Lieutenant and pulled rank, saying I was under his command while on his station. I stuck to my guns and he eventually backed off. Back at Wittering I reported this occurrence and, to cover me in future, I was given a letter from the Ministry confirming the position.

I was glad to return to Wittering for a well-earned four-day rest for the aircraft and me. I also greatly appreciated the hardworking ground crew who kept the 190 in such good trim.

30 August: These were training flights in making blind approach and landings, using a variation of the American Lorenz system: all dots and dashes!

31 August: Back to routine test work. What an anti-climax this was after that fortnight with the 190.

Summary for:- August 1943
Unit:- AFDU   Duxford
Date:- 7/9/43
Signature:- H.L.Thorne

1. Anson	–40
2. FW 190	12–35
3. Oxford	8–10
4. Hurricane	1–05
5. Spitfire V	2–35
6. Phoenix	1–15
7. Typhoon	–35
8. Spitfire VIII	–35
9. Mustang III	1–05
10. Mustang X	–25

Signed: *R.A. Mitchell* S/Ldr
O/C Flying AFDU

YEAR	1943	AIRCRAFT		Pilot or 1st Pilot	2nd Pilot, Pupil or Pass.	DUTY (Including Results and Remarks)	Flying Time		Passenger
MONTH	DATE	Type	No.				Dual	Solo	
September	1st	Spitfire Vb	AF8	Self		Cine films		-20	
	2nd	Spitfire Vb	AF8	Self		Cine films		1-20	
		Spitfire IX	AF10	Self		Test harness		-20	
		Spitfire IX	JF359	Self		Test harness and fuel injection pump		-15	
		Spitfire XII	EN222	Self		Local air test		-20	
	3rd	FW 190	PM679	Self		Local		-15	
	4th	FW 190	PM679	Self		To Aston Down		-40	
		FW 190	PM679	Self		Low aerobatics and beat-up		-20	
	5th	FW 190	PM679	Self		To Benson		-20	
		FW 190	PM679	Self		Trials at 26,000ft v. PRU Mosquitos		-55	
	6th	Spitfire XI	PRU	Self		Local at Benson		-35	
		FW 190	PM679	Self		Benson to Coltishall		-50	
		FW 190	PM679	Self		To base		-40	
	8th	Spitfire XII	EN222	Self		Co-op Lancaster		-50	
		Proctor	220	Self		To Farnborough		1-00	

	Proctor	220	Self		To base		1-10	
12th	Oxford	BG549	S/Ldr Mitchell	Self	To Cranfield		-50	
	Spitfire Vc	AB169	Self		To base		-20	
13th	FW 190	PM679	Self		Air test		-20	
	Oxford	BG549	S/Ldr Mitchell	Self	To Great Massingham		-30	
	Spitfire Vb	AF2	Self		To base		-30	
14th	FW 190	PM679	Self		To Syerston		-40	
	FW 190	PM679	Self		Co-op Lancaster & return to base		1-15	
15th	FW 190	PM679	Self		To Rednal		-55	
	FW 190	PM679	Self		Dog fight and demonstration		-20	
	FW 190	PM679	Self		Aerobatic demonstration		-15	
16th	FW 190	PM679	Self		To Hibaldstow		-50	
	Oxford	BG549	Self	F/Sgt Helens	To Wittering		-40	
17th	Oxford	BG549	Self	F/Sgt Helens	To Hibaldstow		-40	
19th	FW 190	PM679	Self		To Eshott		1-00	
21st	Oxford	BG549	F/O Barr	Self	To Wittering		-30	
23rd	Spitfire L2C		Self		Films at 3G		-30	
	Seafire L2C		Self		Films at 3G		-20	
	Hurricane IV		Self		Films at 3G		-25	
24th	Hurricane IV		Self		Films at 3G		-20	
	Oxford	BG549	Self	S/Ldr Hobhouse	To Farnborough		-50	
	Oxford	BG549	Self	S/Ldr Hobhouse	To base		-50	
25th	Boston		F/O Gough	Self	To Eschott			1-15
26th	FW 190	PM679	Self		To base		1-05	
					GRAND TOTAL TO DATE 880 hours 45 mins	3-30	9-15	
						60-00	808-00	16-15

2 September: I cannot remember much about the harness. Apart from light aircraft – Phoenix, Magister, etc. – we always wore a parachute that buckled at the front. The metal tags on the safety straps pushed into spring-loaded slots in a circular box. The straps were released by turning the front face of the box through 45° and striking it with the heel or palm of the hand.

As I said earlier, Merlin-engined aircraft, the Spitfire, Hurricane and Defiant, suffered the disadvantage of loss of power under negative 'G' Various temporary expedients were tried and it took a long time to catch up with the Luftwaffe's fuel injection system.

4 September: After visits to some of the 11 Group fighter stations made famous in the Battle of Britain, Command decided that the 190 should continue with demonstrations at OTUs, PR Units and some light bomber airfields.

5 September: Benson was a most interesting visit. The 190 evoked the usual interest from all personnel but here I had the pleasure and honour to meet Air Commodore Sir John Boothman, the AOC (Air Officer Commanding) PRU. He was a member of the pre-war Schneider Trophy team. He was most interested in the 190 and spent some time sitting in the cockpit while I explained things. He asked whether it would be possible to fly it during my visit but fully understood my position when I told him about the Air Ministry letter. As I was sure that an exception would be made, I suggested that his adjutant telephone the Air Ministry. Of course, there was no hesitation in granting his request.

I then had the pleasure of giving him further instruction and off he went, to return some time later and make a perfect landing. He thanked me most profusely and allowed me to fly any PRU aircraft of my choice. Again, I missed the chance to fly a Mossie but I did fly a PRU Mark XI Spitfire. With no guns and polished, it was a joy, reckoned to be so fast and able to fly so high that it could not be caught.

6 September: The end of another week on detachment.

8 September: Another first flight. The little Percival Proctor was a small 4-seater cabin plane, used for training and communications.

15 September: The Station Commander at RAF Rednal was Group Captain Richard Atcherley, one of identical twins, both Group Captains in the RAF. They were well known for their practical jokes, often at the expense of the gate guards. Richard, too, said he would like to fly the 190 but accepted my refusal with good grace. He survived the war but was lost some years later when crossing the Mediterranean flying a Meteor. Rednal was a fighter Operational Training Unit, so my dogfight would have been versus Harvards.

16 September: Oh dear! Our 2nd Wedding Anniversary and I was off on another week of detached duty. I managed to sneak back to Wittering in the Oxford and have a night at Easton with Estelle after all.

19 September: During this flight to Eshott the engine of the Focke Wulf started to run rougher than usual; compared with a Merlin, it always felt rough. Despite the efforts of my ground crew, they failed to cure the trouble and the next flight in the Oxford to Wittering was to fetch an ignition harness that had been stripped from a crashed aircraft. This was fitted to PM679 but failed to effect any improvement. Rather than using a 'Queen Mary' road transport, which meant dismantling the 190. I volunteered to fly it back to Wittering a few days later, on the 26th, following a route and height which kept me within gliding distance of one of the many airfields on the route. Fortunately, the BMW 801 engine kept running and I landed safely and very relieved at Wittering. When the engine was dismantled, a hole the size of a half-crown (nearly 2 inches) was found in the crown of one of the pistons.

23 September: The L2C was actually a Seafire of the Fleet Air Arm, courtesy of NAFDU, and is correctly named in the second entry.

It was difficult and tiring to hold a 3G tight turn, hence the short flights.

25 September: F/O Gough was second in command of 1426 and he came with me to Escott to offer help with the 190 and fly as escort back to Wittering.

Summary for:- September 1943	1. Spitfire II & V 2–30
Unit:- AFDU Wittering	2. Spitfire IX –35
Date:- 15/10/43	3. Spitfire XI –35
Signature:- H.L. Thorne	4. Spitfire XII 1–10
	5. Seafire L2C –50
	6. FW190 10–40
	7. Proctor 2–10
	8. Hurricane –45
	9. Oxford 5–55
	10. Boston 1–15

Signed: *S.H. Dyson* S/Ldr
O/C Flying AFDU

YEAR	1943	AIRCRAFT		Pilot or 1st Pilot	2nd Pilot, Pupil or Pass.	DUTY (Including Results and Remarks)	Flying Time		Passenger
MONTH	DATE	Type	No.				Dual	Solo	
October	8th	Oxford	V3791	Self	1 passenger	To Duxford		-30	
		Oxford	V3791	Self	1 passenger	To Farnborough		-45	
		Oxford	V3791	Self	1 passenger	To Duxford		-45	
		Oxford	V3791	Self	1 passenger	To base		-30	
		FW 190	PM679	Self		Air test		-10	

	15th	Oxford	V3791	Self	F/O Garvey	To Swinderby & return		-35	
	24th	Spitfire VIII	JF816	Self		Escort ME109F of 1426 Flt		1-00	
	27th	Oxford	V3791	Self		To Hucknall		-30	
						GRAND TOTAL TO DATE 880 hours 45 mins			

27 October: I cannot remember why I did so little flying this month. It may have been bad weather or the time I spent in the Officers' Hospital at Ely, under observation for a touch of stomach trouble. The continuing engine trouble with the FW190 obviously curtailed my flying programme severely.

Summary for:- October 1943	1. Oxford	3-35
Unit:- AFDU Wittering	2. FW190	-10
Date:- 1/11/43	3. Spitfire VIII	1-00
Signature:- H.L. Thorne		

Signed: *T.S. Wade* S/Ldr
O/C Flying AFDU

After several short changes of O/C Flying, during which I often had to perform that function, Squadron Leader T.S. Wade took over the appointment and remained with AFDU until the end of the European war. Trevor Wade, from his build, was always known as Wimpy, in reference to the shape of the Wellington bomber, also nicknamed the Wimpy, both, I believe, taken from a cartoon character, J. Wellington Wimpy, in an American comic strip.

Trevor Wade, Wimpy, was a terrific character himself; someone should have written a book about him. He was, without doubt, the best aerobatic pilot I ever met. On bad weather days, he would perform over the airfield at very low level and we all turned out to watch. It was said that, when his wife was in a local nursing home awaiting the arrival of their first baby, he gave them a show that caused several ladies to give birth then and there. We became good friends and when their baby was christened at the Wittering Chapel, Estelle and I were guests. No baby had his head wetted as thoroughly as that one.

The district around the airfield, which bordered the Burghley estate, abounded with game, which we shot at every opportunity. On one occasion, Wimpy and I were driving in a lane just outside the boundary fence poaching, with some success, when we were caught by a gamekeeper, who bravely attempted to stop us. Wimpy kept going and the man hurriedly moved aside. This occurrence was duly reported to the Unit Commanding Officer, Allan Wright. He had us up on the carpet but, of course, we denied any knowledge of the matter and so it was duly reported back.

| YEAR | 1943 | AIRCRAFT | | Pilot or 1st Pilot | 2nd Pilot, Pupil or Pass. | DUTY (Including Results and Remarks) | Flying Time | | Passenger |
MONTH	DATE	Type	No.				Dual	Solo	
November	3rd	Master		Self	F/Lt Taylor	Dual instruction		-25	
		Oxford	BG549	F/O Walker	Self	To Hucknall		-25	
		Oxford	V3791	Self		To base		-30	
	5th	Spitfire IX	JK359	Self		Fuel consumption test		-15	
		Spitfire IX	JK359	Self		Fuel consumption test		-30	
		FW 190	PM679	Self		Air test		-15	
		Spitfire XII	EN222	Self		Engine cutting trial		-15	
	6th	Spitfire VIII	JF816	Self		Cine gun		-25	
		Spitfire V	AF9	Self		Cine gun		-20	
	7th	Spitfire XII	EN222	Self		Cutting test		-20	
		Spitfire IX	JF359	Self		Fuel consumption test		1-35	
	18th	FW 190	PM679	Self		To Tangmere		-55	
	19th	FW 190	PM679	Self		Co-op Typhoons		-45	
	20th	FW 190	PM679	Self		Co-op Typhoons		-45	
	23rd	FW 190	PM679	Self		To Dunsfold		-20	
	24th	Auster I		Self		To Redhill		-25	
		Auster I		Self		To Dunsfold		-25	
		FW 190	PM679	Self		Co-op Mustangs		-50	
		Auster		Self		To Redhill		-25	
	25th	Auster		Self		To Dunsfold		-25	
		FW 190	PM679	Self		To North Weald		-40	
		FW 190	PM679	Self		Co-op Mustangs		-40	
	26th	FW 190	PM679	Self		Co-op Mustangs		1-00	
	29th	FW 190	PM679	Self		To Hartford Bridge		-45	
	30th	FW 190	PM679	Self		Co-op Bostons		1-30	
		FW 190	PM679	Self		To Wittering		-40	
						GRAND TOTAL TO DATE 896 hours 30 mins	3-30	9-15	
							60-00	823-45	16-15

3 November: I always enjoyed a trip in a Master; it was so easy to fly.

Flying Officer Walker, with Flying Officer Hugh Godefroy (Canadian) and I were regular members of the Detached Affiliation Flight. F/O Walker had quite a reputation with the WAAFs; it was said he took out a different one every night.

5 November: These fuel consumption tests were of the new Negative G carburettor.

I believe a 'new' engine had been fitted on the 190; one taken from another lost 190 that was damaged on landing.

The engine cutting involved deliberate mishandling of the throttle control while applying Negative G.

7 November: For fuel consumption tests the aircraft was fitted with a Kent Flow-meter by the Kent Company at Luton. The test would be at varying heights and throttle settings. From the longer duration of this flight I assume that this one was at a higher altitude.

24 November: Another visit to the old Squadron, back in 11 Group after their rest. They were now flying Spitfire IXs and could meet the dreaded 190s on better than even terms. Consequently, they were much happier but only two or three pilots were from the 'old lot'. Where did that Auster I come from? I assume I borrowed it from one of the army co-op units at Dunsfold, another first flight in the logbook.

30 November: I was really glad to be back at base after my longest period of detachment, from November 18th to November 30th. It was 12 days of hard going. The Mustang and Boston boys really kept me busy despite some days of doubtful weather.

Summary for:- November 1943	1. Master	-25
Unit:- AFDU Wittering	2. Oxford	-55
Date:- 5/12/43	3. Spitfire IX	2-20
Signature:- H.L. Thorne	4. Spitfire VIII	-25
	5. Spitfire XII	-35
	6. Spitfire V	-20
	7. FW190	9-05
	8. Auster	1-40

Signed *T.S. Wade* S/Ldr
O/C Flying AFDU

YEAR	1943	AIRCRAFT		Pilot or 1st Pilot	2nd Pilot, Pupil or Pass.	DUTY (Including Results and Remarks)	Flying Time		Passengerw
MONTH	DATE	Type	No.				Dual	Solo	
December	1st	FW 190	PM679	Self		To Wittering		-40	
	10th	FW 190	PM679	Self		Air test		-15	
	11th	Oxford	V3791	Self	F/Lt Aalpoel	BAT practice		1-00	
	31st	Mustang III	FZ107	Self		Experience on type		1-00	
						GRAND TOTAL TO DATE 899 hours 25 mins	3-30	9-15	
							60-00	826-40	16-15

1 December: I am puzzled by this entry. The previous day, November 30th, my logbook shows a return to Wittering and again today, December 1st. The flying times are the same, so it appears that there must be a missing entry. Gremlins again!

11 December: This marked a spell of very bad/severe weather so a spell of blind landing practice was sensible. In the event, I spent the following ten days as a guest of Rolls-Royce at Hucknall on an engine-handling course. This was followed by a week's leave, which Estelle, Gill and I spent in Redditch with her family and friends. We were very welcome as we were well loaded with pheasants and partridges!

31 December: I had flown the Mustang III and the Mustang X back in August. I believe they were basically the same version, the Mk X being the type converted by Rolls-Royce in England and the Mk III the final American-produced machine, with Rolls-Royce Merlin engines produced under licence by Packard and Ford. The modifications changed a fairly ordinary fighter into the world-beater it became. My flight on December 31st marked the start of major trials in which I was heavily involved. FZ107 was actually delivered to AFDU four days earlier, on December 26th.

Summary for:- December 1943   1. FW190   -55
Unit:- AFDU Wittering   2. Oxford   1-00
Date:- 1/1/44   3. Mustang III   1-00
Signature:- H.L. Thorne

Signed *T.S. Wade* S/Ldr
O/C Flying AFDU

So ended 1943, an eventful year for me, flying many new types and thoroughly enjoying flying the Focke Wulf FW190. By the end of the year its reputation as a killing machine (the Germans called it the Würger, the Butcher Bird, or shrike) had become somewhat tarnished. Later Marks of the Messerschmitt ME109 were now a more formidable proposition. Spitfire IXs, XIIs, VIIIs, XVIs and the XIVs, now strongly supported by the Mustang, were more than a match for the best the Luftwaffe could muster.

| YEAR | 1944 | AIRCRAFT | | Pilot or 1st Pilot | 2nd Pilot, Pupil or Pass. | DUTY (Including Results and Remarks) | Flying Time | | Passenger |
MONTH	DATE	Type	No.				Dual	Solo	
January	1st	Mustang III	FZ107	Self		Speed runs		-40	
	2nd	Mustang III	FZ107	Self		Speed runs		-45	
		Oxford	V3791	Self	A/C Roscorla	To Romford & back to base		1-20	
	3rd	Proctor	DX220	Self	Cpl Mauker	To Luton		-30	
		Proctor	DX220	Self	Cpl Mauker	To base		-40	
	4th	Spitfire VII	BS229	Self		Dive break test		-55	
		Mustang III	FZ107	Self		Climbs to 20,000ft		-35	
	5th	Mustang III	FZ107	Self		Climbs and speed runs		-45	
	7th	Spitfire IX	BS552	Self		Comparative speeds and climbs		-35	
		Spitfire IX	BS552	Self		Comparative speeds and climbs		-55	
	8th	Spitfire V	AD318	Self		To Wescott, compass test		-35	
		Spitfire V	AD318	Self		To base		-35	
	9th	Proctor	DX220	Self		To Langley		1-00	
		Proctor	DX220	Self		To base		1-00	
	10th	Mustang III	FZ107	Self		Rate of roll		-50	
		Mustang III	FZ107	Self		Dives, climbs & turning circles		-40	
	18th	Mustang III	FZ107	Self		Speed runs		-10	
	21st	Mustang III	FZ107	Self		Speed runs		-45	
		Mustang III	FZ107	Self		Fuel consumption test		1-10	
	22nd	Mustang III	FZ107	Self		To Cranfield and back		-35	

23rd	Mustang III	FZ107	Self		To Cranfield		-25	
	Mustang III	FZ107	Self		To base		-25	
	Mustang III	FZ107	Self		Comparative turning circles		-30	
	Spitfire IX	JL359	Self		Comparative turning circles		-40	
25th	Spitfire IX	BS582	Self		Air test		-30	
	Spitfire IX	JL359	Self		Fuel consumption test		-25	
26th	FW 190	PM679	Self		Air test		-20	
28th	Tempest	JN737	Self		Zoom climbs		-25	
29th	Tempest	JN737	Self		Speed runs		-40	
	Tempest	JN737	Self		Operational climb		-45	
30th	Spitfire IX	MH415	Self		Cutting		-20	
					GRAND TOTAL TO DATE 920 hours 30 mins	3-30	9-15	
						60-00	847-45	16-15

2 January: This entry is unusual as we actually landed at Romford but it is recorded as a single flight. I have noticed that this happened on one or two occasions.

3 January: Our ground crews really enjoyed a flight now and then.

4 January: The Mk VII was basically a Mk VIII with a pressurised cabin for flying at high altitude. It had elongated wings and some had cabin heating. By this stage in the war there was very little need for high-altitude work and only a few were built.

7 January: The last four flights would have taken place with the Spit IX and the Mustang III starting side by side or in formation so that direct comparisons could be made.

8 January: An excuse to land at Westcott and scrounge a lift to Poletrees to see Mum, Gwen and family. Joe again took me back and I obtained a temporary pass for him. He was able to look inside 'my' Spit, then watch while I started the engine, taxied out and took off. Afterwards he was escorted out by the guardroom staff. It made his day and was good for many pints at the local Crooked Billet pub.

10 January: These tests would have been made in conjunction with a Spit IX, probably flown by S/Ldr Wade (Wimpy). On the 23rd, I flew the Spit IX for the comparative turning circles.

21 January: The speed runs were carried out at intervals of 2,000 feet with the throttle set to maximum cruising first, then at full throttle. On the first run at ground level, flying straight and level, I recorded an indicated speed of 455mph, my fastest so far. At such low level the impression of speed was terrific. I wonder what went wrong on the first flight – ten minutes would be just up and down; probably weather conditions were no good.

28 January: My first flight in a Tempest I, the successor to the Hurricane and Typhoon. It was powered by a Napier Sabre engine of 2,400hp with a speed of nearly 450mph. Later versions had a Bristol Centaurus radial engine, first designated the Tempest II and later, the Fury. Its final top speed was nearly 500mph.

Summary for:– January 1944	1. Mustang	8-15
Date:– 3/1/44	2. Oxford	1-20
Unit:– AFDU Wittering	3. Proctor	3-10
Signature:– H.L. Thorne	4. Spitfire VII	-55
	5. Spitfire IX	4-10
	6. Spitfire V	1-10
	7. FW190	-20
	8. Tempest	1-45

Signed *T.S. Wade* S/Ldr
O/C Flying A.F.D.U

YEAR	1944	AIRCRAFT		Pilot or 1st Pilot	2nd Pilot, Pupil or Pass.	DUTY (Including Results and Remarks)	Flying Time		Passenger
MONTH	DATE	Type	No.				Dual	Solo	
February	1st	Mustang III	FZ107	Self		Test long-range tanks		-35	
		Mustang III	FZ107	Self		Comparative v. Tempest		-45	
	2nd	Tempest	JN737	Self	A/C Roscorla	Comparative v. Mustang		-50	
		Mustang III	FZ107	Self	Cpl Mauker	Fuel consumption and firing		2-20	
	3rd	Mustang III	FZ107	Self	Cpl Mauker	Fuel tank change-over test		1-10	
	4th	Mustang III	FZ107	Self		Climb to 35,000ft		1-30	
		Mustang III	FZ107	Self		Cine gun		-15	
	5th	Mustang III	FZ107	Self		Assistance to Typhoon		-15	

		Mustang III	FZ107	Self		To Poddington		-25	
		Mustang III	FZ107	Self		To base		-20	
	6th	FW 190	PM679	Self		Air test		-15	
	7th	Mustang III	FZ107	Self		Comparative v. FW 190 & escort		1-35	
		FW 190	PM679	Self		Comparative v. Mustang		-30	
		Mustang III	FZ107	Self		Night flying trials		1-05	
	8th	Mustang III	FZ107	Self		Clims to 33,000ft & cine gun		-50	
		Mustang III	FZ107	Self		Comparative v. '190		-45	
	9th	Spitfire IX	JL359	Self		Fuel consumption		-25	
		Mustang I	AM107	Self		Compass test		-20	
	10th	FW 190	PM679	Self		Comparative v. Tempest		-30	
		Spitfire Vb	AB169	Self		To Cranfield		-25	
		Mustang III	FZ107	Self		Test bubble hood		-30	
		Spitfire Vb	AB169	Self		To base		-35	
	15th	Spitfire IX	BS552	Self		Air test		-20	
		Mustang III	FZ107	Self		Consumption test		1-00	
	18th	Spitfire XII	EN222	Self		Air test		-15	
	20th	Mustang III	FE107	Self		Fuel consumption		-40	
		Mustang III	FZ107	Self		Speed runs and climbs		1-05	
		Mustang III	FZ107	Self		Fuel consumption		-55	
	22nd	Mustang III	FZ107	Self		To Gravesend		-50	
		Mustang III	FZ107	Self		To base		-35	
	24th	Mustang III	FZ107	Self		Climbs		-35	
		Oxford	V3791	Self	F/Sgt Bristow	To Cranfield		-30	
		Oxford	V3791	Self	F/Sgt Bristow	To base		-30	
	28th	Mustang III	FZ107	Self		Comparative v. ME 109G		1-05	
	29th	FW 190	PM679	Self		Comparative v. Spitfire L2C		-30	
						GRAND TOTAL TO DATE 945 hours 30 mins	3-30	10-20	
							60-00	871-40	16-15

2 February: The fuel tanks of a Mustang held 176 gallons against the Spitfire's 96, giving the Mustang an endurance of a little over 3½ hours at normal cruising speed.

5 February: First trip. The ASI (Air Speed Indicator) had failed so I led the pilot in for his landing.

6 February: We are still trying our best to get that engine right.

7 February: To the best of my knowledge the Mustang was never flown operationally at night. However, with its long range there was always a possibility of having to land after dark, so we still had to check that everything was in working order.

10 February: 'Bubble hood.' This was the same type of canopy as was fitted to the Spitfire IX. It was called the Malcolm hood; it bulged outwards and gave much improved all-round visibility.

22 February: To Gravesend. This was a winter cross-country exercise when I chose to fly there in order to visit my brother-in-law, LAC Ron Davies, who served in the RAF Regiment. It took me some time to locate him in an open anti-aircraft gun-pit on airfield defence duty. Although I arrived across the Thames in a blinding snowstorm, I treated them to 10 minutes of beat-up and low-level aerobatics. Stupid really, as gunners were notoriously trigger happy and quite likely to shoot at one of ours. Ron was frequently in action and probably saw more of the Luftwaffe than I did in this vulnerable and dangerous area of Britain.

28 February: The ME 109G, known as the 'Gustav', was the latest version of that excellent fighter and still able to give a good account of itself in the hands of an experienced pilot.

29 February: This was co-operation with NAFDU against a Fleet Air Arm fighter designated an L2C but actually a Seafire, used effectively as a carrier-borne fighter.

Summary for:- February 1944		
Unit:- AFDU Wittering	1. Mustang III	18-00
Date:- 1/3/44	2. Mustang I	-20
Signature:- H.L. Thorne	3. Tempest V	-50
	4. FW190	1-45
	5. Spitfire IX	-45
	6. Spitfire V	1-00
	7. Spitfire XII	-15
	8. Oxford	1-00

Signed *T.S. Wade* S/Ldr
O/C Flying AFDU

| YEAR | 1944 | AIRCRAFT | | Pilot or 1st Pilot | 2nd Pilot, Pupil or Pass. | DUTY (Including Results and Remarks) | Flying Time | | Passenger |
MONTH	DATE	Type	No.				Dual	Solo	
March	1st	Mitchell	208	F/Lt Lane	Self	Ait test		-35	
		Tempest V	737	Self		Air test		-20	
	2nd	Typhoon	512	Self		Test drop tanks		-40	
	3rd	Typhoon	512	Self		Test drop tanks		-55	
	4th	Typhoon	512	Self		Cutting tests		-30	
	5th	Spitfire IX	BS552	Self		Comparative v VII		-25	
		Spitfire VII	BS229	Self		Comparative v IX		-45	
		Spitfire VC	372	Self		Comparative v VII		-50	
	7th	Spitfire VC	372	Self		Test dive brakes		-50	
		Spitfire VC	372	Self		Test dive brakes		-25	
	9th	Spitfire XIV	RB179	Self		Air test		-15	
	13th	Typhoon	512	Self		Comparative v Tempest		-30	
		Tempest	737	Self		Comparative v Typhoon		-45	
	14th	Tempest	737	Self		Beat-up		-20	
	15th	Spitfire VII	BS229	Self		Test dive flaps		-35	
	16th	Tempest	737	Self		Comparative v Typhoon		-55	
		Oxford	V3791	Self		To Wakely		-10	
		Oxford	V3791	Self		To base		-15	
	17th	Spitfire	AB169	Self		Air test		-30	
	18th	FW 190	PM679	Self		Comparative v. Spitfire XIV		-35	
	19th	FW 190	PM679	Self		Air test		-10	
	22nd	Tempest	737	Self		Guns and camera		-40	
	25th	Spitfire	MH415	Self		Rate of roll		-35	
		Tempest	737	Self		Rate of roll		1-05	
		Spitfire	179	Self		Rate of roll		-25	
						GRAND TOTAL TO DATE 959 hours 30 mins	3-30	10-20	
							60-00	885-40	16-15

1 March: This was my first flight in a B25, known in the RAF as the Mitchell. A twin-engined light bomber with a fair turn of speed and good bomb-carrying capacity, 208 had been equipped with a 75mm gun, taking the length of the fuselage and loaded from a position at the rear. It was intended for use as a tank buster. Before it could prove its worth, it was overtaken by the use of rockets. When fired from the Mitchell the recoil was almost enough to stall the aircraft.

F/Lt 'Cappy' Lane was an Australian, seconded to AFDU almost entirely for Mitchell trials. He remained in England after the war; a qualified solicitor, he became an assistant to the Public Prosecutor at Scotland Yard. He was one of those who attended my farewell party in 1948.

4 March: Great care had to be taken when changing from main to drop tanks on the Typhoon. Wrong action could produce an air lock, causing the engine to cut out. It was sometimes difficult to effect a restart. I did not enjoy these tests or fancy the possibility of having to force-land a Tiffie with a dead engine.

5 March: I do not remember that there were any remarkable differences between a Mk VII and a Mk IX. At the higher altitudes, the extra wing area of the VII may have given a better turning circle.

7 March: With four 20mm cannons, the VC was essentially a ground attack machine so it made sense to reduce speed in the dive. The dive brakes were flap-like panels on top and bottom of the wings, which could be extended in the dive.

19 March: During my flight on the 18th, I was still not happy with the BMW 810 engine of the 190 so, after adjustments, I carried out an air test. Shortly after take-off the engine died and I was lucky enough to be able to force-land successfully on the airfield.

Summary for:- March 1944	1. Spitfire V	2–35
Unit:- AFDU Wittering	2. Spitfire VII	1–20
Date:- 6/4/44	3. Spitfire IX	1–00
Signature:- H.L. Thorne	4. Typhoon	2–35
	5. Tempest	4–05
	6. Spitfire XIV	–40
	7. FW 190	–45
	8. Oxford	–25
	9. Mitchell	–35

Signed *T.S. Wade* S/Ldr
O/C Flying AFDU

YEAR 1944		AIRCRAFT		Pilot or 1st Pilot	2nd Pilot, Pupil or Pass.	DUTY (Including Results and Remarks)	Flying Time		Passenger
MONTH	DATE	Type	No.				Dual	Solo	
April	4th	Mustang III	FZ107	Self		Dives		-50	
	5th	Mustang III	FZ107	Self		Night flying test		-30	
	13th	Tempest	JN737	Self		Fuel consumption		1-00	
		Oxford	V3791	Self		To Cranfield		-30	
		Oxford	V3791	Self		To base		-40	
	15th	Spitfire	BS229	Self		Bombing		1-10	
		Spitfire	BS229	Self		Bombing		1-00	
	17th	Oxford	V3791	Self	F/Lt Roy Hussey	Dual instruction		-40	
	18th	Spitfire VII	BS229	Self		Bombing		-45	
	19th	Spitfire VII	BS229	Self		Bombing		1-05	
	20th	Spitfire VII	BS229	Self		IIL sight setting		-30	
		Oxford	V3791	S/Ldr Wade	Self	To Cranfield		-40	
		Mustang III	FZ107	Self		To base		-30	
	21st	Hellcat	?	Self		Experience on type		-30	
	22nd	Mustang III	FZ107	Self		Climbs to 35,000ft		-50	
	23rd	Mustang III	FZ107	Self		Dives		-35	
		Spitfire VII	BS229	Self		Bombing		-35	
		Proctor	DX220	Self	F/O 'Zip' Zobell	To Sutton Bridge		-30	
		Proctor	DX220	Self	'Zip'	To base		-30	
	26th	Spitfire VII	BS229	Self		Bombing		1-05	
		Proctor	DX220	Self	F/Lt Hussey	To Tangmere via Langley		1-30	
		Proctor	DX220	Self		To base		1-15	
	27th	Spitfire XIV	RB179	Self		Tank dropping		-30	
		Spitfire IX	MH415	Self		Cine gun – gyro gun sight		-20	
		Spitfire IX	JL359	Self		Cine gun gyro gun sight		-25	
	28th	Firefly	?	Self		Local		-45	
		Spitfire IX	MH415	Self		Target for gyro gun sight		-25	
	30th	Proctor	BX220	Self		Local		-10	
						GRAND TOTAL TO DATE 979 hours 15 mins	3-30	10-20	
							60-00	905-25	16-15

13 April: Hooray! Hooray! I'm 24 today!

17 April: The memory of this young man will live with me always; Roy Hussey was young, tall, handsome and so full of life. After a few weeks with us, resting from operations, he was returned to a squadron, posted to Italy and, almost immediately shot down and killed.

21 April: Another first in my logbook, courtesy of NAFDU. The Hellcat was a descendant of the Grumman Martlet. With its powerful Wright double-row Cyclone radial engine, it proved a very formidable fighting machine. With the Corsair it transformed the position in the Far East against the Japanese.

23 April: On one of the Mustang trials, in company with a Spitfire XIV flown by Susie, we checked the operational ceiling and the maximum ceiling. We both reached somewhere in the region of 41,000 to 44,500 feet. At that height the cold was intense and we both went into steep dives to get down into warmer climes.

Flying the Mustang, I half rolled and pulled back into an almost vertical dive. An American test pilot had done this manoeuvre and was believed to have hit the sound barrier; he failed to recover from the dive and was killed. Forewarned, I started my pull-out in time but must have hit a speed close to 700 mph.

Sutton Bridge was one of the WREN Fleet Air Arm units, which manned the dive screens in and near The Wash bombing ranges. 'Zip' Zobel was a Canadian and many years later we made contact through his seeing a particular photograph in *Aeroplane* magazine. We corresponded until his death in the 1980s.

27 April: To extend the range of fighters in general and Spitfires in particular, they were fitted with external fuel tanks that could be jettisoned. The tanks were torpedo-shaped under each wing and/or shipped under the belly. The latter were shaped to follow the profile of the aircraft. We did tests to ensure that, when released, they fell clear and did not cause any engine cut.

MH415 is the Spitfire that survived the war and later was bought by Connie Edwards, a West Texas cattle rancher. After my daughter, Penny, who also lives in Texas, tracked him down, he invited us to pay him a visit in January 1998 to see MH415 and the other aircraft in his collection, ME 109s, Mustangs and others. I spent the day stroking my old plane and taking loads of photographs and was able to sit in the cockpit again. How the memories flooded back. The story of my trip was told in the Redditch local and British national daily papers in February 1998.

28 April: Firefly, another first for my logbook, courtesy of NAFDU. A Fleet Air Arm machine made by Fairey Aviation and powered by a Rolls-Royce Griffon engine, it was a powerful addition to our carrier-borne strike and reconnaissance force.

Target for gyro. The Gyro gunsight replaced the manually adjustable sight which provided a fixed red dot aiming point and which had been in use since the war started. The Gyro sight dot was pulled by the gyros in reaction to 'G' applied. It transformed the art of air fighting by constant correction to deflection and turned ordinary shots (like me) into aces.

Summary for:– April 1944	1. Spitfire VII, IX & XIV 7–50
Unit:– AFDU Wittering	2. Mustang III 3–15
Date:– 3/5/44	3. Tempest 1–00
Signature:– H.L. Thorne	4. Hellcat –30
	5. Firefly –45
	6. Oxford 2–30
	7. Proctor 3–55

Signed *T.S. Wade* S/Ldr
O/C Flying AFDU

YEAR	1944	AIRCRAFT		Pilot or 1st Pilot	2nd Pilot, Pupil or Pass.	DUTY (Including Results and Remarks)	Flying Time		Passenger
MONTH	DATE	Type	No.				Dual	Solo	
May	1st	Proctor	DX220	Self	F/Lt Hussey	To Langley		1–00	
		Proctor	DX220	Self		To Gravesend		–40	
		Proctor	DX220	Self		To base		–50	
	3rd	Fulmar	?	Self		Local		–40	
		Mustang III	FZ107	Self		Air test & target		–15	
		Mustang III	FZ107	Self		Comsumption above 25,000 feet		1–00	
	6th	Spitfire VII	BS229	Self		Bombing with photos		–50	
		Spitfire IX	MH415	Self		Bombing		–45	
	7th	Spitfire IX	MH415	Self		Bombing		–30	
		Spitfire IX	MH415	Self		Bombing		–30	
		Mustang III	858	Self		Turning circles		–35	
	8th	Spitfire IX	MH415	Self		Bombing		–55	
		Spitfire IX	MH415	Self		Bombing		–40	
	10th	Mustang III	FZ107	Self		Comparative turns		–20	
		Mustang III	858	Self		Comparative turns		–20	
	11th	Spitfire XIV	RB179	Self		To Pershore		–30	
		Spitfire XIV	RB179	Self		To base		–30	

	12th	Spitfire IX	BS552	Self		Bombing		-55	
	14th	Spitfire VB	AD318	Self		Film RP (rocket projectile)		-55	
	18th	Spitfire IX	JL359	Self		Air test		-15	
		Spitfire IX	BS552	Self		Bombing		1-00	
	20th	Spitfire IX	BS552	Self		Bombing		-30	
	22nd	Spitfire IX	JL359	Self		Air test		-10	
		Spitfire IX	MH415	Self		Bombing		-55	
		Spitfire IX	BS552	Self		Tank dropping		-10	
		Spitfire IX	BS552	Self		Tank dropping		-15	
		Proctor	DX220	Self	Cpl ?	To Desford		-25	
		Proctor	DX220	Self	Cpl ?	To Derby		-15	
		Proctor	DX220	Self	Cpl ?	To base		-30	
	23rd	Spitfire IX	BS552	Self		Tank dropping		-10	
	24th	Spitfire IX	BS552	Self		Bombing test		-15	
		Spitfire IX	MH415	Self		500lb bomb with photographs		-45	
		Spitfire IX	BS552	Self		Bombing test		-10	
		Spitfire IX	BS552	Self		Bombing		-35	
	25th	Spitfire IX	BS552	Self		Bombing		-30	
	26th	Tempest V	EN757	Self		Comparative v. Mustang		-45	
		Spitfire IX	BS552	Self		Bombing		-50	
	29th	Spitfire IX	BS552	Self		Bombing		-40	
	30th	Spitfire IX	BS552	Self		Weather test		-15	
		Spitfire IX	BS552	Self		Bombing		-45	
	31st	Spitfire IX	MH415	Self		Bombing		-45	
		Spitfire IX	BS552	Self		Bombing		-45	
						GRAND TOTAL TO DATE 1,003 hours 30 mins	3-30	10-20	
							60-00	929-40	16-15

3 May: First trip of the day. Another first flight in a Fleet Air Arm aircraft. The Fairey Fulmar was a smaller and faster version of the Fairey Battle and was used as an FAA carrier-based fighter.

11 May: The trip to Pershore was for the fitting of a modified radar set by RAE Malvern.

14 May: There was increasing interest in the use of rockets for ground attack. These were carried on rails under the aircraft wings. With a 6 lb. warhead, they proved a devastating weapon when fired against tanks and thin-skinned transport. They were used with great effect when fitted to the Typhoon and Tempest.

22 May: To Desford. A visit to my old EFTS (Elementary Flying Training School). A busy day, seven flights.

23 May: It didn't take me long to drop the tank!

24 May: The most accurate way to drop a bomb from a fighter was in the steepest possible dive, sighting the gun sight at the target. The boys in the squadrons were nervous about this method, as there was a belief that the bomb would hit the aircraft or at least the propeller. To disprove this we fitted a camera in the fuselage, pointing sideways, behind the pilot's head. The pilot, S/Ldr Wade, flew the bombing aircraft and I as his No. 2 maintained close formation, with a sighting spot painted on the wingtip, lined up with the bomb. While I maintained position, Wimpy dropped the bomb. Fortunately, our photographs proved that the bomb fell away clear of the aircraft; otherwise we would both have been blown to kingdom come!

29 May: These bombing runs were done from different starting heights, speeds and angles of dive to determine the most accurate methods. It proved best to start at 8,000 ft, over-fly the target until it reappeared behind the wing, perform a half-roll or stall turn into a dive at 70°, locate the target with the gunsight and release the bomb. At this point a Spitfire would reach a speed of nearly 500 mph, so recovery should commence immediately!

31 May: Hurrah!! I passed 1,000 hours today!

Summary for:- May 1944	1. Spitfire V, VII, IX, XIV	16-40
Unit:- AFDU Wittering	2. Mustang III	2-30
Date:- 3/6/44	3. Tempest	-45
Signature:- *H.L. Thorne*	4. Fulmar	-40
	5. Proctor	3-40

Signed *T.S. Wade* S/Ldr
O/C Flying AFDU

YEAR	1944	AIRCRAFT		Pilot or 1st Pilot	2nd Pilot, Pupil or Pass.	DUTY (Including Results and Remarks)	Flying Time		Passenger
MONTH	DATE	Type	No.				Dual	Solo	
June	2nd	Spitfire IX	BS552	Self		Bombing		-40	
	3rd	Spitfire XIV	RB179	Self		Bombing		-30	
	4th	Spitfire XIV	RB179	Self		Speed climb to 30,000 feet		-30	
	5th	Oxford	V3791	Self		Air test		-10	
	7th	Spitfire IX	BS552	Self		To Tangmere		-50	
		Spitfire IX	BS552	Self		Duty, to base		-50	
	9th	Spitfire IX	BS552	Self		Local		-15	
	10th	Spitfire IX	BS552	Self		Bombing		1-00	
	11th	Spitfire IX	BS552	Self		Bombing		-55	
	12th	Spitfire IX	JL359	Self		Air test		-10	
	14th	Spitfire IX	JL359	Self		Air test		-20	
	15th	Spitfire XIV	RB179	Self		Blind take-off		-15	
		Spitfire VII	BS229	Self		Bombing		-25	
	16th	Spitfire V	372	Self		Air test		-15	
	17th	Spitfire IX	BS552	Self		Bombing		-35	
		Spitfire IX	BS552	Self		Bombing		-30	
	18th	Spitfire IX	BS552	Self		Bombing		-35	
		Spitfire IX	BS552	Self		Bombing		-50	
	19th	Spitfire IX	BS552	Self		Bombing		-20	
	20th	Oxford	V3791	Self	WAAF	To Catfoss		1-00	
		Oxford	V3791	Self	WAAF & F/Lt Hussey	To base		1-00	
	24th	FW 190	PM679	Self		Air test. Pranged on take-off		-05	
		Spitfire VII	BS229	Self		Air test		-10	
		Spitfire IX	BS552	Self		Bombing		-50	
						GRAND TOTAL TO DATE 1,016 hours 30 mins	3-30	10-20	
							60-00	942-40	16-15

5 June: From 12.00 hours until dawn on June 7th, covering D–Day (June 6th), the Normandy invasion, all non–combatant aircraft were grounded. At units like AFDU, potentially operational aircraft, our Hurricanes, all Marks of Spitfire and Mustang, Typhoon, Tempest, Boston and Mitchell, were painted with wide black and white stripes on wings and fuselage. It was not until the public announcements were made on the 6th that we knew for sure what was happening. Of course, we already had a good idea, as on the evening and well into the night, Estelle and I, with Mr and Mrs Walker, stood in the garden watching streams of aircraft passing over, all heading south. First came hundreds of troop-carrying Dakotas (DC3s) then the glider tugs and finally the Fortresses, Halifaxes and Lancaster heavy bombers. From before dawn on June 6th, from dozens of airfields in the South of England, the light bombers and fighters, the Spitfires, Typhoons and Tempests of the RAF and the Mustangs, Thunderbolts and Lightnings of the USAAF, flew in their thousands to maintain constant cover and absolute air supremacy over the beachheads. The constant drone of engines was incredible. It was a sight and sound that would never be forgotten by those of us who witnessed it.

7 June: On D-Day plus one I was given permission to fly into the Active war zone. At Tangmere airfield I talked to pilots of the Canadian Wing, whose Mark IX Spitfires had been equipped with the new Gyro gunsight. In an encounter over the beachheads they shot down 10 out of 12 JU88s.

Both my outward and return flights took me across the Channel to witness the incredible sight of hundreds of ships and thousands of aircraft but I was under strict orders not to cross the French coast, so my dream of firing a few shots at an enemy aircraft was not to be realised. But I can say that I was there, saw it all and would certainly have bought the T-shirt!

9 June: A note regarding my flight on the 9th said it was a quick flip over Colley Weston to Easton on the Hill and our rented part of Chain Cottage. By then our host Fred Walker could be seen pushing Gill around the village, first in a pram and later in a pushchair, despite earlier misgivings about a baby on the premises. The Walkers were very upset when, in the spring of 1945, I was posted to Tangmere. At their request I posted a notice in the Officers' Mess offering our rooms to any other couple who had a young baby. Estelle and I were amazed ten years later, back in Worcestershire, to meet the landlord of our local pub, the Neville Arms, and learn that he and his wife, Mr. and Mrs. Hayden-Jones, had taken up the offer and spent two or three happy years there with their baby Jennifer.

19 June: Our continuous programme of bombing flights attempted to improve the method and accuracy of fighter dive-bombing. After take-off we usually flew to the Holbeach or Wainfleet bombing ranges in The Wash, the large bay on the East Coast. On towers at various points, facilities were set up to measure dive angles, release heights and accuracy of bomb drop.

This equipment was operated by WRENs of the Fleet Air Arm, under the command of a WREN officer, popularly known as a Queen Bee or Wasp, depending on their personality. It was a lonely spot and most weekends our chaps and the NAFDU pilots were invited over for dances and social evenings. Being a sedate old married man, I only attended once that I can remember but several of our pilots went often. Romances blossomed and I believe that our Canadian, F/Lt W. A. (Bill, but known as Otto) Waterton, married one of the WREN officers.

20 June: To Catfoss. I believe my passenger was ACW M.S. (Peggy) Snashall, our Orderly Room secretary and assistant to F/Lt Simms, the Adjutant. I kept in contact later and visited her many times. On our first meeting after the war, she congratulated me on receiving an AFC and would not believe it when I said I had not received the award as she had typed the citation. It would seem that a change of CO caused the medal to go to one of his favourites.

24 June: This was the last attempt to get 'my' 190 flying again. The airscrew pitch control on the 190 was by an electrically operated unit called the *kommandgerat*. On this flight it developed a fault which caused the pitch to change from fine (for take-off) to full-course, thus stalling the engine. Luckily I was over the airfield boundary on the downwind leg and was able to make an emergency landing. However, as I did not fancy a deadstick touchdown with a closed canopy, I operated the hood jettison device, which was the only damage. So in fact, this was not a prang.

As our programme with PM679 was virtually complete and as other 190s were now falling into our hands, it was decided not to attempt further repairs. PM679 was sent to Colley Weston to be used by 1426 Flight for spares. I was very lucky to survive the two forced landings, as similar trouble at 1426 Flight caused their 190 to catch fire and crash on 13th October 1944. The pilot, F/Lt E.R. Lewendon, was killed.

Summary for:- June 1944	1. Spitfire	10-45
Unit:- AFDU Wittering	2. FW 190	-05
Date:- 3/7/44	3. Oxford	2-10
Signature:- *H.L. Thorne*		

Signed *T.S. Wade* S/Ldr
O/C Flying AFDU

8

MUSTANGS AND OTHERS

| YEAR | 1944 | AIRCRAFT | | Pilot or 1st Pilot | 2nd Pilot, Pupil or Pass. | DUTY (Including Results and Remarks) | Flying Time | | Passenger |
MONTH	DATE	Type	No.				Dual	Solo	
July	8th	Spitfire Vb	AD318	Self		Camera		-45	
		Spitfire Vb	AD318	Self		Camera		-45	
	9th	Spitfire Vb	AD318	Self		Air to ground firing		-55	
	10th	Spitfire VII	BS229	Self		Air test		-30	
	11th	Spitfire Vb	AD318	Self		Air to ground firing		-45	
	12th	Oxford	V3791	Self	Lt Wurley	Local		-25	
		Spitfire Vb	AD318	Self		Weather test		-20	
	13th	Proctor	DX220	Self	S/Ldr Murray	To Thorney Island		1-20	
		Proctor	DX220	Self		To base		1-05	
	14th	Tempest	JN757	Self		Speed runs and climbs		-25	
		Tempest	JN757	Self		Speed runs and climbs		-40	
	15th	Spitfire Vb	AD318	Self		Guns and camera		-40	
		Proctor	DX220	F/Lt Lane	Self	Weather test		-15	
	16th	Spitfire Vb	AD318	Self		Film smoke from Hellcat		-20	
		Spitfire Vb	AD318	Self		Guns and camera		-40	
		Spitfire Vb	AD318	Self		Film smoke from Hellcat		-15	
		Spitfire Vb	AD318	Self		Film smoke from Hellcat		-15	

		Spitfire Vb	AD318	Self		Cannons and camera		-35	
	17th	Spitfire IX	MH415	Self		Bombing		-35	
	18th	Spitfire Vb	AD318	Self		Cannons and camera		1-10	
		Mustang III	FZ107	Self		Air test		-30	
	19th	Mustang III	FZ107	Self		Bomb dropping		-35	
		Mustang III	FZ107	Self		Bomb dropping		-30	
	20th	Spitfire IX	MH415	Self		Bombing		-45	
	22nd	Mustang III	FZ107	Self		Local		-20	
	23rd	Oxford	V3791	Self	F/Lt Hill	Observe nickel dropping		-45	
		Mustang III	FZ107	Self		Observe nickel dropping		-35	
	26th	Mustang III	FZ124	Self		Target & tests on gyro gun sight		-45	
	27th	Mustang III	FZ124	Self		Guns & sighting test		-35	
	28th	Mustang III	FZ124	Self		Guns & sighting test		-30	
	29th	Mustang III	FZ107	Self		Observe nickels		-45	
	30th	Mustang III	FZ107	Self		Handling for bombing		-50	
	31st	Spifire IX	BS552	Self		Bombing		-50	
						GRAND TOTAL TO DATE 1,037 hours 25 mins	3-30	10-20	
							60-00	963-35	16-15

12 July: The Oxford flight was for a local army officer ('Brown Job') from the searchlight post.

14 July: It was about this time that the first V1 flying bombs started to be used against England. The Tempest was one of the planes that were fast enough to catch a V1 in level flight, hence the continued interest in top speeds.

15 July: Weather tests in July? Must have been a period of anticyclonic gloom!

16 July: The first flight was cut short when I saw a black stream of oil pouring back from the NAFDU Hellcat's engine cowling. The Fleet Air Arm pilot just managed to land before the engine seized up. The trouble proved to be nothing serious, just a loose filler cap.

These flights were for the deliberate ejection of smoke for the purpose of laying down a smoke screen.

19 July: This was low-level bombing using 20 lb. smoke bombs. For these trials we did not use the Holbeach coastal ranges but a disused, small grass airfield. A very low approach at a fast cruising speed was exciting but the accuracy was poor.

23 July: I am puzzled by this entry as nickel (code name for strips of aluminium foil) was used by bombers to confuse radar. I can only assume that this was a co-operation exercise with Bomber Command.

28 July: On a nice, bright, sunny summer day it was very pleasant to buzz around in a Mustang but with the moulded bubble or teardrop canopy, it could get very warm in the cockpit. I used to wear a pair of white drill overalls and on one occasion I wore only a pair of trunks underneath. Due to a minor fault I had to land away from base to get it fixed, which should have taken only a few minutes. In fact, it took three hours and I was stuck with the aeroplane, unable to visit the Officers' Mess for a drink or a snack. It taught me a sharp lesson and I did not repeat the lightweight dress code!

Summary for:- July 1944	1. Spitfire	10-05
Unit:- AFDU Wittering	2. Mustang	5-55
Date:- 4/8/44	3. Proctor	2-40
Signature:- H.L. Thorne	4 Tempest	1-05
	5. Oxford	1-10

Signed: *T.S. Wade* S/Ldr
O/C Flying AFDU

Certificate for a 'Mention in a Despatch'. This one was awarded for flight testing various Allied fighters but particularly flying a captured German Focke Wulf 190A-3 fighter under operational conditions in comparative trials against Allied, RAF and FAA fighter aircraft and flying combat demonstrations at various UK fighter airfields.

By the KING'S Order the name of
A/Flight Lieutenant H. L. Thorne,
Royal Air Force Volunteer Reserve,
was published in the London Gazette on
8 June, 1944,
as mentioned in a Despatch for distinguished service.
I am charged to record
His Majesty's high appreciation.

Archibald Sinclair.

Secretary of State for Air

AFDU Officers' Mess, Wittering, August/September 1944. Dinner to welcome new W/Co Alan Wright and to say goodbye to W/Co Blackadder. Top of tableL W/Co Allan Wright. Left, from top: Station Commander; G/Cpt Gillam?; S/Ldr T.S. 'Wimpy' Wade (DFC, AFC, killed April 1951); NAFDU Officer F/Lt H.L. 'Len' Thorne; F/Lt W.A. 'Otto' Waterton (GM, AFC & Star) (Canadian);
F/O Roy Hussey; F/O Bob Henderson; 'Boffin' Mr. Gould. Right: W/Co Blackadder, 'The Bladder'; F/Lt 'Simmie' Simms (Unit Adjutant); F/Lt Lang (Unit Eng. Officer); F/Lt 'Cappy' Lane (Australian); F.O Chadwick (Photographic Officer); F/Lt A.W. 'Bill' Burge (New Zealand). Another Boffin.

| YEAR | 1944 | AIRCRAFT | | Pilot or 1st Pilot | 2nd Pilot, Pupil or Pass. | DUTY (Including Results and Remarks) | Flying Time | | Passenger |
MONTH	DATE	Type	No.				Dual	Solo	
August	3rd	Spitfire V	AD318	Self		Air test		-10	
	4th	Spitfire IX	BS552	Self		Bombing		-45	
		Spitfire IX	MH415	Self		Bombing		-45	
	6th	Spitfire V	AD318	Self		Photography		-35	
	7th	Spitfire IX	MH415	Self		Bombing		-40	
	9th	Spitfire V	AD318	Self		Photography		-20	
		Spitfire IX	251	Self		1 x 500lb bomb & 2 x 250lb bombs		-55	
		Proctor	DX220	Self	F/Lt Simms, LAC Hunt	To Doncaster		-45	
		Proctor	DX220	Self	F/Lt Simms, LAC Hunt	Doncaster to Wittering		-35	
	10th	Spitfire XIV	650	Self		To Westcott		-40	

		Spitfire XIV	650	Self		To base		-30	
	11th	Mustang III	FZ107	Self		Bombing		1-00	
		Proctor	DX220	Self	Mr Gould	Farnborough via Sutton Bridge		1-40	
		Proctor	DX220	Self	Mr Gould	To base		-50	
	12th	Mustang III	FZ107	Self		Bombing		1-05	
	13th	Boston	BZ363	Self		Local		-40	
	14th	Spitfire XIV	RH179	Self		Test curved windscreen		-30	
		Spitfire XIV	RM689	Self		Test curved windscreen		-30	
	17th	Spitfire V	AD318	Self		Film Corsair		1-00	
		Spitfire V	AD318	Self		Film Corsair		-10	
	20th	Spitfire IX	MH415	Self		Air test		-10	
	23th	Spitfire V	AD318	Self		Film Corsair		-30	
	24th	Tempest	757	Self		Local		-35	
	25th	Mustang III	FZ107	Self		Local		-35	
		Mustang III	FZ107	Self		Bombing		1-10	
	26th	Spitfire V	AD318	Self		Film Corsair		-45	
	27th	Boston III	?	Self		Local		-30	
	29th	Anson	184	Self	LAC Hunt	To Doncaster		-35	
	30th	Anson	184	Self	LAC Hunt	To base		-35	
	31st	Spitfire IX	JL359	Self		GGS dive bombing		-45	
						GRAND TOTAL TO DATE 1,057 hours 10 mins	3-30	11-20	
							60-00	982-20	16-15

9 August: We photographed the bomb release at various heights and speeds.

A Spitfire IX flew perfectly with ½ ton of bombs, a 500 pounder under the belly and a 250 pounder under each wing, with a full load of fuel and ammunition.

The Doncaster trip was interesting as we landed on what is now Doncaster horseracing track.

10 August: Another trip to see the old folks at home but I was somewhat delayed by the interest shown in my Mk XIV Spitfire, at that time the latest model and probably the most advanced fighter in the world. With its high speed, phenomenal rate of climb and an operational ceiling of over 40,000 feet, it attracted attention from all ranks at Westcott. An OUT using Wellingtons for operational training, their usual sight of a fighter was a ME109 or a FW190 attacking them.

Before returning to base I gave them a short aerobatic display, ending with a battle climb up and out of sight.

11 August: Our test programme on the Mustang III was more or less finished and it, too, was relegated to carrying bombs and rockets. We gave it the thumbs-up in every respect and it went into service with the RAF and USAAF in ever-increasing numbers. In the opinion of most of the fighter pilots I knew, the Spitfire prevented us from losing the war and the Mustang enabled us to win it.

Many of our experimental flights involved mathematical calculations to ascertain heights and true air speeds. The latter varied by approximately 1.5% according to altitude. Mr Gould was a civilian technician, attached to the unit; we became good friends.

13 August: After many trips as a passenger I finally flew the Douglas Boston as pilot. (Strange that no one volunteered to be a passenger on this trip. Cowards!) The Boston was another very pleasant aircraft to fly and, with its tricycle undercarriage, easy to handle on the ground. The two powerful Wright Cyclone radial engines made this a really potent aeroplane.

14 August: Night flying. The windscreen of Spitfires was normally a thick flat piece of bulletproof, laminated plastic to protect the pilot from injury to the head and upper body in the event of a head-on attack, or return fire from the rear gunner of an enemy bomber. RM689 was used as an experimental aircraft with a modified curved windscreen, which was tried out by the pilots of AFDU in various daylight conditions. I cannot think why it was thought necessary to test it out at night as, at that stage of the war, there was no way that a Spitfire could again be used at night.

Wimpy Wade and I undertook the night flying trial, taking turns in the two aircraft. I flew RM689 first then we swapped and it was Wimpy's turn in the modified machine. After a midnight take-off, we flew to The Wash to fire all guns and cannon. The muzzle flash severely affected our night vision. Again on landing there were streams of sparks from the exhaust stubs when the throttle was closed. Despite this I made both landings without any trouble but Wimpy held off too high on his first approach and had to go round again. On his second attempt he hit the ground hard and bounced badly; at full throttle, he failed to make sufficient allowance for torque and pulled away in a vicious left-hand turn. Where his port wingtip hit the ground it left a 30-yard furrow but he got away with it. On the third approach he did better and got down without further damage. Badly shaken, the only time I ever saw him in that state, he needed a drink but, as the Officers' Mess was closed, we repaired to Chain Cottage. There, with some help from a sleepy Estelle, we saw off a bottle of gin.

There is an interesting follow-up to this story: My friend Peter Arnold, the Spitfire historian, let me know that two of the Spits that I had flown during the war had survived. The Mk IX, MH415, which I went to see in America, and Mk XIV, RM689, which was used by Rolls-Royce as their showpiece. On June 27 1992 it was being flown at a display at RAF/BAe Woodford in Cheshire by David Moore, a pilot with Rolls-Royce; he apparently left it too late pulling out of a loop. The aircraft went into a high-speed stall and crashed into the runway and burst into flames, killing the pilot. The aircraft was a complete write-off. Some years later I was amazed to learn that Rolls-Royce had preserved the wreckage and that it was to be sent to Filton, Bristol, to be restored, hopefully to flying condition. [The rebuild was still ongoing in 2012.]

17 August: The Corsair flights were used in the making of a propaganda film.

29 August: My 1937 Vauxhall 14, as I mentioned earlier, was, without doubt, the worst car I ever owned, trouble almost from the word go. It was the first model to be fitted with independent front suspension, two large cylinders filled with oil and 'splash' lubricated bearings. When the units leaked the needle roller bearings dried out and broke.

LAC Hunt was our unit driver, a skilled mechanic trained by Rolls-Royce car division. He located and offered to fit two new units, which we had to collect from a breaker's yard in Doncaster, LAC Hunt's home town. We flew there in the Anson but, by the time we had obtained the units, it was too late to return to Wittering so we stayed the night at his house. All against regulations but after all, I was the Flight Commander! Some time later these units again failed and Estelle's uncle, George White, replaced the needle bearings with externally lubricated phosphor bronze bushes, manufactured in his engineering factory, Edward White & Son in Redditch; this cured the trouble.

Summary for:- August 1944	1. Spitfire	1-00 N.F.
Unit:- AFDU Wittering	2. Proctor	8-40
Date:- 3/9/44	3. Mustang	3-50
Signature:- H.L. Thorne	4. Tempest	3-20
	5. Boston	-35
	6. Anson	1-10

H.L Thorne F/Lt for S/Ldr
O/C Flying AFDU

W.F. Blackadder W/Com.
O/C AFDU

During July our Wing Commander had strongly recommended me for the award of an AFC (Air Force Cross) but, as I said in the note at the end of June, I did not get on very well with W/Co Blackadder (disrespectfully known as The Bladder) who, I always wondered, might have switched the award to another pilot.

| YEAR | 1944 | AIRCRAFT | | Pilot or 1st Pilot | 2nd Pilot, Pupil or Pass. | DUTY (Including Results and Remarks) | Flying Time | | Passenger |
MONTH	DATE	Type	No.				Dual	Solo	
September	3rd	Spitfire V	731	Self		GGS electric ranging		-30	
		Spitfire V	731	Self		GGS electric ranging		-20	
	4th	Boston III	BZ363	F/Lt Lane	Self, W/C Blackadder	To Farnborough		-30	
		Boston III	BZ363	F/Lt Lane	Self, W/C Blackadder	To base		-30	
	5th	Boston III	BZ363	F/Lt Lane	Self, W/C Blackadder	To Ouston		-45	
		Boston III	BZ363	Self		To base		-55	
	6th	Spitfire V	AD318	Self		Air to ground firing		-40	
	7th	Spitfire IX	251	Self		To Langley		-40	
		Spitfire IX	251	Self		To base		-40	
	9th	Spitfire IX	JL359	Self		Bombing		1-05	
	10th	Boston III	BZ363	Self	Sgt Jardine	Aerial photography		-40	
		Boston III	BZ363	Self	Sgt Jardine	Aerial photography		1-05	
	13th	Boston III	BZ363	Self	F/Lt Henderson	To Catfoss & Swanton Morley		1-30	
		Boston III	BZ363	Self	F/Lt Henderson	To base		-20	
	15th	Typhoon	MN418	Self		Test contacting altimeter		-10	
		Mustang III	FZ107	Self		Test Divewright		-30	
		Typhoon	MN433	Self		Test contacting altimeter		-10	
	17th	Mustang III	FZ107	Self		Bombing		-40	

	29th	Spitfire IX	ML421	Self		To Farnborough		-40	
		Spitfire IX	ML421	Self		To base		-45	
		Boston III	BZ363	Self	F/Lt Waterton	To Millfield		1-05	
		Boston III	BZ363	Self		To base		-55	
	30th	Boston III	BZ363	Self	F/O Gendle	To Acklington		1-05	
		Boston III	BZ363	F/Lt Lane	Self, F/O Gendle	To Catfoss		-40	
		Boston III	BZ363	F/Lt Lane	Self, F/O Gendle	To base		-35	
						GRAND TOTAL TO DATE 1,074 hours 45 mins	3-30	11-20	
							60-00	999-55	16-15

3 September: This was an attempt to adapt the gyroscopic gunsight for bomb aiming.

5 September: I took over to fly the Boston solo back to Wittering. No passengers; they all ran away when I took over.

10 September: A passenger at last, brave fellow he must have been; anyway he flew with me twice!

13 September: Bob Henderson was another youngster who spent a few weeks at AFDU as a rest from operations.

15 September: I cannot remember what the piece of equipment on the Typhoon was but it did not take long to test it, so I guess it was a landing aid.

29 September: Bill (W.A.) Waterton had joined AFDU some months earlier. Another Canadian, an excellent and 'exact' pilot, he specialised in flying the Typhoon and Tempest. After many bombing trips he did a great deal of work in developing the RP (Rocket Projectile) as a war-winning weapon. By reason of his large 'Kaiser Bill' moustache, he was known by all as Otto. We, too, became very good friends. Bill was a frequent visitor at Chain Cottage.

After the war he remained in England for some years and he married his WREN officer. In the early 1950s he joined Gloster Aircraft Co., succeeding Bill Greenwood as Chief Test Pilot. He was responsible for the test programme on the

Javelin all-weather aircraft. Following a partial break-up on a high-speed run, he deliberately chose to crash-land, at great risk to himself, rather than bale out, so that the aircraft would be available for examination. The aircraft caught fire but, in spite of the risk, Bill returned to the fuselage to retrieve the flight records. He was awarded the George Medal.

Due to his outspoken comments in a book that he wrote about the aircraft industry, he was not popular with the company and returned to Canada. Following our final meeting at Gloster Aircraft in 1954, we remained in contact by letter. W.A. Waterton, GM, AFC & bar, died in 2006.

Summary for:- September 1944	1. Spitfire	5-20
Unit:- AFDU Wittering	2. Typhoon	-20
Date:- 1/10/44	3. Mustang	1-10
Signature:- *H.L. Thorne* F/Lt	4. Boston	10-45

Signed *T.S. Wade* S/Ldr
O/C Flying AFDU

YEAR	1944	AIRCRAFT		Pilot or 1st Pilot	2nd Pilot, Pupil or Pass.	DUTY (Including Results and Remarks)	Flying Time		Passenger
MONTH	DATE	Type	No.				Dual	Solo	
October	2nd	Spitfire XIV	RB179	Self		Dive bombing		-50	
		Mustang III	FZ107	Self		Dive bombing		-40	
	3rd	Spitfire XIV	RB179	Self		Dive bombing		-40	
		Spitfire XIV	RB179	Self		Dive bombing		-25	
		Spitfire XIV	RB179	Self		Dive bombing		-25	
	5th	ME109G	TP814	Self		Local experience on type		-20	
		Spitfire IX	BS552	Self		Tank dropping		-55	
	6th	Spitfire IX	MJ421	Self		Aileron test		-25	
		ME109	TP814	Self		Local		-20	
	10th	ME109	TP814	Self		Local		-20	
		Spitfire IX	MJ421	Self		Bombing		-30	
	13th	Spitfire IX	251	Self		Air test		-15	
		Spitfire IX	251	Self		GGS tracking		-30	
	24th	Spitfire IX	MJ421	Self		Local		-15	
		Tempest	808	Self		Bombing, dives		-35	
	25th	Spitfire IX	MJ421	Self		Bombing at Holbeach		-35	

27th	Spitfire IX	MJ421	Self		Bombing		-50	
	Spitfire IX	MJ421	Self		Bombing		1-00	
28th	Spitfire IX	MJ421	Self		Bombing		-30	
29th	Spitfire IX	MJ421	Self		Bombing		-30	
	Spitfire IX	MJ421	Self		Bombing		-25	
30th	Spitfire IX	MJ421	Self		Bombing		1-00	
	Spitfire IX	MJ421	Self		Bombing		-45	
31st	Spitfire IX	MJ421	Self		Bombing		-45	
	Spitfire IX	MJ421	Self		Bombing		-50	
					GRAND TOTAL TO DATE 1,089 hours 20 mins	3-30	11-20	
						60-00	1014-30	16-15

5 October: This was my first flight in the Messerschmidt 109G, known as the Gustav, the most advanced model of the 109 at that time. It was superior in many respects to the Spitfire Mk V, many of which were still in service, but the Griffon Spitfires (Mks XII and XIV) and the Mustang III all outclassed the Gustav. Used by the Luftwaffe in its dive and zoom tactics, the Gustav was still a formidable opponent. I did not like flying the 109; for me the cockpit was cramped and, with its up-and-over canopy, claustrophobic.

10 October: Further experience on type. As I was flying without an escort, I stayed close to base. With its narrow undercarriage, great care had to be taken when taxiing.

24 October: This aircraft would have been the Tempest V with a Napier Sabre liquid-cooled engine. Like the Typhoon, the Tempest picked up speed very quickly in a dive and great care was necessary in the recovery.

31 October: What a week! I came to hate this experimental bombing; high-level flight starting at 15,000 feet, releasing at 12,000 feet and dive bombing starting at 8,000 feet to low level, ending with cannon firing for ground attack.

Summary for:- October 1944	1. Spitfire	12-20
Unit:- AFDU Wittering	2. Mustang	-40
Date:- 1/11/44	3. ME 109G	1-00
Signature:- *H.L. Thorne* F/Lt	4. Tempest	-35

T.S. Wade S/Ldr
O/C Flying AFDU

| YEAR 1944 | | AIRCRAFT | | Pilot or 1st Pilot | 2nd Pilot, Pupil or Pass. | DUTY (Including Results and Remarks) | Flying Time | | Passenger |
MONTH	DATE	Type	No.				Dual	Solo	
November	1st	Spitfire IX	JL359	Self		Guns and camera		-55	
	2nd	Spitfire IX	MJ421	Self		Bombing		-25	
		Spitfire IX	MJ421	Self		Bombing		-40	
	4th	Spitfire IX	MJ421	Self		Bombing		-25	
	5th	Spitfire XVI	DV295	Self		Speed runs		-40	
	6th	Spitfire IX	MJ421	Self		Bombing		-30	
		Spitfire IX	MJ421	Self		Bombing		1-00	
	9th	Hurricane	397	Self		Photography		-20	
	10th	Mustang III	FZ107	Self		To Manston		-45	
		Meteor I	K	Self		Local experience on type		-30	
		Anson	184	F/Lt Lane	Self	To base		1-35	
	13th	Spitfire XVI	PV295	Self		Speed run		-15	
	14th	Spitfire XVI	PV295	Self		To Grimsburgen, Brussels		1-55	
	15th	Spitfire XVI	PV295	Self		Grimsburgen to Antwerp		-15	
	18th	Spitfire XVI	PV295	Self		Antwerp to Wittering		1-40	
	20th	ME 109G	TP814	Self		Air test		-10	
	22nd	ME 109G	TP814	Self		Crashed on take-off		-05	
		Spitfire IX	MJ421	Self		Weather test		-25	
		Spitfire 21	LA201	Self		Preliminary handling		-30	
	27th	Spitfire IX	MJ421	Self		Marker bombing		-25	
	30th	Spitfire IX	PV295	Self		Observe Lancaster marker bombs		-45	
						GRAND TOTAL TO DATE 1,103 hours 30 mins	3-30	11-20	
							60-00	1028-40	16.1

AFDU 1944 in front of a Mk 1 Tempest. Above: formal and hatted. Below: casual. Standing: 'Zip' Zobell (RCAF); F/Lt W.A. 'Bill' Reid; F/Lt C.E.O. 'Cappy' Lane (RAAF); F/Lt W. 'Otto' Waterton (RCAF); F/O H.W. 'Chas' Charnock. Seated: F/Lt Collins; F/Lt Simms; S/Ldr T.S. 'Wimpy' Wade; W/Cdr Allan R. Wright; S/Ldr 'Sawn off' Joce; F/Lt Chadwick; F/Lt H.L. Len Thorne.

Bud and Ian 'Bill' Burge.

Left to right: F/Lt H.L. Thorne, S/Ldr T.S.
'Wimpy' Wade, F/Lt H.S. 'Susie' Sewell, Cpl
Green, on a very cold day in winter 1944.

5 November: With increased production of Spitfires and Merlin-engined
Mustangs, demand for Merlins and Griffons outstripped Rolls-Royce production
capacity. The American car firms Packard and Ford produced Merlins under
licence. The Spitfire Mk XVI was powered by a Packard Merlin and had American
armament of .5 mm Browning machine guns instead of 20 mm Hispano cannons.
Broadly similar to the Spitfire Mk IX, it was still checked for performance.

F/Lt Thorne and his ME109 at Wittering, 22nd November 1944. Port oleo collapsed on take off.

10 November: For a few hours I was attached to the famous 616 Squadron, which had also been known as 'Bader's Bus Company' earlier in the war. Written on the Squadron bulletin board during 1941 was 'Bader's Bus Company – daily tickets to the Continent – Return tickets only!'

That autumn the Luftwaffe brought their first jet-engined fighter, the ME262, into service. It was an outstanding aircraft capable of speeds far in excess of any piston-engined machine. It was imperative to get the RAF jet into service for operational and prestige purposes. The first Gloster Meteors underwent handling trials at A&AAE, Boscombe Down, and were immediately passed into service with 'A' Flight, 616 Squadron.

Flying our first jet was a revelation, no torque, therefore no swing on take-off, no vibration and little or no engine noise. The engines of the Meteor Mk I had very poor performance at low speed, so take-off procedure was very different. Brakes held full on, throttle fully open; when maximum revs had built up, release brakes and allow the aircraft to roll forward. When speed built up, stick back to raise nose wheel, followed by becoming airborne. Maintain level flight until speed built up to 200 mph, then commence climb. In other respects the Meteor was an easy aeroplane to fly, with excellent forward visibility.

14 November: This was a flight and landing in mainland Europe. After D-Day increasing numbers of enemy aircraft fell into Allied hands as the ground forces advanced towards Germany. I was sent over to test fly a number of ME109s which were intended to be 'playthings' for senior officers. Great care was needed, as many of these machines were booby-trapped. My flight had to be planned with care, as some of the Channel ports, including Calais, Cherbourg and Dunquerque, had been bypassed but still held enough ammunition to give a hot reception to any Allied aircraft that flew too close. It had been a very wet autumn and the steel mesh decking (Somerfield Tracking), which made the runways, was underwater. Landing and take-offs left wakes rather like speedboats. Conditions were primitive and I spent 2 or 3 nights in partially destroyed buildings around the airfield perimeter; the least damaged had been made into temporary living quarters and messes. The Wehrmacht forces had been pushed back to the River Scheldt but small groups, known as Werewolves, were active at night.

A number of ground staff personnel were killed at night by these silent assassins. It became obvious that under these conditions there was no chance of doing any test flying. I therefore flew north to Antwerp in the hope of an improvement but still no flying.

Living conditions were much better here as I was billeted in the Hotel Century, right in the city centre. The Germans had left behind some excellent chefs and a very good orchestra that played background music in the evenings. The most requested tune was, of course, the German war song, Lilly Marlene. We were under strict orders not to go sightseeing alone but always in threes or more. The danger here was not Werewolves but prostitutes, who were missing their German customers. I spent one pleasant evening in a nearby nightclub, listening to music and watching the very attractive girls performing. With a couple of American officers and one Brit I went into Brussels one morning for sightseeing and shopping. Luxury goods, clothes and furs could be bought very cheaply but perfume and jewellery were not particularly cheap. Those in the know took home two items that were in great demand, real coffee and toilet soap.

During my stay in Antwerp a number of V1s fell in the area; one in particular, during the night, fell near enough to break crockery and glass in the hotel. The weather continued to make test flying impossible so on the sixth day I decided to return to Wittering. When I asked the flying control, he initially refused to give me a clearance but finally agreed, making it clear that it was my own responsibility. After take-off I climbed to 12,000 feet into clear air and set an estimated course to the west. When I judged my position to be mid-Channel, I called Wittering control for a homing. They suggested that there was better weather at some southwest airfields, particularly Hurn.

This posed a problem as I was carrying a few parcels to be posted in England to wives and girlfriends of the chaps in Antwerp, plus some presents like perfume for Estelle. It was essential to land at base where there were no customs checks, so I carried on with the homing to Wittering and only saw the ground when I landed. Our ground staff stripped gun panels to quickly remove any incriminating material, plus my own parachute bag, which was hanging behind the armour plate that protected my head. On the outward flight I had carried a drop tank under each wing, which contained not petrol but many gallons of Mitchells and Butlers' Best Bitter for the Grimsburgen messes! So ended an adventurous week.

18 November: Looking back I find it incredible that I undertook these flights with nothing more than a set of maps and an absolute faith in radar and our ground controllers.

22 November: Probably my nearest brush with death. On take-off, just before 'unsticking' at around 120 mph, the port oleo support strut broke and the left leg of the undercarriage collapsed. The port wing hit the ground, causing the aircraft to do a complete cartwheel. By good fortune it came to rest the right way up but badly damaged. It was a frightening situation as the fuselage 'kinked' just behind the cockpit, jamming the canopy closed. With fuel and coolant dripping, I was very relieved that help came quickly and I was released, badly frightened. Flying Officer Chadwick, the Unit photographic officer, was on hand to take the picture that has since appeared in many magazines and newspapers. There was no attempt to repair TP814 as many captured 109s were now available. It came to rest in one of the 1426 Flight hangars at Colley Weston, to be cannibalised for spares.

Following the rules, I flew again immediately after the crash and suffered no noticeable ill effects.

The Mk 21 was meant to be a big step forward, with a more powerful Griffon engine, four 20 mm cannons, cut down rear fuselage for better visibility and contra-rotating airscrews, each of three blades. Problems in controlling the increased torque with a single 11-foot-diameter airscrew were the reasons for changing to contra-rotating airscrews.

I went on to make eleven or so flights in the Mk 21 covering all aspects of the test programme and, at the CO's request, wrote the draft report. For the first time there was an adverse report on a Spitfire. AFDU received LA201 towards the end of 1944. It was only 10/12 mph faster that the Mk XIV but apart from improved aileron control, it otherwise felt unstable, particularly in the horizontal plane. As a gun platform it proved poor and sighting was difficult. My comments were upheld by other Unit pilots and it was generally felt that the Mk 21 should not go into service, the Mk XIV being a much better aircraft. However, extensive modifications were made and a few months later the Spitfire Mk 21 was accepted for service.

27 November: These bombs emitted coloured smoke which was released slowly after impact. They were intended for target marking.

Summary for:- November 1944	1. Spitfire	10-45
Unit:- AFDU Wittering	2. Hurricane	-20
Date:- 4/12/44	3. Mustang	-45
Signature:- H.L. Thorne F/Lt	4. Meteor	-30
	5. ME109G	-15
	6. Anson	1-35

Signed *H.L. Thorne* F/Lt
for O/C Flying A.F.D.S.

In the absence of Squadron Leader Wade I was given an acting rank as O/C Flying. The Unit was upgraded to Squadron status and became AFDS.

| YEAR | 1944 | AIRCRAFT | | Pilot or 1st Pilot | 2nd Pilot, Pupil or Pass. | DUTY (Including Results and Remarks) | Flying Time | | Passenger |
MONTH	DATE	Type	No.				Dual	Solo	
December	1st	Spitfire XVI	PV295	Self		Bombing		-35	
		Spitfire XVI	PV295	Self		Bombing		1-00	
		Spitfire XVI	PV295	Self		Bombing		1-00	
	4th	Spitfire XXI	LA201	Self		Climbs and speeds		-45	
	5th	Spitfire IX	JL359	Self		Bombing		-40	
		Spitfire V	AD318	Self		Air test		-20	
	6th	Spitfire XXI	LA201	Self		Comparative v. Tempest		-45	
	7th	Spitfire IX	JL359	Self		Bombing		-35	
	17th	Typhoon	MN974	Self		Rocket projectiles (RPs)		-55	
		Spitfire XVI	RB179	Self		Rocket projectiles		1-05	
	18th	Typhoon	MN974	Self		Rocket projectiles		1-00	
	31st	Mustang	FZ107	Self		Fire bombs (napalm) at Colleyweston		-25	
		Mustang	FZ107	Self		Fire bombs at Colleyweston		-25	
						GRAND TOTAL TO DATE 1,113 hours 00 mins	3-30	11-20	
							60-00	1038-10	16-15

1 December: The development of bombing by fighters was something that had to be done. I hated it! Our lovely Spitfires were not meant to be used in this way. Ground attack, whether by the use of bombs, rockets, machine gun or cannon fire, was a most dangerous action. German light ack ack was most efficient and the casualties were horrendous.

6 December: Comparative testing embraced all aspects of fighter use: mock combat, turning circles, rates of roll, climbs, dives, speed runs, operational and absolute ceiling.

17 December: Rocket Projectiles were carried on rails under each wing, four each side, and were fired electrically. They had been in use for some time and it was our job to improve aiming techniques. Those first RPs were the forerunners of the air-to-ground and air-to-air missiles that are in use today.

18 December: The RPs could be fired selectively in pairs, fours or eights. Firing all eight at once was equivalent to a destroyer's broadside.

31 December: Earlier in this year AFDU commenced experiments on the use of fire bombs. I have the doubtful honour of being the first, or at least one of the first, to demonstrate this diabolical weapon. It was primarily intended for use against the Japanese in the Pacific war and would need to be effective against fox-holes and slit trenches.

The first efforts were somewhat primitive: a 250-gallon drop tank under each wing of the aircraft was filled with jellified benzole. [Later known as napalm.] Two hand grenades were strapped to each tank, the firing pins attached by wires to the bomb-rack.

On an unused part of Colleyweston airfield fox-holes and slit trenches were dug and human dummies were placed in them. I was ordered on this cold and very windy day to release the tanks in front of senior officers of Allied and American Army and Air Forces to demonstrate the effect. Despite the adverse weather conditions I made a successful run in but, at the first attempt, one tank failed to release immediately. However, when I made a climbing turn away, the second tank dropped. It fell on to the parade ground of a nearby American army camp, bursting into a spectacular ball of fire. I visualised with horror burnt and dead American soldiers but, luckily, being a Sunday, they were all off camp.

Against my will I was ordered to try again and at the second attempt, again, only one tank released. I pulled up into a very gentle climbing turn and flew to the Wainfleet bombing range. I admit to being worried (scared stiff!) that the grenade pins had pulled out and I was about to be cremated or blown to bits. All was OK; after a very tight turn the second tank fell harmlessly into the sea. By then the weather had deteriorated and further tests were abandoned – thank goodness! I assume the one tank test had been enough, as the system was adopted and has, unfortunately for the victims, been used ever since.

Summary for:- December 1944	1. Spitfire	6-45
Unit:- AFDS Wittering	2. Typhoon	1-55
Date:- Jan 1944	3. Mustang	-50
Signature:- *H.L. Thorne* F/Lt		

H.L. Thorne F/Lt, Acting S/Ldr
For O/C Flying AFDS

During the first week in December our CO, I believe it was Wing Commander Allan Wright, decided that a Unit dance, to be held in the hangar, was a good idea. As we now knew that we would be moving to Tangmere, the dance would be a farewell to Wittering. For some unknown reason, I was made responsible for arrangements. A sub-committee was formed from the NCOs and with a lot of help from F/Lt Simms, the Adjutant, things got underway. A dance band was borrowed from a nearby airfield, I believe it was Oakington; flags, bunting and Christmas decorations appeared by the cartload. Bars were set up in two corners, a raised platform was built for the band, refreshments were arranged from the various messes and the Tannoy was modified for the occasion. The bare hangar walls were covered in flags and overhead decorations hid the roof. A nominal charge of two shillings (10p) was made for admission. I only vaguely remember the actual dance but apparently it was a great success.

9

THE WIND-DOWN

YEAR	1945	AIRCRAFT		Pilot or 1st Pilot	2nd Pilot, Pupil or Pass.	DUTY (Including Results and Remarks)	Flying Time		Passenger
MONTH	DATE	Type	No.				Dual	Solo	
January	9th	Spitfire 21	LA201	Self		Formation flying		-35	
	14th	Spitfire 21	LA201	Self		Air test		-30	
	15th	Mustang IV	704	Self		Handling		-45	
		Mustang IV	704	Self		Handling		-25	
	17th	Tempest V	EN529	Self		GGS tracking		-20	
		Mustang III	410	Self		Comparative v. Spitfire 21		1-15	
	21st	Tempest V	EN529	Self		GGS tracking		-45	
	27th	Mustang III	410	Self		Comparative v. Spitfire 21		1-25	
	29th	Spitfire 21	LA201	Self		Sighting test		-25	
		Spitfire 21	LA201	Self		Sighting test		-25	
						GRAND TOTAL TO DATE 1,119 hours 40 mins	3-30	11-20	
							60-00	1044-50	16-15

15 January: This Mk IV was the best version of the Mustang. It had the one-piece moulded canopy and, with the cut-down rear fuselage, gave truly all-round visibility. A modified tail unit greatly improved stability and with six .5-inch machine guns it was a formidable aircraft. With its 6-hour endurance it was certainly one of the most successful weapons in shortening the war.

29 January: It was in this test that the poor stability of the Mk 21 showed up most.

Summary for:- January 1945   1. Spitfire   1-55
Unit:- AFDS Wittering   2. Mustang   3-40
Date:- 3/2/45   3. Tempest   1-05
Signature:- *H.L. Thorne* F/Lt

H.L. Thorne F/Lt, pp S/Ldr
O/C Flying AFDS

During this winter period there was extremely cold weather with several heavy
snow falls. This explains the lack of flying activity during December and January.
There was one particular day when Wimpy and I had to use a car to carry out an
inspection at Colley Weston and he demonstrated his complete recovery from his
night flying fright. We were on the country road south of Wittering, Wimpy at the
wheel, driving at high speed over ice-covered surfaces. I expected to end up in
a ditch but we got away with it; the drive scared the pants off me worse than any
flying experience. Wimpy at his best!

| YEAR | 1945 | AIRCRAFT | | Pilot or 1st Pilot | 2nd Pilot, Pupil or Pass. | DUTY (Including Results and Remarks) | Flying Time | | Passenger |
MONTH	DATE	Type	No.				Dual	Solo	
February	1st	Spitfire 21	LA201	Self		Cine camera		-35	
	3rd	Spitfire IX	JL359	Self		Cine camera		-25	
	4th	Spitfire IX	JL359	Self		Cine camera		-25	
		Mustang III	FZ107	Self		To Tangmere		-45	
		Mustang III	FZ107	Self		To base		-45	
	7th	Spitfire 21	LA201	Self		Cine camera		-30	
	9th	Spitfire IX	BS552	Self		To Boscombe Down		-40	
		Spitfire IX	BS552	Self		To base		-45	
	10th	Spitfire IX	MJ421	Self		GGS tracking		-40	
	14th	Spitfire IX	MJ421	Self		GGS tracking		-25	
		Tempest V	EN529	Self		GGS tracking		-25	
	18th	Spitfire IX	RR228	Self		(Cine camera) handling		-35	
		Spitfire IX	RR228	Self		Handling		-20	
	19th	Spitfire IX	PV295	Self		Cine camera		-40	
		Mustang IV	704	Self		Target		-35	
	21st	Boston	BZ363	Self		Air test		-20	
		Spitfire XIV	253	Self		Gunsight test		-15	
	24th	Boston	BZ363	Self		To Tangmere		-50	
		Anson	?	S/Ldr Wade	Self	To base		1-00	

								-40	
		Spitfire 21	LA201	Self		To Tangmere		-40	
		Anson		Self	F/Lt Cull	To base		1-00	
	28th	Meteor III	EE263	Self		Local		-35	
						GRAND TOTAL TO DATE 1,132 hours 50 mins	3-30	11-20	
							60-00	1058-00	16-15

4 February: I had flown FZ107 on and off since December 31st 1943, completing the test programme and much flying purely for pleasure. It was with a sense of regret that I flew it for the last time. Goodbye to a friend.

24 February: This was the start of our move to Tangmere. After D-Day this airfield was almost empty, all the operational units, aircraft and personnel had moved to the Continent. It was decided by the Air Ministry that various fighter test and experimental units would be merged into one organisation under the heading CFE (Central Fighter Establishment). Among the units was AFDS (now with squadron status), A & AEE (Aeroplane & Armament Experimental Establishment from Boscombe Down), FLS (Fighter Leaders School), part of RAE (Royal Aircraft Establishment from Farnborough) and others.

It was with great regret on all sides that Estelle and I left our rooms at Chain Cottage and started a search for new accommodation. With so many people moving to 'Tangers' this was not easy and we spent the first few weeks in one room in a council house at East Wittering with Mr and Mrs Kirby and their 12-year-old daughter. I remember only one feature of this house: in the front room was an Anderson air-raid shelter. We were pretty relieved to move into a furnished bungalow, near the seafront, in Bracklesham Bay towards the end of March. 'Veronica', a wooden bungalow just a stone's throw from the beach, was very much a holiday home but ideal for us, with the spring and summer to come.

28 February: The Meteor Mk III, with more powerful engines, was a great improvement on the earlier version of the aircraft.

Summary for:- February 1945		1. Spitfire	6-55
Unit:- AFDS Tangmere		2. Mustang	2-05
Date:- 2/3/45		3. Tempest	-25
Signature:- H.L.Thorne		4. Boston	1-10
		5. Anson	2-00
		6. Meteor III	-35

Signed: *T.S. Wade* S/Ldr
O/C Flying AFDS

| YEAR | 1945 | AIRCRAFT | | Pilot or 1st Pilot | 2nd Pilot, Pupil or Pass. | DUTY (Including Results and Remarks) | Flying Time | | Passenger |
MONTH	DATE	Type	No.				Dual	Solo	
March	1st	Meteor III	EE263	Self		Air test		-20	
		Meteor III	EE263	Self		Air test		-25	
	4th	Spitfire IX	MJ421	Self		Weather test		-30	
		Spitfire 21	LA215	Self		Gun platform		-40	
	17th	Spitfire IX	PV295	Self		Air test		-25	
		Anson		Self	Sgt Leslie	To Boscombe Down		-40	
		Anson		Self		To base		-40	
	22nd	Mustang IV	204	Self		Target		-30	
						GRAND TOTAL TO DATE 1,137 hours 00 mins	3-30	11-20	
							60-00	1062-10	16-15

1 March: Fun and games on the first flight: the starboard engine suffered a flame-out and I had to make my first single-engine approach and landing in a twin. To my relief it turned out to be a piece of cake. A minor fault corrected for the second flight but I did not go far from the airfield.

Summary for:- March 1945   1. Spitfire   1-35
Unit:- AFDS Tangmere   2. Mustang   -30
Date:- 2/3/45   3. Meteor   -45
Signature:- H.L.Thorne   4. Anson   1-20

Signed: *T.S. Wade* S/Ldr
O/C Flying AFDS

| YEAR | 1945 | AIRCRAFT | | Pilot or 1st Pilot | 2nd Pilot, Pupil or Pass. | DUTY (Including Results and Remarks) | Flying Time | | Passenger |
MONTH	DATE	Type	No.				Dual	Solo	
April	3rd	Spitfire IX	JL359	Self		Air test		-30	
	4th	Mustang III	890	Self		Handling at 25,000ft		1-25	
	5th	Mustang III	754	Self		Air test		-30	

	7th	Auster I		Self		To Westcott		1-15	
		Auster I		Self		Westcott to base		1-00	
	14th	Spitfire XIV	JL356	Self		Local		-30	
						GRAND TOTAL TO DATE 1,141 hours 25 mins	3-30	11-20	
							60-00	1066-35	16-15

4 April: This was not really a test flight. Climbing all the way to the south coast, at 25,000 ft I could see across the Channel to Cherbourg and the last of the Normandy invasion shipping.

7 April: Many items of food, including eggs, were still rationed. The flight was one of a number that I made to collect a crate of 12 dozen eggs from my sister's farm, for the Officers' Mess.

On April 20th the European war came to an end and our work at AFDS came almost to a standstill. Like many servicemen, our own futures were in doubt and CFE in general and AFDS in particular were swamped by an influx of officers from Europe. The new CFE set-up was still being organised and a commanding officer had yet to be appointed. Wing Commander Douglas Bader, recently returned from his POW days at Colditz Castle, paid an escorted visit to Duxford and hoped to get the post. I was told that he was very disappointed to be passed over. Wing Commander Ronald (Razz) Berry, a hero of the Battle of Britain and the siege of Malta, was appointed commanding officer.

Summary for:– April 1945	1. Spitfire	1–00
Unit:– AFDS Tangmere	2. Mustang	2–10
Date:– 30/5/45	3. Auster	2–15
Signature:– H.L. Thorne		

Signed *H.L. Thorne*, F/Lt Acting S/Ldr
O/C Flying AFDS

I was going through a bad time, worried about the future and stale from 4½ years of flying. In the absence of a commanding officer, O/C Flying (Wimpy) had already gone to become chief test pilot at Hawkers, Langley and with so many pilots returning from the hard fighting in Germany, I had many extra duties with which to cope. I received much help from the adjutant, F/Lt Simms and his staff but towards the end of April I asked for a transfer to other non–flying duties. For the rest of the month and until early July I was appointed range instructing officer at the bombing and firing ranges between Bracklesham and Selsey Bill. I still paid regular visits to Tangmere in my now nominal position of Flight Commander. I did several days as Duty Officer and, surprisingly, I was appointed Officer for the Defence at a Court Martial.

Aircraft parked overnight had locking toggles placed to prevent wind damage to the control surfaces, i.e. ailerons, rudder and tail plane; these had to be removed before flying. The Court Martial followed a fatal accident involving two Typhoons. The first had taken off and, the pilot realising something was wrong with the controls, immediately managed to go round for an emergency landing. Meanwhile a second Tiffie had taken up position ready for take-off and the first plane landed on it, killing both pilots. The station's senior engineering officer, a wing commander, was held responsible and charged with negligence. He could have had a civilian defence counsel but elected to take his chances with me. He was found guilty but got off lightly with an admonishment, so perhaps I did some good.

So, from mid-April to July I became range instructing officer, telling senior officers of the Fighter Leaders School what they were doing wrong when carrying out ground attacks. In dive bombing it was essential, in order to achieve reasonable accuracy, to dive at or near 70° and this took a lot of determination and practice.

Fortunately I did not know the rank of any particular officer and they did not know that they were being bawled out by a mere Flight Lieutenant. The range control tower was a 60-ft-high open scaffolding tower with facilities such as radio, sight screens and plotting at different levels. The control room was on the top platform and you got there by open ladders from level to level. It was some weeks before I overcame my fear of heights and being shamed by the ground staff boys before I made the climb with my eyes open.

From our bungalow in Bracklesham Bay there were two routes to the range control tower. The first was by road, a long way round through Earnley and including some tortuous lanes, back to the farm where the tower was situated. An easier and nearer way was by foot and bicycle along a path which followed the coast, a distance of about two miles. Near the control tower a tidal brook ran inland but it could be crossed by a plank bridge about 15 inches wide. I usually used my bike and did not dismount for the plank but just gave the handlebars a lift and sailed straight across. One morning the handlebars pulled out and I went sideways into the very stagnant and weed-filled brook. I rescued the bicycle and went on to the farm, looking like the old man of the sea and stinking worse than the farm dung heap. When the lads at the tower could stop laughing, they hosed me down under the farm pump while one of them went by road in the Jeep to collect my No. 2 uniform. Luckily no one had a camera handy, so my mishap was never recorded on film and was known only to the control tower staff and Estelle.

The Jeep is another story. The range not only had orthodox flat and angled targets but also had lines of vehicles arranged nose to tail to imitate an enemy convoy. Crashed vehicles – cars, pickups and lorries – which were damaged beyond repair, were brought from all over the country on 'Queen Marys', low loading vehicles. Usable equipment such as batteries was salvaged and fuel and oil was supposed to be drained from tanks and engines. The vehicles were placed on the range as targets for ground attack. It happened that one of the range officers was a skilled car mechanic and he rescued a Jeep that was not too badly damaged. With spares from other machines he rebuilt the Jeep to provide the boys with unrecorded and unlicensed transport to get around the lanes to country pubs. Petrol, which was strictly rationed, was always to be found in newly delivered, written-off transport.

The range extended along the coast for some two or three miles and inland from the beaches for about 1½ miles. It was, of course, strictly out of bounds to all civilians and unauthorised service personnel. I always thought that wild mushrooms were only a late summer or autumn crop but some fertile areas of the range abounded with them that spring. We used to take square sheets of balloon fabric, of which the targets were made, and fill them in the early morning before flying commenced with newly gathered mushrooms. Our local pub, the Bracklesham Bay Hotel, was always good for a bottle of whisky or gin in return for a large bag of mushrooms.

Meanwhile the ranges were being extensively used. Although the Germans had been defeated, the Japanese were still fighting with their usual fanaticism. It was vital to keep up the pressure on land where General Slim and his 'forgotten' army were pushing the Japanese out of the Malayan peninsula. Likewise, the Americans and some units of the Royal Navy were island-hopping towards Japan. The pilots at the Fighter Leaders School were trained to the highest possible standard of bombing, gunfire, rockets and napalm dropping before being posted to the Far East. Inevitably, there were a number of accidents and particular care was necessary when using Typhoons and Tempests for dive-bombing. These aircraft accelerated quickly to speeds in excess of 500 mph and it was vital to effect the recovery from the dive in good time with height to spare. I well remember with sadness the one fatal accident that I witnessed; I believe the aircraft was a Typhoon. The pilot left it too late to pull out of the dive and went straight into the ground. He was, of course, killed and all efforts to recover the aircraft failed because it continued to sink into the sandy foreshore faster than a digger could dig down.

The spring that year (1945) gave us some very good, warm weather. Baby Gill loved the beach but needed careful watching as she was apt to run straight into the sea fully dressed! We were very popular with family and friends and our spare bedroom was in constant demand. For most it was their first seaside holiday for six or more years. Among our visitors was Mrs Simms, the adjutant's wife. I made frequent trips to Tangmere to work with 'Simmy' in the affairs of AFDS but in truth he and Peggy Snashall did most of the work. I sometimes put in an appearance at the FLS debriefing but was careful not to let them know what my function was at the range. It was an interesting experience, which I thoroughly enjoyed.

Estelle and I paid weekly visits to Selsey village and got to know the brave fishermen who went out to gather the fruits of the sea, particularly shellfish. The shellfish were kept alive until the day of the week when crabs and lobsters were cooked, ready for delivery to the markets in Chichester. I had a standing order for these items, for delivery to the Tangmere Officers' Mess and for one or two of the officers who lived out. Among them was Wing Commander 'Razz' Berry, who I came to know very well. On one of the Selsey trips I went on a no-cooking day and so bought half a dozen live and very lively crabs in a wooden box, which I placed in the annex of the bungalow while I boiled a large pot of water. Unfortunately, the crabs got loose and were running around happily. In my frantic efforts to catch them I was lucky not to lose one or two fingers!

I made friends with Mr Dormer, who opened his small butcher's shop in East Wittering on two days a week. We did quite well for meat, which, of course, was strictly rationed. More mushrooms and an occasional petrol coupon worked wonders! Friday was a special day. Estelle walked to West Wittering to the baker's shop, to collect her allowance of the finest jam doughnuts I ever tasted. Each member of the family was allowed just four each week.

By and large I really enjoyed this interlude in my service but it could not last. At the end of June a professional instructor was posted in and I returned to AFDS normal duties. I still spent most of the time with administration, with just one flight on June 30th in my favourite plane, the Mk IX Spitfire, No.JL356. I spent 50 minutes firing rocket projectiles.

On July 9th I made a 25-minute local flight in a Meteor III, No. EE243, then on the 12th I made a 1 hour, 10 minute flight in an Auster, taking as my passenger Lieutenant Colonel Sanderson, our next-door-neighbour at Bracklesham, a retired army officer and a gentleman of the old school. I gave him a trip round the locality, which he thoroughly enjoyed.

On July 13th I did a local GGS (Gyro gunsight) test for one hour in the Tempest V, No. EN529. I little thought that this would be my last flight as the Flight Commander and Acting O/C Flying at AFDS. One of the new boys took over, recently returned from a hectic tour in Europe, Flight Lieutenant Fifield.

The last of the piston-engined fighters, the Mk 22 Spitfire and the Tempest V version, known as the Fury or Sea Fury, were undergoing trials. A little later the last of the true Spitfires, the Mk 24, appeared. Later still the almost completely redesigned aircraft appeared. It would have been the Mk 25 but, with its wide track undercarriage and straight-edged laminar flow wing, like the Mustang and the German FW190, it was so different that the RAF version was renamed the Spiteful. Not many were built and most of them went to the Fleet Air Arm, where they were known as the Seafang.

Later versions of the Meteor were also undergoing trials. In fact, in 1946 a new High Speed Flight was formed, commanded by Group Captain R.A. (Batch) Atcherley, one of the pre-war team. My old friend Bill Waterton was a member of the team. That year a successful attempt by Edward Donaldson in a Meteor F Mk 4 briefly held the world speed record, following the success of the same plane in 1945, piloted by H.J.Wilson. On the coastal path between Rustington and Littlehampton in Sussex there is a bronze plaque confirming the event. Also appearing at AFDS was the single-engined jet, the DeHavilland Vampire. Sadly, I did not get to fly these new machines, something I now regret.

Summary for:- June, July 1945	1. Spitfire IX	-50
Unit:- AFDS Tangmere	2. Meteor III	-25
Date:- July 31st 1945	3. Auster	1-10
Signature:- H.L. Thorne	4. Tempest V	1-00

Signed *H.L. Thorne*, Acting pp S/Ldr
O/C Flying AFDS

F/Lt Herbert Leonard Thorne, AE, MiD, 1945.

This certificate was awarded for flight testing under operational conditions the Spitfire Mk XXI in comparative trials against various RAF, FAA and USAAF fighters, for evaluating suitability for service use and for preparing and rendering a report and recommendations to the Air Ministry.

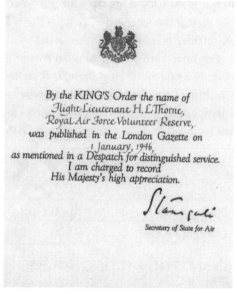

By the KING'S Order the name of
Flight Lieutenant H. L. Thorne,
Royal Air Force Volunteer Reserve,
was published in the London Gazette on
1 January, 1946,
as mentioned in a Despatch for distinguished service.
I am charged to record
His Majesty's high appreciation.

Secretary of State for Air

Towards the end of July 1945 I received a telephone call from a friend, a former AFDU Flight Commander, Wing Commander Ron Brown, to say that there was a vacancy at Staff level in the Air Ministry. The chosen candidate was to be attached to the MOS (Ministry of Supply) as a liaison officer between the service and the aircraft manufacturing companies. Although I thought my educational background would mar my chances, Ron suggested that I attend an interview with his Group Captain. So, in August on VJ Day, I presented myself to Thames House South in

London. To my surprise I was offered the posting, on condition that I remained in the Service for at least three years. I remember walking back to the car park, watching the crowds on the Embankment setting off fireworks, dancing and singing to celebrate the victory over Japan.

As there was no Service accommodation in London it meant a move from Bracklesham and finding some furnished quarters in the London area. We found a furnished house on the south side of Slough, very near to the Eton College playing fields and only two miles from Windsor. The location was very handy for us to visit Doris, my eldest sister and her policeman husband Percy Climer, who was stationed in Slough. I had lived with them from 1934 to 1939, finished my grammar school education at Slough Secondary School and started my working life at the High Duty Alloys factory in the town, so I had many friends there. As Estelle had worked as a secretary in the CID police office she, too, had many friends in the vicinity. Shortly after we took up residence in Slough my old school friend Freddy Deeks and Dorothy were married on 18th May 1946, Gill's third birthday. We remained lifelong friends.

On November 15th I flew a Spitfire VB from Hendon to West Raynham and back, each flight lasting 50 minutes.

In order to maintain our pilot pay status we were required to fly a certain number of hours annually. A special unit was based at Hendon, from which we could take our pick of the several aircraft types there. The aforementioned flights were some of these; there were others not recorded.

On June 13th 1947 I flew an Auster Autocrat accompanied by a Staff Pilot, making a one-hour local flight at Rearsby. Following a meeting at Auster Aircraft Company I was offered a flight in a new machine just off the production line. After a buzz round with the company's pilot, I was free to do my own thing. This was my last recorded flight as a member of the RAFVR.

	Flying time		
	Dual	Solo	Passenger
Night Flying	3-30	11-20	
Daylight Flying	60-00	1074-50	16-15

GRAND TOTAL FLYING HOURS: 1149 hrs. 40 minutes.

I was released from active service on 2nd September 1948, although I remained a serving officer until the end of November and was able to continue wearing my uniform until then. This was also the day on which our second daughter, Penelope, was born.

For the next 33 years my time was fully occupied earning a living in civvy street and I was unable to take an interest in flying. After my retirement at the end of 1981 I was able to join a flying club at Wellesbourne, Warwickshire. In anticipation of my eagerness to fly again, earlier that year Estelle had given me a one-hour flight as a birthday present; but it was 1984 before I made further flights on a regular basis.

APPENDIX 1

LIST OF AIRCRAFT FLOWN

De Havilland Tiger Moth DH 82	Biplane Trainer	Gipsy Major		At EFTS Desford Sept/Nov. 1940
Miles Master Mk I	Low-wing Monoplane Trainer	Rolls-Royce Kestrel Series 1		At SFTA Hullavington Nov/April '40/41
Miles Master Mk 2	Low-wing Monoplane Trainer	Rolls-Royce Series 2		Instruct Bomber S/Ldr. Duxford '42
Miles Master Mk 3	Low-wing Monoplane Trainer	Twin Row Wasp Radial		Instruct Bomber S/Ldr. Duxford '42
Hurricane I		Rolls-Royce Merlin III	8 machine guns	SFTS Hullavington '40/41
Hurricane IV		Rolls-Royce Merlin XX	4 machine guns & 2 x 20mm. Cannons	AFDU Duxford '42
Spitfire Mk I		Rolls-Royce Merlin III	8 machine guns. OTU	1st solo Speke '41
Spitfire Mk IIa		Rolls-Royce Merlin III	8 machine guns. OTU	41 Sqdn. Catterick '41
Spitfire Mk IIb		Rolls-Royce Merlin III	8 machine guns. OTU	41 Sqdn. Catterick '41
Spitfire Mk Vb		Rolls-Royce Merlin III	4 machine guns and 2 20mm cannon	41 Sqdn. Catterick and W. Hampnett '41
Spitfire Mk Va		Rolls-Royce Merlin III	8 machine guns	41 Sqdn. Catterick and W. Hampnett '41
Spitfire Mk Vc		Rolls-Royce Merlin III	2 machine guns and 4 cannon	Duxford
Spitfire Mk VI		As Mk Vb but with pressurised cabin		AFDU Wittering
Spitfire VII		As Mk above but with elongated wings for super high altitude		

All following Spitfires at AFDU Duxford or Wittering

Spitfire Mk VIII LF	Redesigned Mk Va but with Merlin 66 2-speed 2-stage blower for best performance to 30,000 ft
Spitfire Mk VIII HF	As above but with max. performance up to 40,000 ft
Spitfire Mk IX LF	As Mk VIII LF
Spitfire Mk IX HF	As Mk VIII HF. The best of all the Spitfires
Spitfire Mk XI	Similar to Mk IX HF but without armament for PRU
Spitfire Mk XII LF only	Similar to Mk IX LF but with the new Rolls-Royce Griffon engine

Spitfire MkXIV HF	As above but super performance up to 40,000 ft. Ceiling 43/44.000ft
Spitfire Mk XVI	Similar to Mk IX HF but with American Packard built Merlin engine and .5 colt machine guns
Spitfire Mk XVIII	Similar to Mk XIV but without armaments for PRU
Spitfire Mk XXI	As Mk XIV but with more powerful engine and 5 bladed airscrew

Miles Magister	Monoplane Trainer	Gipsy Major		602 Sqdn. Kenley '41/42
Stinson Reliant	American 4 seater light passenger plane	Engine: Lycoming		AFDU Duxford '42/43
Boulton Paul Defiant	Night Fighter	Rolls-Royce Merlin		AFDU Duxford '42/43
Blackburn Skua	Naval Fighter reconnaissance aircraft	Radial engine		AFDU Duxford '42/43
Airspeed Oxford	Twin-engined Trainer	Cheeta Radials		AFDU Duxford '42/43
North American Mustang Mk I (P51)		Alison water cooled	Armament 8.5 colt m/g.	17.6 42, evaluation
North American Mustang Mk III (P51a)		Packard Merlin 66		AFDU Duxford and Wittering
North American Mustang Mk X (P51d)	As above but with Bubble canopy			AFDU Duxford and Wittering
North American Mustang Mk IV	As above but with Tear Drop canopy and 'cut down' rear fuselage			AFDU Duxford and Wittering
Wellington Bomber		Twin Bristol radial or RR Merlin engines		Fighter Affiliation at Lakenheath
Aerocobra	American Fighter	Alison in line		August.42 for evaluation
Gloster Gladiator	Biplane fighter	Radial		Jan.'43 to Little Rissington for breaking up
American Thunderbolt (P47)	Popularly known as 'The Jug'	Wright double row cyclone		Experience on type. Feb '43
Hawker Typhoon		Napier Sabre		Evaluation and comparative performance April '43
Heston Phoenix	4 seater light communication aircraft	Gypsy VI		
Grumman Martlet	American naval fighter	Wright Cyclone		Experience on type, an unusual one for my logbook
Focke Wulf FW 190	German Fighter	BMW 801 Radial		Aug.43. Comparative trials and Demonstrations began.
Percival Proctor	Light comm. Aircraft	Gypsy Queen		Sept '43
Auster	Army co-op aircraft	Cirrus		Nov '43
Tempest I		Sabre		Performance testing Jan. '44
Tempest V		Bristol Centaurus		Performance and dive bombing Oct. '44

John Timmis, Len Thorne and Ron Rayner at Hullavington, 1991.

Len Thorne and Ron Rayner off for a flight with Bristol University Air Training Squadron instructors at Hullavington.

Len settling in to an ME109G at Duxford, after its rebuild, identical to the one which he flew in 1944 and crashed when the port oleo collapsed on take-off. 'They wouldn't let me fly it in case I broke the bloody thing again!'

Len Thorne in 1996 being shown the 'taps' on Messerschmitt Bf 109 G-2 trop 10639 (G-USTV) at Duxford Airshow.

Grumman Hellcat	US Naval fighter	Double Row Wasp		Another odd one for my logbook
Fairey Firefly	Naval fighter/Bomber	RR Griffon		Another odd one for my logbook
Firefly Fulmar	Naval fighter/Bomber	RR Merlin		Another odd one for my logbook
US Boston (also known as the Havoc)	Fighter/bomber	Twin Wright Cyclones		Evaluation and communications
Gloster Meteor Mk I		RR B 23 Jet		Attached to 616 Sqdn. Manston Nov '44 for experience with Sqdn.
Gloster Meteor Mk III		RR B 23 Jet		Testing. Moved to Tangmere. Feb '45
German Messerschmidt Me 109 G (known as the Gustav)		Daimler Benz DB 605		Nov. '44 comparative testing
Mustang IV	Packard or Ford Merlin 66 built under licence			Some testing, mostly bombing
Auster Autocrat				At Rearsby factory, experience on type; my last flight as an RAF pilot.

Flown as a civilian pilot

Piper PA 38 Tomahawk	Flown as a member of Wellesbourne Aviation Flying Club
A glider	At Bidford Gliding Club
Cessna C152	At Wellesbourne Club
Katana DV 20	At Wellesbourne Club
Slingsby Firefly	For aerobatics to celebrate my 80th birthday
Robin	
Warrior	Flown for BBC in connection with a News 24 item about FW 190s being built at Gamelsdorf, Germany

Flown as second pilot

Avro Anson (later flown as first pilot)
Avro Lancaster
Percival Q 6 (later flown as first pilot)
NA Mitchell B25 twin-engined day bomber

Flown as passenger

DC 3 Dakota
DC 4 (I believe it was called the 'Pionnair')
DC 8 DC10
Fuji Twin
DH Rapide
BAC 111
Boeing 727
Boeing 737
Boeing 747
Boeing 767
Concorde (most of this flight was spent on the Flight deck with the crew)
Airbus (various versions)
Tristar
Bristol Britannia (the Banana Bomber of Monarch Airlines)

APPENDIX 2

AERODROMES AT WHICH I LANDED OR FROM WHICH I OPERATED

Desford (Leics)	30-09-1940	Thornaby	24-06-1941
Elementary Flying Training School (EFTS)		*41 Sqdn Advance Base*	
Braunston (Leics)	01-10-1940	Greatham (Durham)	24-06-1941
Derby	08-11-1940	*(Satellite to Thornaby)*	
Satellite for practice navigation			
		Redhill (Surrey)	27-06-1941
Cosford (Salop)	13-11-1940	*11 Group, for operations over France*	
For first solo cross-country flight			
		Kenley (Surrey)	11-07-1941
Hullavington (Wilts)	11-12-1940	*602 Sqdn operational base & sector station*	
Service Flying Training School (SFTS)			
		North Weald (Essex)	21-07-1941
Chipping Norton (Oxon)	05-04-1941	Merston (Sussex)	22-07-1941
Babdown Farm (Glos)	30-03-1941	Tangmere (Sussex)	24-07-1941
Satellite for night flying training		White Waltham (Berks)	24-08-1941
		Little Rissington (Glos)	10-10-1941
Upavon (Wilts)	07-04-1941	Hendon (Middx)	01-11-1941
Hawarden	25-04-1941	Manston (Kent)	08-11-1941
Near Chester, OTU for Spitfire training		Shoreham (Sussex)	07-12-1941
		Leysdown (Kent)	07-12-1941
Speke (Liverpool)	25-04-1941	Llandow (Glam. S Wales)	17-12-1941
Sealand		Martlesham Heath (Suff)	29-12-1941
Temporary use due to bombing of Hawarden		Bircham Newton (Norfolk)	24-02-1942
and Speke		Langham (Norfolk)	24-02-1942
		West Raynham (Norfolk)	24-02-1942
Catterick (Yorks)	11-06-1941	Duxford (Cambs)	29-03-1942
Homebase of 41 Squadron		*This was only a visit; I was not posted to*	
		AFDU Duxford until May '42	
Acklington (Northumbs.)	11-06-1941		
Leeming Bar (Yorks)	17-06-1941	Marham (Norfolk)	12-05-1942
Spitfire Vb M Unit		Waddington (Lincs)	16-05-1942

Syerston (Notts)	17-05-1942	Warboys (Hunts, now	
Scampton (Lincs)	30-05-1942	Cambs)	01-10-1942

Famous as the home base of the Dam Busters

		Burtonwood (Ches)	23-10-1942
		Langar (Notts)	15-10-1942
Matlask (Norfolk)	02-06-1942	Lichfield (Staffs)	15-10-1942
Woodhall Spa (Lincs)	04-06-1942		

*A Wellington OTU, handy for visiting my
brother's family*

Bottesford (Lincs)	07-06-1942		
Digby (Lincs)	09-06-1942		
Reading (Berks)	10-06-1942	Fulbeck (Lincs)	26-11-1942
Ludham (Norfolk)	18-06-1942	Foulsham (Norfolk)	07-12-1942
Honnington (Suffolk)	19-06-1942	Hunsden (Herts)	13-02-1943
Stradishall (Suffolk)	21-06-1942	Bovingdon (Herts)	13-02-1943
Boscombe Down (Wilts)	22-06-1942	Wittering (Cambs)	15-02-1943
Fowlmere (Cambs)	23-06-1942		

*The base for AFDU from March '43 to
Feb '45*

Lympne (Kent)	25-06-1942		
Wyton (Cambs)	28-06-1942		
Waterbeach (Cambs)	28-06-1942	Ridgewell (Essex)	03-03-1943
Oakington (Cambs)	28-06-1942	Gransden Lodge (Cambs)	24-03-1943
Methwold (Norfolk)	29-06-1942	Colleyweston (Northants)	29-03-1943
Feltwell (Norfolk)	01-07-1942		

*Joined to Wittering by a 3-mile runway cut
between the two airfields to form an emergency
landing strip for aircraft in trouble*

Lakenheath (Suffolk)	01-07-1942		
Heston (Middx)	27-07-1942		
Farnborough (Hants)	29-07-1942		
Dishforth (Yorks)	04-08-1942	Coltishall (Norfolk)	20-04-1943
Middleton St. George		Ibsley (Hants)	20-04-1943
(Durham)	05-08-1942	Hixon (Shrewsbury,	
Hucknall (Notts)	19-08-1942	Shropshire)	03-05-1943

Rolls-Royce Aero Engine Division

		North Luffenham (Rutland)	13-05-1943
		Woolfox Lodge (Lincs)	14-05-1943
Mildenhall (Suffolk)	20-08-1942	Worthy Down (Hants)	21-05-1943
Upwood (Cambs)	21-08-1942	Manby (Lincs)	25-05-1943
Colerne (Wilts)	24-08-1942	Westcott (Bucks)	05-06-1943
Cranfield (Beds)	27-08-1942		

*A Wellington OTU, nearest airfield for visiting
the family at Poletrees Farm, Brill*

Nottingham	02-09-1942		
Tempsford (Beds)	03-09-1942		
Chelveston (Northants)	03-09-1942	Hockley Heath (Warks)	05-06-1943
Topcliffe (Yorks)	06-09-1942		

*A small grass field for emergency landings –
and visits to the folks in Redditch*

Skipton (Yorks)	10-09-1942		
Northolt (Middx)	16-09-1942		
Thurleigh (Beds)	23-09-1942	Castle Bromwich (W. Mids)	20-06-1943
Langley (Bucks, now Berks)	24-09-1942		

*The airfield adjoining the Hawker Aircraft
factory. My nearest place for visiting the family
at Slough*

*Adjoining the Spitfire production factory; also
useful for visits to Redditch*

		Church Fenton (Yorks)	27-06-1943
		Pershore (Worcs)	11-07-1943
Wolsingham (Durham)	09-11-1942		

*The flying field for RRE (Radar Research
Establishment) at Malvern, Worcs*

Henlow (Beds)	13-11-1942	
Bourne (Lincs)	27-11-1942	

Northcotes (Lincs)   17-07-1943
Newmarket (Suffolk)   06-08-1943
A wartime FFTS in the middle of Newmarket
racecourse

Hornchurch (Essex)   18-08-1943
Biggin Hill (Kent)   15-08-1943
Exeter (Devon)   22-08-1943
Portreath (Cornwall)   23-08-1943
Aston Down (Glos)   04-09-1943
Benson (Oxon)   05-09-1943
The base for PRU where I met Air
Commodore John Boothman, winner for
Britain of the Schneider Trophy in 1931

Great Massingham (Norfolk) 13-09-1943
Rednal (Shropshire)   15-09-1943
Hibaldstow (Lincs)   17-09-1943
Eshott (Northumberland)   19-09-1943
Dunsfold (Sussex)   23-11-1943
Hartford Bridge (Hants)   29-11-1943
The first airfield to have FIDO (Fog Intensive
Dispersal by Oil) Oil was sprayed under
pressure from pipes laid each side of the
runway and ignited. Landing was a most
frightening experience

Luton (Beds)   03-01-1944
Podington (Beds)   05-02-1944
Gravesend (Kent)   22-02-1944
Spanhoe (Northants)   16-03-1944
Sutton Bridge (Lincs)   23-04-1944
Catfoss (Yorks)   20-06-1944
Thorney Island (Sussex)   13-07-1944
Doncaster (Yorks)   09-08-1944
Another horseracing track used as an EFTS
during the war

Ouston (Northumberland)   05-09-1944
Swanton Morley (Norfolk) 13-09-1944
Millfield (Northumberland) 29-09-1944
Grimburgen, Belgium   14-11-1944
A large airfield used until a month earlier by
the Luftwaffe; now the base for hundreds of
USAAF & RAF fighters

Antwerp, Belgium   15-11-1944
Rearsby (Leics)   13-06-1947
My final recorded flight as a pilot in the RAF.

Len on a visit to Old Warden, sitting in the cockpit of a Spitfire that had flown in from Duxford.

Swapping memories with Stuart Waring, right, and Andy Sephton, pilot with the Shuttleworth Collection.

Len with Connie Edwards and Spitfire IX MH415 in Big Spring, Texas, December 2000. Len flew this aircraft as a fighter bomber in 1944. The story of the visit to Texas was covered in the *Daily Express* and on BBC News.

APPENDIX 3

CIVILIAN FLYING

Postwar as a Civilian

West Raynham – *a cross-country test flight*
Leicester East – *an away from base landing lesson*
Wellesbourne – 08-07-81
My base as a member of Wellesbourne Flying Club
Bidford (Bickmarsh) – 18-07-81
My one and only flight in a glider

For my birthday in 1981, Estelle's present was a voucher for an introductory flight at Wellesbourne. Prior to this I had made a trial flight in a glider from Bickmarsh near Bidford-on-Avon. Following my introductory flight I made four other trips in 1984, 1985 and 1992 but it was not until I lost Estelle in 1997 that I joined Wellesbourne Aviation Flying Club. Originally I flew with the Avon Club but did not enjoy the high wing Cessna 196 so I changed clubs and started off flying the PA38 Tomahawk.

I started out to retrain and attain a PPL (Private Pilot's Licence) but, even though I got a 50% waiver from the CAA in respect of flying hours, I would still have had to take full and regular medicals, all ground lectures and exams. My friend Rick Ions advised me that, as he was quite willing and happy to fly as my safety pilot, I would be better just to carry on with flying for fun. The following is a record of my civil flying, ostensibly as a pupil but actually flying as the pilot:

1981				
18th July	Glider	With Don Carey	From Bickmarsh	40 mins
1984	Introductory flight from Wellesbourne (date not recorded)			
8th Dec	Fuji	To take grandson Andrew for a first flight on his 11th birthday. Granddaughter Rowena came too.		40 mins
1985				
12th May	PA38 G.BKCY	With Rick Ions	From Wellesbourne	1-00 hr.
1992				
18th June	"	"	"	40 mins
Sept	"	"	"	1-00 hr.

1997				
29th Aug	"	"	"	1-00 hr.
3rd Sept	Cessna 196	With David ?	"	1-00hr.
11th Sept	PA38 G.BKCY	With Rick Ions	Cross country	1-00 hr.
9th Oct	"	"	Cloud & instrument flying	55 mins
15th Oct	"	"	Touch & Go	55 mins
22nd Oct	G.BRNJ	"	Cross country	1-00 hr.
29th Oct	"	"	Cross country & T&G	55 mins
7th Nov	"	"	T&G Use of RT	45 mins
14th Nov	"	"	Cross country	1-00hr.
21st Nov	"	"	Tight turns and stalls	1-00 hr.
1998				
28th Feb	"	"	Cross country to Waddesdon	1-05 hrs
4th Mar	"	"	Cross country in Cotswolds	1-05hrs
12th Mar	"	"	Touch & Go	-50 mins
20th Mar	"	"	Advanced handling	1-00hr.
21st May	Katana DV20	"	Handling new type	1-00hr.
20th Aug	PA38 G.BKCY	"	Local. Pinpoint navigation	-55 mins
27th Aug	"	"	To & land at Leicester East	-35 mins
27th Aug	"	"	Return to base	-35 mins
8th Sept	Cessna 152	With Paul Western	Aerobatics	1-05 hrs
'Orrible! I do not recommend aerobatics in this high-wing aeroplane.				
17th Sept	PA38	Self, Rick Ions	Cross country to Waddesdon & Quainton	1-05hrs
27th Sept	Concorde	Pilot Unknown	Took nephew Robin Thorne; with 98 other passengers, to Paris, landing at Charles de Gaulle Airport after flying supersonic. I was given VIP status when they found I had been a WWII pilot and was invited onto the flight deck for the latter part of the trip and landing, sitting at the back of the cockpit. Overnight stay in Paris. A truly memorable experience.	1-00 hr.
28th Sept	Airbus 300		Return to London Heathrow	1-00 hr.
1st Oct	PA38	Self, Rick Ions	Low level to Staverton and the Severn Estuary	1-00 hr.
19th Oct	PA38	Self, Rick Ions	Avon Valley, Wyre Piddle, River Severn & Malvern	1-00 hr.
2nd Nov	PA38	Self, Rick Ions	Very poor weather. Flew locally, Astwood Bank & Studley	-40 mins
Nov	Airbus		(Passenger) To Malta	4-00 hrs
Nov	Airbus		(Passenger) Return to Birmingham	4-00 hrs

1999				
Apr	Boeing 767		To Austin, Texas via Chicago (Passenger)	9-20 hrs
Apr	Boeing 767		To Birmingham	7-40 hrs
2000				
10th Mar	PA38	Self, Rick Ions	Base to Broadway, Evesham local round home	1-00 hr.
17th Mar	PA38	Self, Rick Ions	Cross country to Waddesdon; Navigation, instrument & cloud flying	1-00 hr.
24th Mar	PA38	Self, Rick Ions	Show off over Bidford & to Gill's school children at Flyford Flavell School	-55 mins
30th Apr	Cessna	Self, Rick Ions	With Club group. Started fly-out to Duxford; aborted by bad weather	-30 mins
5th May	PA38	Self, Rick Ions	Advanced handling	1-00 hr.
19th May	PA38	Self, Rick Ions	Speed turns. Round Walkmills Farm. Took photos of home (Wood Lane)	1-00hr.
7th Jun	Firefly Slingsby	Self, Adrian Burt	Aerobatics to celebrate my 80th birthday	1-00 hr.

Having undergone surgery for bowel cancer only months before I had decided that, providing I survived the operation and reached my 80th birthday, I wanted to do an aerobatic flight. Once I had been given the all clear from the cancer, my doctor was quite happy for me to give it a go. The flight became a sponsored stunt, engineered by daughter Gill, to raise money towards the provision of a new playground for the Children's Ward at the Alexandra Hospital, Redditch. The flight was covered by local media. I performed loops, rolls, steep turns, climbs, an inadvertent stall and spin and a roll off the top. I thoroughly enjoyed myself. The BBC gave a DVD of the event to me. Generous sponsorship by family, friends and neighbours raised £1,600 for the appeal.

8th Dec	Boeing 747	Passenger	To Austin, Texas via Chicago	10-00 hrs
During my holiday in the US in December, staying with younger daughter Penny and husband Phillip in Austin, Texas, we drove to West Texas to visit Connie Edwards, a cattle rancher and oil man, at Big Spring. Among his collection of World War II aircraft was a Mk IX HF Spitfire MH415. This was the same aeroplane I had flown during the war, as a fighter bomber. It was a thrill to sit again in the cockpit, which was still familiar to me after all that time. Many photographs were taken, some of which appeared in the *Daily Express*.				
2001				
12th Jan	Boeing 747	Passenger	To Birmingham	8-30 hrs
19th Jun	PA38	Self, Rick Ions	Trip over the Cotswolds	1-00 hr.
6th July	PA38	Self, Rick Ions	Local Flying	1-00 hr.
21st Aug	Robin	Self, Rick Ions	Familiarisation to new type	1-00 hr.
1st Sept	Robin	Self, Rick Ions	Gloucester & Severn Estuary	1-00 hr.

25th Sept	Robin	Self, Rick Ions	'High' flight to 8,600 ft.	1-05 hrs
In the course of this flight, I flew over Alcester, Warwickshire, then across to Malvern to fly down the length of the east side of the hills.				
5th Oct	Robin	Self, Rick Ions	To Aylesbury & Waddesdon	1-05 hrs
2002				
22nd Feb	Robin	Self, Rick Ions	Local flying	-42 mins
2nd Mar	Robin	Self, Rick Ions	To Waddesdon & Aylesbury	1-00 hr.
2nd Mar	Warrior	Self, Rick Ions and two BBC interviewers		-40 mins
This flight was to record an interview about my wartime flying in the Focke Wulf FW190. It was paid for by the BBC and was filmed with me flying the Warrior and back at home. It was shown on BBC News 24 with other interviews made in Germany. Again, the BBC kindly gave me a DVD.				
April	PA38	Self, Rick Ions	Local training	-50 mins
7th July	Robin	Self, Rick Ions	Flew over Alexandra Hospital to view the new children's playground	1-05 hrs
31st Aug	Robin	Self, Rick Ions	Cross country to Malvern for another view of the hills.	1-05 hrs
17th Sept	PA38	Self, J. Jackson	Visit to Kemble airfield, club and microlight hangar	-50 mins
17th Sept	PA38	Self, J. Jackson	Return to base	-35 mins
27th Sept	Robin	Self, Rick Ions	Local flying	1-00 hrs
11th Oct	Robin	Self, Rick Ions	Flew down the western scarp of the Cotswolds	-50 mins
2003				
25th Apr	Robin	Self, Rick Ions	Local flying	1-00 hrs
9th Jun	Robin	Self, Rick Ions	Flew over Burcot Grange near Bromsgrove and home (New End)	-40 mins
			GRAND TOTAL OF ALL FLYING HOURS AS PILOT	**1,186 hrs 42 mins**

During the last year I started to have difficulty in judging distances due to a developing cataract in my right eye. After two anything but smooth landings I decided very reluctantly to hang up my flying helmet. I remained an honorary member of Wellesbourne Aviation Flying Club and still looked in occasionally for a chat with Rick and other members of staff.

I flew nearly 70 different types and marks of aircraft, making over 2,000 flights. I made 1,400 Spitfire flights in approximately 150 individual machines, from the Mk 1 to the Mk 21. What a delight and privilege that was.

APPENDIX 4

SOME RECOLLECTIONS OF THOSE I HAVE KNOWN

I read the book *Aces High* by Christopher Shores and Clive Williams and from it I extracted the names of some of those men I knew personally: they were heroes to me and many others. Originally, just for my own interest I called on my memory for comments about them and if I am able to give some further information as to what happened to them later, they are listed below.

David Atcherley. I met David Atcherly but I did not know him well personally. However, I knew his twin brother R.A. (Richard), popularly known as 'Batchy', fairly well. I met him at Kenley, Duxford, and when he was Station Commander at Rednal OTU. It was there I met David during my visit there to demonstrate PM678, the FW190 A3 I was showing. They were great jokers. A story told is that when David paid a visit to Rednal, he passed out of the main gate and when Richard followed a few minutes later the sentries were taken to task for not seeing him return.

S/Ldr Ivor Badger. From 1945 to the end of 1948 I was on Air Ministry staff attached to the Ministry of Supply at Millbank in RDQF, later RDQB, as a liaison officer to the aircraft manufacturing firms. S/Ldr Badger was also in RDQB and we often joined up for some visits. I remember him as having been a Halton apprentice and he had fitted various items to his car, in fact a journey in his motor was the first time I had experienced a car heater. One of our visits to AVRO at Chadderton was during the harsh winter of 1946/47 and we only made it as far as Potterspury near Towcester on the A1 and had to spend the night at a nearby pub, of which the landlord was a retired ex warrant officer. We drank steadily and at midnight mine host said, 'I'm going to bed. Help yourselves to drink and put the money in the till. If there is a knock at the door, it will be the local copper. Let him in, give him a drink and send him on his way.'

G/Cpt. F.V. (Francis Victor) Beamish. One of the four Beamish Brothers from Eire who fought with great distinction for the RAF. He was our station commander at Kenley in 1942, a keen sportsman and a real disciplinarian but with fairness and a sense of humour. He flew frequently on operations, either with the squadrons or independently with the wing or squadron commander. On one such trip he and his colleague spotted and reported the German ships *Scharnhorst* and *Gneisenau* on their Channel dash in the winter of 1942. On 28th March 1942 he led the wing on one of the dreaded trips to Lille. They were heavily engaged and the G/Cpt. was badly hit and disappeared into the Channel. I was on the fighter sweep from Hardelot, south to Le Tréport. We saw no enemy fighters but when we landed we found out that the G/Cpt. was missing. We were immediately ordered to fly a search so we patrolled the Channel until dusk and again the following morning in the hope of finding him. He was never seen again. On the same operation my friend right from training days, Sgt Desmond O'Connor, was also lost. Shortly before this sad day, 'FV' interviewed me for a commission; on his recommendation it was gazetted on May 1st after I had been presented to King George VI during a visit to Kenley.

W/Cdr Roland Beamont. We met when he paid a visit to AFDU at Tangmere in 1945 and he later became CO of the unit. We also met later at English Electric.

W/Cdr Ronald (Razz) Berry. He was also at Tangmere in 1945 and was the first CO of the newly formed Central Fighter Establishment, which combined various test and experimental units. Razz was largely responsible for welding the new set-up into one body. During the spring I had a break from flying and for two months became the range instructing officer at Selsey bombing and firing range. Razz and his family were some of the customers for the Selsey shellfish, crabs and lobsters newly caught and cooked I got hold of at that time.

W/Cdr Blackadder (popularly known as 'the Bladder'). We got off on the wrong foot when he was appointed to command AFDU in 1944. He ordered me to 'show him the taps' of the FW190 so that he could fly it. I gave him the complete run through, warning him to be particularly careful, when landing, to maintain the correct speed and not to hold off too high. He did just that and dropped like a brick and hit the ground tail first. Although the damage was repairable it still put the aircraft out of action for some days. He always held this against me and seemed to blame me for the mishap. In my opinion he was not universally popular in the Unit and did not stay very long.

Eric Bocock. 'B' Flight commander in 602 Squadron at Kenley. Although I was the senior NCO pilot in 'A' Flight Eric signed my logbook a number of times.

W/Cdr Finlay Boyd was wing leader at Kenley in 1942 but I do not remember him staying very long. He was flying with 'Francis Victor' (above) when they spotted the two German ships in their Channel dash. I have a vague memory that he brought with him a reputation for violent weaving when in enemy territory. This made life very difficult for his number two, not only to stay with him but also because it used too much fuel making those violent manoeuvres.

W/Cdr John Braham. As mentioned earlier, in June 1942, when I had settled in at AFDU, Duxford, the CO encouraged me to take a living out pass and find accommodation so that my wife could join me. I said this might be difficult as she was of an age when she had to do war work. The Wingco said, 'No problem. Take some leave, get her pregnant and get her released.' It did not come to that. The Superintendent was a friend and he released her on condition that she did war work near Duxford. The first accommodation we had was at the Duxford vicarage, the vicar being the Reverend Dr Braham, the very proud father of John. John's wife Joan and his baby son, Michael, also lived at the vicarage. Consequently we got to know them very well. Among my treasured memorabilia is a photo of them on their wedding day.

Harry Charnock. He was always known as 'Chas'. Perhaps he is the most interesting of all those on my list. Probably not known by many people but to me he was something special. It says in *Aces High* that he was court-martialled for a 'flying offence'. I think the offence was to fly under Tower Bridge. His exploit was seen and reported. In the book it says that he re-joined the RAF on the outbreak of war. However, my memory tells me that at the time I heard he was actually called up into the army. When it was discovered that he was a qualified pilot he transferred to the RAF. He spent several months with us at AFDU, Wittering in the winter and spring of 1944, first still only a flying officer but later as a Flt. 'Loot'. He was completely mad and proved a perfect foil for Wimpy (T.S. Wade) and I could tell many stories about their activities. For instance, on the north side of Wittering there is a smallish lake on which, at that time, was a small sailing dinghy. One cold cloudy day, when flying was cancelled, Wimpy and Chas (even more so) got well tanked up during lunchtime in the mess. Egged on by the rest of us they took to the water and were soon in trouble when they were raising the sail. The sheet came off the top pulley. Chas attempted to climb the mast and the boat capsized, flinging them into the lake. They struggled to the bank, sent someone to fetch blankets and towels then, cheered on by the unit WAAFs, stripped starkers amid much merriment.

I was able to live out at that time in the nearby village of Easton on the Hill and my wife and I loved to entertain the boys at home. Chas was always interested in the well-kept garden and liked to try the flowers as an addition to his diet: he said that he preferred the Wisteria. Before I left the RAF at the end of 1948, I threw a farewell party at the Old Queen's Head just off the Victoria Road. Chas was one of my guests. He was then in civvy street, married and with small children. He was much subdued, not the Chas I remembered.

Air Commodore Al Deere. My squadron commander at Kenley, with 602 AA Squadron from July '41 to the end of that year. I was then a very 'sprog' Sgt Pilot with only a short experience in 41 Squadron. Al was my hero and, although I was only an NCO when I served with him, we kept in contact and were friends up to his death. He was an excellent leader, and helped us through our learning curve at what became a very difficult time with the advent of the Focke Wulf FW190. One episode stands out in my memory. At the end of December '41 we were ordered to Martlesham Heath to cover a minesweeping operation in the North Sea; we were told that an important convoy was coming through. The weather was awful and our first and only patrol on December 30th showed no sign of ships. The following day it was worse and there was no possibility of flying.

Remember that 602 was a Scottish outfit and most of the lads had dates for the Hogmany festivities at Kenley, some had even arranged for wives and girlfriends to stay over. Permission to fly back and return early on New Year's Day was refused and the Scots were royally teed off. We were finally released late in the afternoon and transport was laid on but only to take us into Ipswich. I remember that with the boys of 485, we drowned our sorrows in one of the town's pubs and were still hard at it when the landlord called time. When we showed no sign of leaving he called for help from the local police. Two brave special constables tried to evict us and were shut into a revolving door, which was kept spinning until we were ready to leave. A strong complaint was made by the chief constable to the station commander, who demanded names. These were not forthcoming and before any other action could be taken we were back at Kenley. The station commander explained to the police that we were on operational service engaged with the enemy. It was eventually agreed that an apology should be made and Al and Hawkeye Billy Wells went back by road and did it personally.

Hugh Dundas. I met (then) S/Ldr (Cocky) Dundas late in 1941 when I was at Duxford. I had gone to a mess party at Fowlmere, just the other side of Cambridge and he was another of the guests. There were also quite a number of American officers there. As the evening progressed many, including Hugh, got well oiled and things got a bit wild. The high point was to take a pair of scissors and cut off ties just below the knot. As I could not afford to buy a new tie (I was a newly commissioned P/O), I took mine off and put it in my pocket out of harm's way. When it happened to one of the Yanks, he was very annoyed and caught 'Cocky' from behind, took hold of his tunic tails and ripped his beautifully tailored garment from bottom to top, straight up the seam.

Charles Dyson. He was for three months our O/C flying at AFDU Wittering in 1943. He was a bit 'toffee nosed' having, I believe, come from the Indian Air Force. He was the CO when I took over the FW190 to take it around Fighter Command for demos. As I had no Pilot's Notes I spent two or three days carefully studying the beast before taking to the air. As Air Ministry were rather anxious to get the tour under way, Charles tried to bully me into action. He got rather annoyed when I refused to be rushed.

W/Cdr Donald Finlay. I first came into contact with Donald when he was 11 Group Engineer Officer. He paid regular visits to the Squadrons, including 602 at Kenley. It was his practice to take one of the aircraft for a test flip and have a few words with the pilot afterwards. I normally flew LOA and he selected this machine and talked to me on several occasions. After I had moved to AFDU he joined us for a short time as CO in place of Campbell-Orde, who was sent to the US. Donald was a fitness fanatic and turned us out for PT and cross-country runs at the crack of dawn. As it was winter when he was there, this was not exactly popular with the pilots. He also picked on me for flying duties and one morning he decided on a formation climb through 20,000 feet of cloud. By the time we came out at the top, I was seeing double but I was still tucked in behind his wing. On another occasion he took up the Mosquito, which we were testing, and made me his navigator through a series of turns and twists over mid-England. I bumped into him later when he was CO of an OTU which I visited with the FW190. Despite all this we got on very well.

Brendan Paul Finucane. At the time of his death in July 1942, he was the top-scoring fighter pilot with 32 kills. He became CO of 602 Squadron just after Christmas 1941. I was tour expired in mid-May and he left soon after to become wing leader as stated earlier in the book. I only learned much later that doubts were cast on some of his claims but in my experience they were all true. By April I had been promoted to F/Sgt and became senior NCO pilot in 'A' Flight. As such I flew as a sub-section leader and on a number of operations I flew as Paddy's number two. I was Blue 3 on 28th March 1942, but missed most of the action in which Red Section was involved. It was on this operation, in the afternoon, that Group Captain Francis Victor Beamish was lost. Immediately after landing Paddy had us back to search the Channel until it became too dark to see. We returned for night landings and were back again at dawn the next morning. Sadly FVB was not found.

16th April was a big show when Le Havre was attacked. It was almost a rehearsal for Dieppe. The action was intense, the Huns up in force, the book shows Paddy having a half share in an FW190 confirmed, I had the other half but Paddy very generously withdrew his claim to give me my second confirmed victory. The previous day we did a deep penetration to Lille. A visiting doctor from Farnborough, a pilot with some experience but too many years, persuaded Paddy to allow him to fly with us. Paddy placed him as my number two, saying, 'Fly with Len Thorne, he is very experienced, you will be safe with him.' Wrong. As we crossed the coast the doctor, G/Cpt. Hugh Corner, and I were dropped on by two 190s and despite my calls to break, he failed to do so and was shot down. Paddy called the squadron to close on us but they were too late to help. I had to face a court of enquiry, but was exonerated from blame on the say-so of Paddy. There was a censure for allowing

GC Corner to fly on that operation. Although I was exonerated, I still blamed myself, then and ever since for his death.

Although I was still (not for much longer) an NCO, I got to know Paddy very well. My wife (we were married Sept 1941) lived at Slough and Paddy's fiancée, a girl-next-door romance, lived at Kingston. On days off, we travelled together on the train from Victoria. On these occasions Paddy always wore a mac to hide his decorations. I thought he was a great guy, a real hero and I was devastated when his death was announced, we all were.

In 2004, a Dublin radio station put out a one hour broadcast on him entitled 'In Search of Paddy Finucane'. I had been interviewed by phone and so had a small part in the story. Paddy's elder brother, Kevin, tipped me off and so I heard and taped the programme.

Hugh Godefroy. Then a flying officer, he had joined AFDU a few weeks before me. He was an excellent pilot and with F/Lt Denis Clive was detached to Farnborough to carry out comparative tests on the first FW190 to fall into our hands. This was the one that landed at Pembrey when the pilot, after bombing Portland, flew red on black and thought he was back in France. On returning to Duxford Hugh joined F/O. Walker and me to form the fighter affiliation flight under the command of S/Ldr. Jock Murray, DFM, DFC. We toured many Bomber Command airfields to teach the bomber boys how to 'corkscrew' in order to evade Luftwaffe attacks. Poor sods – little did they know! I remember that Hugh acquired an Alsation puppy, naturally called Spit and took him with him tucked into a parachute bag that he carried on his lap.

S/Ldr Reg Grant. The Australian CO of 452 Sqdn. We met often at briefings before ops. My enduring memory of him dates from Christmas Eve 1941. My newly wedded wife had come over to Kenley just for the night so that we could attend a dance at Croydon airport. A small group of us went to Croydon by train and found ourselves in a carriage with, sitting opposite, several beligerent army chaps. There were five of us, myself and wife, my friend Dessie O'Connor, Reg Grant and one of his 452 pilots. The squaddies who had been in the Dunkirk evacuation, despite the presence of my wife, were all set for trouble. (One of our pilots had been badly beaten up only the week before.) Reg, who was quite a small man, faced them when they said, 'Where were the airforce when we were being dive bombed?' He said we were there further into France trying to stop the enemy before they got to the coast. He finally silenced them by saying that unlike those who escaped, many of our chaps, including his only brother, were shot down and killed there.

Lt Giles Guthrie. He was my counterpart in the NAFDU (Naval Air Fighting Development Unit). During my time at Duxford I had a sleeping out pass and we had rooms at a huge old farmhouse house in Duxford village. It belonged to a young couple, farmer Guy Smith and his wife Ynez. She had been a dancing instructress with one of the London big bands and loved to give parties for the officers and their wives. Giles and his lovely wife, Rhona, frequently attended and always stayed at College Farm both for Ynez's and for mess parties, so, although we were not exactly in their social class, we got to know them very well and were never conscious of the social distinction. Many years after the war, I attended a Birmingham Chamber of Commerce lunch at the county cricket ground. Giles, who was then the chief executive of British Overseas Airways, was the guest speaker, he spotted me at the far end of my table and immediately left his seat to come round and greet me, to the amazement of the assembled company.

Jim Hallowes was briefly O/C Flying at AFDU, Wittering, from March 1943, taking over from Ted Smith, at the time of our move from Duxford to Wittering. He was there until July and I was sorry to see him go. He was a quiet, modest and very likeable man. It was not until some time later that I learned of his most distinguished career. Hallowes was given command of 222 Squadron at North Weald in June 1942. In August he took command of 165 Squadron and led it in the Dieppe operation on the 19th, destroying a Do217 and damaging another and on 8th November he damaged another FW190. Hallowes was awarded the DFC (gazetted 19th January 1943). In October 1943 he took command of 504 Squadron at Peterhead. Hallowes was promoted to acting wing commander in March 1944 and became station commander at Dunsfold. He stayed on in the RAF, in the Secretarial Branch, and retired on 8th July 1956 as a squadron leader, retaining the rank of Wing Commander. He went to work for the Ministry of Transport. Jim Hallowes died in 1987.

P/O Roy Hussey. DFC, DFM. A strikingly handsome young officer posted to AFDU for experience in 1944. He is in the group photograph taken at the Officers' Mess dinner when W/Co Blackadder left, to be replaced by young Allan Wright. He re-turned to 'ops' with 19 Squadron and was sadly killed in an accident coming in to land at Dallachy in Mustang KH440 on February 20th 1945.

'Sandy' Johnstone was our Sqdn. Ldr. He was the C/O of 602 when I joined the squadron at Aire in July 1941. I did not get to know him before our move to Kenley as he was replaced immediately by S/Ldr Meagher. In fact, I did not meet him until long after the war when I attended a reunion in 1995. He very kindly autographed a copy of his book, which is now among my treasures.

W/Cdr John (Johnny) Kent. He was the Kenley wing leader in August 1941. An operation that is still fresh in my mind was on August 7th. 602 were flying as escort cover, flying above and to the right of 6 Blenheims. My logbook read, 'I flew as Red 4 and when about 10 miles west of St Omer Red Section were dived on by 6 Me. 109s, they overshot and the leading e/a was attacked by W/Co Kent, who followed it down. I attacked the 2nd 109, firing a short burst from astern and slightly below. It turned onto its back and went down vertically leaving a trail of white smoke. I later claimed it probably destroyed but the W/Co confirmed that it was seen to crash so my claim was raised to one confirmed destroyed. P/O Thornton was missing.'

S/Ldr Jimmie Lacey was my flight commander very briefly in March 1942. During that month things warmed up and we started intensive operations. But by then, the FW190s were appearing in numbers and our losses started to mount. It was in this month that my friend 'Dessie' O'Connor, from training days, was shot down and killed. I remember Jimmie Lacey as a slim young man with very fair hair and piercing, pale blue eyes, It was many years later in the 1980s that I met him again at a Spitfire society AGM in London: by then he was very ill and died shortly after.

Sgt Bill Loud. Bill became a member of 'A' Flight 602 in March 1942. He flew as my number two several times and may have been in that position when he scored his first success, a 'probable', on May 1st 1942. I was on that show and also claimed a probable as well as a damaged. See also my comment at the end of the Paddy Finucane story.

S/Ldr James MacLachlan. Another of the really notable members of the RAF. His biography, *One Armed Mac* by Brian Cull and Roland Symons, was published in July 2003. I recommend it as a good read. He had two stints at AFDU, the first was as a supernumerary member but it is the second which has remained in my memory. In *Aces High* it says that he joined AFDU in June, but he actually joined at the beginning of May or even the end of April, as we flew together on May 3rd in a Heston Phoenix. As described earlier, it was on this trip that another light aircraft chose to join us in formation. To warn him off, Mac unscrewed his false left arm and shook it at the pilot, out of the port window. The operation with Geoff Page described in *Aces High* was carried out from AFDU in two of the Unit's Mustangs. To enable them to achieve maximum speed both machines were 'hand polished' and we all took turns to help. On 29 June the duo participated in the destruction of six aircraft (four Hs 126s of JG 105, two each, and two KG-6 Ju-88s, sharing one with Page) in a single sortie. On his next mission on 18 July his Mustang FD442 was hit by ground fire when crossing the French coast and crash-landed. MacLachlan was critically injured. He was taken prisoner, and died on 31 July 1943. His loss in their second operation saddened us all.

Johnny Niven. We were together during training from December 1940, through SFTS, Hullavington to Operational Training at 57 OTU, Hawarden. It was there that I really became friendly with John and I have several photos of us together as Sgt Pilots. We were separated while I did my stint at 41 Squadron and I was delighted when we met again in the Segeants' Mess at Kenley in July 1941. We flew in 'A' Flight and later that year John was commissioned and, due to our heavy losses, achieved rapid promotion. He became 'A' Flight commander and thus my immediate commanding officer. He was just 21 and I, with many others, attended his typically Scottish 21st birthday party, which took place just before he gained his commission. I vaguely remember holding him back when he tried to march round the parade ground backwards. Many, many years later we met in one of those coincidences which rarely happen. John was shot down later in the war and I believe was badly injured. During a visit some 20 years ago to Hendon, I was lunching in the restaurant when John walked up and greeted me. Not long before our meeting, he had suffered a serious heart attack and was still not in the best of health. He invited me to visit his home at Inverness for a short holiday. Sadly, before I could make the trip, he suffered a further heart attack and died.

W/Cdr Geoff Page. As mentioned in the recollection of F/Lt James MacLachlan, Geoff was another of the supernumeraries attached to AFDU. He did some general flying but his real purpose was to join S/Ldr MacLachlan in their attack on the German western training bases. We met at various air shows after the war. I made the visit to Capel le Ferne for the commemoration service of the Battle of Britain Memorial some years ago. Geoff was then seriously ill but determined to be there and we had a brief conversation. He managed to autograph my copy of his book *The Guinea Pigs*, which tells the story of his recovery from terrible burns to his face and hands caused when his aircraft was shot down in August 1940. He was cared for by Sir Archibald MacIndoe and was the founder chairman of the Guinea Pig Club.

W/Com John Peel. He was another of the wing leaders at Kenley in 1941. On July 21st I made my 4th operational flight with 602 Squadron, when we escorted 3 Stirlings to bomb the railway yards at Lille. Near the target we were attacked by five 109s and the Wing Commander was badly hit but managed to return to base. F/Lt Glyn Richie was not so lucky, he was shot down and killed. On the return leg very heavy flak was experienced.

Frenchman **Baron Roland François de la Poype** (then Count de la Poype) was the equivalent rank of sergeant and joined us in the Sergeants' Mess at the time when Paddy Finucane was CO. Roly still wore his original dark blue French uniform and cap. To us he was a typical young French officer, tall, slim and handsome, a wow with the ladies and good fun to be with. From time to time Roly received, via Switzerland, large sums of money from his family and would take us to our favourite pub, the Greyhound at Croydon for a right royal party, paying most if not all the cost. We also made forays to the nightclubs of London and on one such occasion Roly and I were more than merry. We had exchanged headgear and were stopped by the Service Police at Waterloo for being improperly dressed. I do not remember the outcome but presumably they did not press the matter. Roly was later commissioned and left the squadron to train and lead a group of

French volunteers for the Russian Front, arriving at Ivanovo on 28th November 1942 with GC 3 *Normandie*. He stayed there for two years, and became Warrant Officer and then Captain. He even became a Hero of the Soviet Union. After the war, he stayed for a while with the 'Neu-Neu' (French shorthand for the group Normandie Niemen) and afterwards he became the Air Attaché in Belgium, and then Yugoslavia.

Australian **Sgt John Sanderson** was a member of 602 before joining 452 Australian Squadron. On one of our ops his Spitfire was badly shot up and I have a picture of Sandy crouched beneath the wing, looking up through a gaping hole where the cannon shells had struck. Luckily Sandy himself was uninjured but he was extremely fortunate to get home.

Herbert Scott Sewell (Susie). Susie was twice a member of AFDU, first at Duxford in 1942 and for a longer stay in the spring and summer of 1943. In 1942, before my wife joined me at Duxford, I lived in mess and came to know Susie well. The following year, when we had moved to Wittering, my wife returned to her home in Redditch for the birth of our first child. She was away from early May until early July and I again moved back into mess. During this period Susie and I became firm friends. He was very good company, an attractive personality, popular with the ladies but also a typical fighter pilot, respected by his fellows. In July he was appointed to carry out comparative testing and demonstrations of the newly acquired FW190 and had made several flights during the month. On July 31st 1943 Susie was carrying out fuel consumption tests on a modified Mosquito and I was flying with him as observer, taking the flow meter readings. When we were over the Thames valley the port engine cut and Susie made a precautionary approach to White Waltham. At the last moment we were baulked by some men on the perimeter trap. Susie opened to full throttle to go round again and the starboard engine cut. The aircraft stalled and crashed on the airfield. We were incredibly lucky to escape with a few cuts and bruises. In fact the 'blood wagon' crew looked quite disappointed when we walked away. Susie was badly shaken and a few days later he was posted on rest and I believe he was off flying for a time. I was told that he served as a Squadron Adjutant before going back to operations in March 1944. I remained in contact and learned that he left the RAF late in 1945. He did not resume his pre-war job as a car salesman in Darlington but after training became a school teacher. After our Mosquito crash I, then also a Flt. Loot, took over Susie's position of unit flight commander and also the appointment to fly the FW190.

S/Ldr T.S. Wade, known to all as 'Wimpy' from his resemblance to the cartoon character. Again, I was not aware of his success as a fighter ace until much later. He joined AFDU in October 1943 as OC Flying, a position he occupied until October 1944. He then spent three months in the USA, returning to AFDU, which had then moved to Tangmere in February. He was there until the end of March 1945. In my humble opinion Wimpy was one of the best Spitfire pilots I knew. His handling was exceptional, he could do everything short of making it sit up and beg. He loved to show off with aerobatics at low altitudes. A favourite trick was to make his final landing approach inverted and roll out when crossing the airfield boundary. He would often perform a slow roll immediately after take-off while retracting his undercarriage. On August 14th 1944 we were testing a Spitfire Mk X1V that had been fitted with a curved windscreen against one with the usual armoured flat panel. One of the trials was at night when we took turns with each aircraft. I flew the 'special' first, then we swapped over and Wimpy flew the trial machine. One of the problems was that on throttling back for landing there were streams of sparks from the exhausts, which played hell with night vision. When Wimpy came in he was blinded and only got down at the third attempt. It was the only time I saw him badly shaken. He needed a drink but as it was then past midnight I had to take him home with me to get one. That machine, RM 689, was the one that crashed at Woodford Airshow killing David Moore.

Wimpy too lived out with his wife. Estelle and I attended the christening of their first baby, a boy. It took place in the chapel at Wittering, with many washings of the baby's head in the mess after the ceremony. We had many adventures together, both in the air and on the ground. Wittering as you probably know is on the edge of the Burghley estate and the area around, at that time, abounded with game. The odd pheasant or partridge was a welcome addition to wartime rations. On one occasion Wimpy and I were driving in his staff car in a lane just outside the boundary and we already had a useful haul when we were caught by one of the gamekeepers. He had to jump for his life when Wimpy took no notice and just kept going. The episode with the sailing boat has already been mentioned in the Charnock story. I could go on for ages about Wimpy, he was a real larger than life character. In May 1949 he set a speed record between London and Paris in the Hawker P1052. On 3rd April 1951 he was killed while test flying the Hawker p1081, the swept wing fighter, when it crashed near Lewes in Sussex. His end when testing the first Hawker Hunter was very sad but almost inevitable. Our orderly room Corporal, WAAF Peggy Snashall, became Wimpy's secretary when he worked at Hawkers.

W/Cdr E.S. 'Hawkeye Billy' Wells. At the time I met him he was the CO of 485 Sqdn. at Kenley, at the same time that his fellow New Zealander, Al Deere was C/O of 602 Sqdn. I flew on many of the shows in which he was involved.

G/Cpt. Allan Wright. Our CO in AFDU, at Wittering and Tangmere, 1944–45. Although already a veteran of much fighting, Alan looked like a shy schoolboy. He retired as a Group Captain in 1967 and lived near Holsworthy in Devon. He featured in a number of television programmes, one of which was Tony Robinson's *Time Team*. His October 1940 recommendation for the DFC read: 'One night in

August 1940, this officer displayed great determination and skill in destroying a Heinkel 111, under difficult conditions. Pilot Officer Wright has consistently shown a keen desire to engage the enemy on all occasions. He has brought down a total of four enemy aircraft and has badly damaged four more.'

APPENDIX 5

LETTERS OF CONDOLENCE

After Len Thorne died on 6th June 2008, we received many letters and cards from his friends and connections in the RAF and Spitfire societies. Here are four.

1. Dr Gordon Mitchell, son of R.J. Mitchell who designed the Supermarine Spitfire.
2. W/Com Gerry Mayhew, Officer Commanding XIII Squadron, ex member of 41 Squadron, RAF.
3. W/Com A.M. 'Andy' Myers, Officer Commanding 41 (R) Squadron, RAF.
4. G/Capt Iain Panton, RAF, retired.

TEL. COTSWOLD
01451 - 822252

'BARN CLOSE'
LOWER SLAUGHTER
CHELTENHAM
GLOS. GL54 2HT

29 June 2008

Gill Griffin,
14, Moat Farm Lane,
Bishampton,
Pershore, Worcs. WR10 2NJ.

Dear Gill Griffin,

It was a great shock to receive your letter of the 26th June telling me the your father (Len) had died on the 6th June.

Over the years I got to know Len very well and always considered him to be one of my special friends. As I presume you know, our interests centered very much in the Spitfire which as you say was his greatest love, as, of course, is mine!

Going back, I remember that in August 1996 I gave a talk to the Redditch Probus Club followed in September 1996 to one at a Centre in Birmingham. For these, Len and your mother kindly put me up for which I was very grateful since it meant I did not have to do the long drive home at night.

I do not remember exactly, but I think it was not long after that your mother died which was such a terrible loss for your father, as it was for me when my wife died 3 years ago.

I should say, of course, that I held Len with my greatest respect for what he achieved in the RAF.

Regarding the book Len was writing, if you have not already got a publisher, it could be worth contacting my Publishers, namely The History Press, The Mill, Brimscombe Port, Stroud, Glos. GL5 2QG, mentioning my name. As their name suggest. Len's book should automatically be at least/of interest to them, though obviously I cannot guarantee this!

I finish by conveying to you my sincere condolences in your sad loss of a specially fine man and father.

Sincerely,

Gordon Mitchell.

From Wing Commander G M Mayhew MA RAF

Officer Commanding XIII Squadron
Royal Air Force Marham
Kings Lynn, Norfolk PE33 9NP

Mrs G Griffin

15 June 2008

Dear Mrs Griffin,

may I offer my deepest condolences on the loss of your father, Len. Having heard of his passing from John Jervis, I wanted to write, as both an ex-member of 41 Squadron and as a serving member of the Royal Air Force today.

As you know, the squadrons have a great pride in their history and especially in the exploits of their courageous and dedicated personnel. Len was one such person and you can rest assured that he will be mourned by those of us who follow in his footsteps. He was obviously a man of great talent, enthusiasm and bravery and our great nation will be forever in his debt.

I'm sure that he's now back with his friends in that big airfield in the sky. We will remember him.

Yours

Gerry Mayhew

OC XIII Squadron

214

⊙ ROYAL AIR FORCE

Number 41 (Reserve) Squadron
RAF Coningsby
Coningsby
Lincolnshire
LN4 4SY

23 June 2008

Dear Mrs Griffin,

    I was saddened to hear of the recent death of your father, a wartime member of No. 41 Squadron. As the present Commanding Officer of the Squadron I would wish to pass on the condolences of the entire Squadron. It is clear from the information passed to me by Mr Jervis and my own examination of the Squadron's records that he was an outstanding pilot and worthy of the title 'one of the few'. I must apologise for not being able to provide any formal attendance at the funeral, you should understand I only received this letter on my return from the USA yesterday evening.

Yours sincerely

A M Myers

A M MYERS
Wing Commander
OC 41 (R) Sqn

PS. Should you or Mr Jervis wish to visit the Squadron at any time, then please ring me. AM.

Group Captain Iain Panton, RAF (Ret'd)

Wednesday 11 June 2008

Dear Mrs Griffin,

Deeply saddened to hear from Ray Brandish of the death of your father, I am writing on behalf of the members of the Stratford upon Avon & District Branch of the Aircrew Association to convey our heartfelt sympathy to you & to all of Len's family at your tragic loss.

Len had been a very supportive & staunch member of the Branch for many years: he was popular, warmly regarded & highly respected by all of us — especially so during the last year when he made such valiant attempts to attend meetings, in spite of his increasingly limited mobility.

To Len his flying days in the Royal Air Force remained a vivid memory undimmed by the passing years. I remember with pleasure many interesting & lively reminiscences shared with Len over a pint of beer: his powers of recall as a raconteur were impressive! Indeed I remember in particular once lending him a book about World War Two fighter aces which he later returned kindly enclosing a sheaf of neatly typed notes of fascinating comments & anecdotes on many aircraft when he'd flown. His indomitably cheerful & friendly manner & his knowledgeable contributions to discussion will be greatly missed by all of us.

We salute the memory of a fine officer who served his country gallantly when it needed him: a firm, convivial friend: & a true gentleman.

Len will long be remembered by all those who had the privilege of knowing him with warm affection & abiding respect — & a smile.

Again, Gill, our deepest sympathy & sincere condolences to you & yours.

Yours sincerely,
Iain Panton

INDEX

If you enjoyed this book, you may also be interested in ...

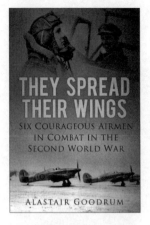

They Spread Their Wings

ALASTAIR GOODRUM

What turns an ordinary man into an extraordinary one? The answer lies in the stories of Fg Offs Howard Clark and Jack Cheney, Wg Cdr Walter Dring, Flt Lt James Crampton, Sqn Ldr Kenneth Summerson and WO Arthur Edgeley; teenage volunteers for wartime aircrew who exchanged school uniform for Air Force Blue and took a giant step into the unknown. This collection of true tales describes training for those coveted 'Wings'; the nervous excitement of that first sortie over enemy territory; and flying into the hell of an enemy flak barrage and fighters.

9780752487588

To Scale the Skies

PETER CORNWELL

With humble beginnings as an RAF apprentice, Johnny Wells progressed to pilot and rose to the higher echelons of command at the Air Ministry. Indeed, Wells ended the Second World War as one of the most successful and highly decorated Typhoon Wing Leaders in the Tactical Air Force. This well-researched account of one man's rise through the ranks of the Air Ministry is finely illustrated with contemporary images and is an excellent testimony of what was required of air pilots during the Second World War. Wells' story is both an inspiration and a gripping account of one man's journey through a service career spanning more than three turbulent decades.

9780752463537

Spitfire's Forgotten Designer

MIKE ROUSSEL

Spitfire's famous designer R.J. Mitchell died in June 1937 and never saw his prototype design become one of the most famous fighter aircraft of the Second World War. Working under Mitchell as chief draughtsman was Joe Smith, who became manager of the design department, and then chief designer after Mitchell's death. This illustrated book celebrates the inspirational and innovative work of Mitchell, Smith and their design team. Including first-hand accounts of members of the design team and apprentices, it reveals a little-known but pivotal figure. Smith's dedication, leadership and the part he played in the development of the Spitfire and post-war jet aircraft have largely been forgotten.

9780752487595

Visit our website and discover thousands of other History Press books.

www.thehistorypress.co.uk